A High School English Teacher's Guide to Writing Literary Analysis

I0894267

A High School English Teacher's Guide to Writing Literary Analysis

Coley Conter, Mary Ehrenworth, and Lauren Gould

Routledge
Taylor & Francis Group
NEW YORK AND LONDON
A Stenhouse Book

Designed cover image: Lauren Gould

First published 2026
by Routledge
605 Third Avenue, New York, NY 10158

and by Routledge
4 Park Square, Milton Park, Abingdon, Oxon, OX14 4RN

Routledge is an imprint of the Taylor & Francis Group, an informa business

© 2026 Coley Conter, Mary Ehrenworth, and Lauren Gould

The right of Coley Conter, Mary Ehrenworth, and Lauren Gould to be identified as authors of this work has been asserted in accordance with sections 77 and 78 of the Copyright, Designs and Patents Act 1988.

All rights reserved. No part of this book may be reprinted or reproduced or utilised in any form or by any electronic, mechanical, or other means, now known or hereafter invented, including photocopying and recording, or in any information storage or retrieval system, without permission in writing from the publishers.

For Product Safety Concerns and Information please contact our EU representative GPSR@taylorandfrancis.com. Taylor & Francis Verlag GmbH, Kaufingerstraße 24, 80331 München, Germany.

Trademark notice: Product or corporate names may be trademarks or registered trademarks, and are used only for identification and explanation without intent to infringe.

Interior illustrations by Lauren Gould

Library of Congress Cataloging-in-Publication Data
Names: Conter, Coley author | Ehrenworth, Mary author | Gould, Lauren author
Title: A high school English teacher's guide to writing literary analysis /
Coley Conter, Mary Ehrenworth, and Lauren Gould.
Description: New York, NY : Routledge, 2026. | Includes bibliographical
references and index.
Identifiers: LCCN 2025029324 (print) | LCCN 2025029325 (ebook) |
ISBN 9781032988733 paperback | ISBN 9781003606567 ebook
Subjects: LCSH: English language--Rhetoric--Study and teaching (Secondary) |
Criticism--Authorship--Study and teaching (Secondary) |
English teachers--Training of
Classification: LCC PE1404 .C63386 2026 (print) | LCC PE1404 (ebook)
LC record available at https://lccn.loc.gov/2025029324
LC ebook record available at https://lccn.loc.gov/2025029325

ISBN: 978-1-032-98873-3 (pbk)
ISBN: 978-1-003-60656-7 (ebk)

DOI: 10.4324/9781003606567

Typeset in Sabon LT Pro
by KnowledgeWorks Global Ltd.

Dedication

From Coley:
To B, for believing in every dream
on my index card.

From Mary:
To Jordan Kravitz and Todd Shy, whose extraordinary teaching
made a reader and thinker of my son.

From Lauren:
To Dad, who taught me the power of a good debate
and the importance of finding my voice.

Contents

Dear Colleagues,

Please consider this an invitation to adapt, expand, and experiment with these lessons to meet the needs of your students *and* help them unlock their potential. We hope to save you some planning time, expand your resources, inspire you to consider new frontiers, and help you achieve your vision.

Lots of the lessons in this book will fit into the typical paradigm of a literary essay, and some of them will push the boundaries that have been predetermined (in high school) for this genre. We know you'll self-select the lessons inside each chapter that fit your sensibility and needs. We invite you to experiment, to play, to try out a few lessons that move you and your high school writers to think deeply about texts and write with voice and purpose.

We have many resources, from charts and tools to mentor texts and student exemplars, available at www.hs-guidetoteaching.org. You may reach us there as well, to celebrate your successes or share student writing.

Our hope, for you and your students, is a literary analysis unit filled with deep thinking, artful writing, and, above all, joy. We can't wait to see where you take these lessons (and your students' writing)!

All the best,

Coley, Mary, Lauren

Introduction: A High School English Teacher's Guide to Writing Literary Analysis

Essays ... do not close down thinking, do not conclude arguments,
but rather open up new thinking, new possibilities,
new perspectives on the world.
—Katherine Bomer

We begin with Katherine Bomer's description of essays (2016), because this book aims to expand what essay writing looks and feels like in English classrooms. This is also why we call this book *literary analysis*, not merely *literary essay*. Literary analysis includes book reviews, video essays, literary criticism, articles, podcasts, braided essays, and beyond. At its core, an analysis is the act and art of thinking deeply about a text. And that's what makes this genre so beautiful.

There is beauty in writing highly analytic, obsessed-with-literary-craft essays that can bring an avid reader deeper into the language of a narrative, so that they delight in the author's phrases and attach meaning to the most nuanced details. And there is also danger: the danger of making the art of talking and writing about books a club that is small and private and intimidating. We teach not only in high schools but also in college and graduate courses, and we see too many young people who are insecure about their ideas and their academic writing, because they feel like they've never really felt secure in this club. And maybe it's because the club hasn't expanded to include them, or the rules of the club keep them from joining. Here, we'll establish a metaphorical literary analysis writing club that all your students can readily step into, one where they can surprise you with their quirky fascinations, their personal insights and connections, and you in turn can teach them the elegance of literary interpretation and writing for other readers.

We want to lure you to conceptualize the process of writing literary analysis so that all your readers learn more about texts *and* more about themselves through the process of annotating, talking, and writing about stories. We're also acutely aware that the terrain of what writers explore when they dive into textual analysis has shifted over the last years in colleges and universities, where students explore identities and cultural heritage and power and representation and discourse, as well as characterization and literary craft and theme. Widening the scope of what readers might find fascinating in a novel means that more readers have more to say, and that literary analyses become more intimate and significant to the writer and to their audience.

Some Important Aspects Particular to Literary Analysis

There are a few ways to adjust a literary analysis unit so that it becomes more engaging and personal, while still instilling the analytical skills and academic vocabulary that will empower your students not only in English classes but also on their high-stakes assessments, applications, and the future analytic writing they do in the world. Literary analysis is a genre like and unlike others, and there are some important aspects of it to consider as you imagine teaching this genre.

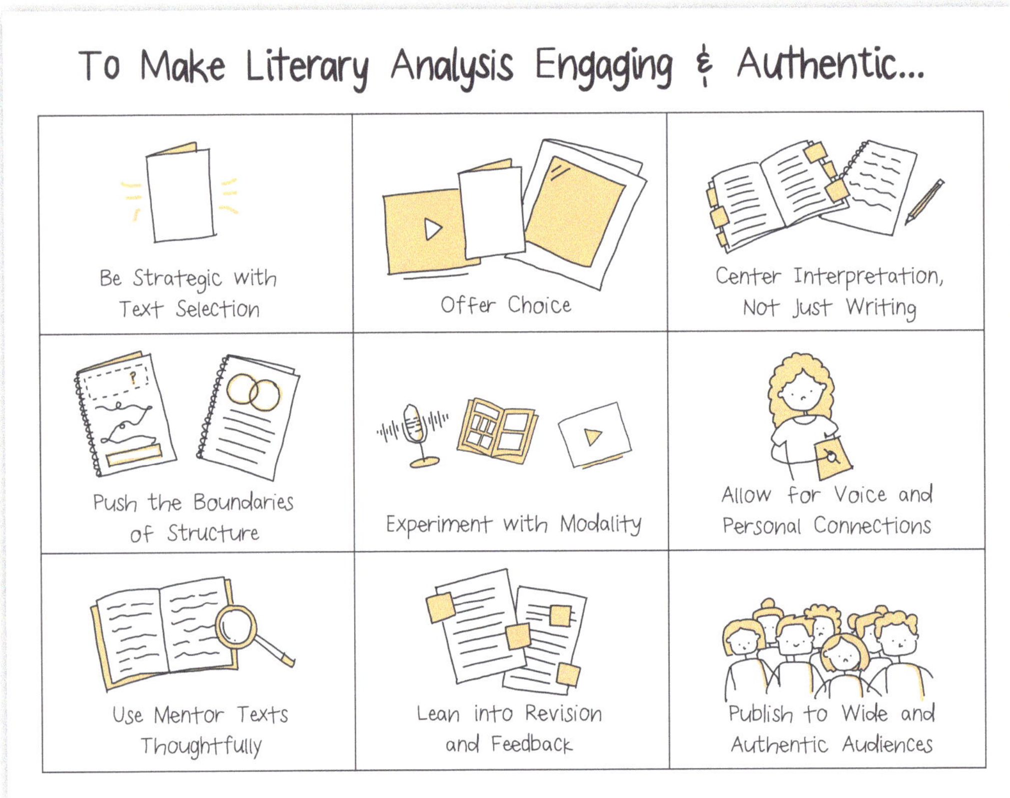

Be Strategic with Text Selection

One way to make literary analysis more engaging and accessible is to give students some choice over what text to write about. Writers will write better when they can choose a text they connect with. Anytime you can offer a menu such as a novel and a few short stories, or two plays with similar themes, it will open choice, and choice increases engagement, which increases insight. Maybe it's a book students have just read in a book club, or a book they've selected themselves.

Of course, it can be powerful for a whole class to write on the same text, for the shared experience. In these instances, if students aren't going to have their choice of text, it's important to give them agency in *how* and *what* they write about the text. Coley remembers her tenth graders writing an essay on *The Great Gatsby* and one student choosing to write about how reading the book ruined her summer. It was a powerful essay. The choice is what made it so.

Know that if a text is challenging for students, it will be harder for them to craft a deep analysis. Often the opposite is the case for easier texts, as long as they have some depth. Armed with this information, you can decide what your goals are. Do you want students to analyze a challenging text? A specific text? Or are your goals more about them working on their writing and analytical skills? All are worthy endeavors, but staying centered on your purpose can help you approach which texts to offer students more mindfully.

We also use the word *text*, and not *book*, purposefully. Analytical writing can happen about any type of text. Kids can analyze the TV show *White Lotus* or a children's book they are now reconsidering, such as *The Giving Tree*, or even Taylor Swift's newest album. Visit our website for student examples of these types of analytical essays. For a deeper dive, we highly recommend Allison Marchetti and Rebekah O'Dell's (2018) professional text *Beyond Literary Analysis*, which celebrates a kind of poststructural approach to text that is inclusive of multiple modalities.

In this book, we model with *The Poet X* by Elizabeth Acevedo (2020), a beautiful novel in verse about a teenage girl trying to find herself and her voice. You might decide to read this novel with your students, or choose another contemporary text. When you invite students to read the geniuses who are writing for teens now, they are more likely to fall in love with reading.

When we teach literary analysis units, we find it's actually easier to model with a text kids are familiar with but that is different from the one they are writing about. This way, they can transfer the strategies you teach them but not the work of your actual thinking. You'll see, as well, that at times we model with a video, which both widens the notion of what we mean by "text" and teaches students to deepen their skills at multimodal analysis.

Explicitly Teach Interpretation

You'll notice that the first three chapters of this book are really about interpretation. Kids can write beautiful analysis when they have a lot to say, and we've found that what they often need are fewer writing lessons and more lessons on interpretation. Part of interpretation is also annotating. Any form of writing about reading deepens readers' engagement with a text (Graham and Hebert 2010).

Writing about reading helps kids notice and track patterns they are interested in or begin to ask questions or start to notice language. Set them up with sticky notes, with colored gel pens, with Moleskine notebooks—make writing about reading integral to the reading process, so that they are tracking several ideas as they read, exploring what might play out well in a discussion or an essay. Then, by the time students are ready to craft a literary analysis, whether it be a podcast, an infographic, or an essay, they've done a great deal of work with the text at hand. They likely have annotations, notebook entries, and reading responses. They've talked about the text during conferences with you and with their peers during a book club or Socratic seminar. This reading work is the key to deep, analytical thinking. It's also writing about reading that will make it less likely that students use AI irresponsibly to write an entire essay: they will have notes and thinking when it comes time to draft. When they realize they've done the heavy lifting—the thinking work—already, they'll realize it's not necessary to outsource to AI.

If you're planning on giving students a prompt, it's best, when possible, to give them access to the prompt early, so they have it in mind as they read. This way, they can start doing more pointed preparation to get ready for this essay. Better yet, ditch the prompt entirely and let students know they'll have to write about what resonated most, or the element they find most interesting. Giving students this frame means they'll read knowing their job is to develop interpretations.

Embrace Authenticity

Another way to think about angling this work toward brilliance is to be unafraid to be innovative and intimate even in this oh-so-academic genre. Teens are flexible. They are good at shifting register. They can write an analysis that has a highly personal or poetic tone, learn a lot about structure and voice and analysis, and then they can do it again in a more distant third-person tone to respond to a prompt when needed. They shift register *all the time* in their complicated lives. This genre is also surprisingly inclusive and flexible when you begin to study published mentors, especially in terms of structure, modality, and voice.

Push the Boundaries of Structure

In this book you'll find lessons that push the boundaries of what an academic literary analysis can be. To engage (and challenge) your students, you could try experimenting with structure. If you traditionally teach "five-paragraph essays," consider how you might outgrow paragraphs and think instead about parts. Then you can move on to investigating the structural choices published authors make in this genre. Can this genre embrace one-sentence paragraphs? Does the thesis need to be the last sentence of the introduction paragraph, or could the essay lead the reader on a journey of thought? For this, we look to mentor texts, the ones that published authors and academics write. With these small shifts, kids can take ownership and make more intentional and authentic decisions within this genre.

While breaking free from the typical essay structure can feel uncomfortable, we lean on the words of John Warner, author of *Why They Can't Write* (2020) and *More Than Words* (2025). He reminds us that "it's very rare to find a five-paragraph essay in the wild; one only finds them in the captivity of the classroom" (2020, 29). The word *captivity* is deliberate, painting a picture of kids in rows of desks all writing the same essay, confined from the capacity of their own minds. We certainly want to teach past compliance. We want a messy classroom where kids are exploring and experimenting and failing and then trying again. Warner's plea, then, is for us to let go of the "fill in the blanks" format and trust our students to go beyond that, even before they have learned all the "rules."

If all of this talk of breaking boundaries makes you anxious, and in the back of your mind a voice is whispering ominously, "What about their state or national assessment?," know that there are ways to raise the level of essays and still adhere to structures you feel comfortable with, and you'll find plenty of those lessons here.

Experiment with Modality

Similar to structure, experimenting with modality can ignite your students as writers. Thinking about modality really means thinking about audience and purpose—and a lot of students will be more excited to dive into this work if they know they are filming video essays in defense of banned literature, or contributing to a website of book recommendations, or engaging in a panel talk around a novel, film, or series. Analysis is analysis is analysis, regardless of how it's being delivered. So, instead of thinking of this work as limited to traditional "for school" literary essays, consider expanding how kids might write or share their brilliant ideas.

For example, this work could be shared as a podcast, with one student interviewing experts, pulling in evidence, and sharing new ideas, or it could be more of a talk show style, where two or three students dish about the text they're reading, analyze the characters, discuss the themes, and connect to other texts. There are so many podcasts like this, dedicated to analyzing each *Survivor* episode or Beyonce's new album, that it shouldn't be hard to find mentors. In fact, it's more likely that your students will host one of these podcasts than it is that they'll write and publish traditional literary criticism.

Students might also choose to write an article, or host a panel, or create a talk for your school board. Don't feel like you have to be an expert at all of these modalities. If students are pulled to make a video essay, they likely have the tools or know someone who does!

Across this book you'll find lessons that can be adapted for different modalities but not lessons that speak to creating in these modalities directly. It was just too big a scope for this book. Just know that you can take a lesson on structure or analysis and apply it to any modality students might be experimenting with. You can find mentors and resources on our website, www.hs-guidetoteaching.org.

Encourage Voice

The voice students bring to a literary essay wholly depends on their intended audience and how much they relate to the book they are reading. But, often in literary analysis, the intended audience is the teacher, and the kids have no choice over the text. In Chapter 1, we make a case for giving students choice (even if it is limited, mitigated choice) over what they write about, and in Chapter 7, we make a case for inviting students to choose an audience for their literary essay, whether it be writing to the author of the book, their peers, someone who dislikes the book, or a specific person in the writer's life. Focusing on purpose will lead to conversations about tone and language and craft—all important parts of writing that are sometimes left out of the equation when it comes to the perceived formal nature of literary essays.

Although the default in formal writing is often to avoid using "I," helping students develop their voices means guiding them to understand when and how to intentionally weave personal stories into this genre. There are a lot of ways to develop voice, and we focus on these strategies in every chapter of this book. And know that at the university level, writing and English professors strive to reinsert "I," to hear the writer in all of their writing. We nudge you again toward John Warner's work (2020) for a spirited plea for high school English to loosen the perceived boundaries of academic writing.

It's easy to push back on this idea, arguing that the personal has no place in literary analysis. Yet to truly engage with a text, students need something to say—something they care about, a question they're wrestling with, or a perspective only they can bring. In that way, literary essays are inherently connected to the self. It can be powerful, even necessary, for analytical writing to begin with an anecdote, draw a parallel between the student's life and a character's, or reflect on emotional or intellectual reactions to the book. Take a look at the start of *So We Read On* (2014), Maureen Corrigan's deep dive into the complexity and emotional power of *The Great Gatsby*:

> Forget *great. The Great Gatsby* is the *greatest*—even if you didn't think so when you had to read it in high school. I didn't think so back then either. As a high-school senior, I couldn't "identify" with the bland Nick or enigmatic Gatsby; nor could I connect with golden girl Daisy, who acted too much like the mean girls in the cafeteria, flaunting their shining hair and their knowingness. I thought *The Great Gatsby* was a boring novel about rich people. (3)

We know this type of writing, the engaging and personal, is part of literary essay and can be taught to students. It may be a new challenge—your writers are used to the "school rules" of literary essay—but with explicit instruction, modeling, and access to mentor texts like this one, students will welcome bringing in their voices. In *Unearthing Joy*, Gholdy Muhammad discusses how we should focus on the connection between joy and learning, not the complicated relationship between test prep or graduation (2023). Teaching students the joy of writing to discover why they love a book, what they think, and in what varied ways they can express their thinking, is going to be so much more joyful for you, as well.

Mapping Your Curriculum

This guide offers more than fifty flexible lessons, giving you plenty of choice as you plan to teach literary analysis. You might select a few favorite lessons to enhance your existing unit, or use this resource as a foundation, picking several lessons from each chapter to create an entirely new unit. These lessons aren't intended to be taught in a strict sequence; instead, they're intentionally designed to honor your agency as a teacher and make the art (and work) of planning a little lighter.

Most lessons in this guide follow a minilesson structure: a short, focused teaching point followed by immediate student practice. Lessons typically begin with a quick demonstration or model, transition into guided practice, and then move students toward independent work. Keeping instruction brief and targeted maximizes student engagement, helps them retain key skills, and provides ample time for authentic writing practice. Lessons help students build momentum and confidence as writers, allowing them to quickly apply new strategies into their own writing.

The chapters in this book are set up so that you can make choices—choices about how long your unit will be and choices about which lessons you might teach the whole class and which you might convert into *micro lessons*, *small-group conversations*, or *independent work in stations*. Converting lessons into shorter formats allows you to condense your unit when you are pressed for time and support students with differentiated instruction.

- *Whole-class lessons* introduce or remind students of a strategy that will make them more powerful. We reserve whole-class lessons for strategies we're sure will benefit all, or almost all, of our writers, though during their independent writing time, students may not always be practicing only this strategy.
- *Micro lessons* make for fast-paced guided practice. When we think of micro lessons, we picture a single period where we might teach a short lesson, give students a chance to try it, teach another, give them a chance to try that, and so on.
- *Small groups* allow for targeted instruction for only a few students, while others are working.
- *Stations* are a kind of midway point between these, where you set up workspaces around the room, so students can choose to study and try certain strategies. To convert any of these lessons into stations you can either a) invite students to read the lesson and play the role of both teacher and student or b) convert the lesson into a short handout with steps.

Literary Analysis Curricular Timelines: Options for Planning Your Unit

7 Weeks

Day	Topic
1	Developing Interpretations
2	
3	
4	
5	Crafting Artful Theses
6	
7	
8	
9	
10	
11	Collecting & Organizing Evidence
12	
13	
14	
15	
16	
17	Writing with Structure
18	
19	
20	
21	Honing & Integrating Evidence
22	
23	
24	
25	Bolstering Analysis, Developing Commentary
26	
27	
28	
29	
30	
31	Craft & Conventions
32	
33	
34	

4 Weeks

Day	Topic
1	Developing Interpretations
2	
3	
4	Artful Theses
5	
6	
7	Collecting Evidence
8	
9	
10	
11	Structure
12	
13	Integrating Evidence
14	
15	
16	Bolstering Analysis
17	
18	
19	Craft & Conventions
20	

2 Weeks

Day	Topic
1	Interpretations
2	Theses
3	Collecting Evidence
4	Structure
5	Integrating Evidence
6	
7	Analysis
8	
9	Craft & Conventions
10	

You'll make different choices about how many of these lessons you'll teach, depending first on whether you are using these lessons as a curriculum or you are inserting them into your existing curriculum, and, second, how many days and weeks you have to teach literary analysis. On our website (www.hs-guidetoteaching.org) we share some detailed calendars for planning literary analysis using these lessons, depending on your time frame.

Teaching and Coaching Inside a Workshop Structure

Teaching inside a workshop structure allows you to demonstrate a strategy or launch an inquiry and then set up students to write for the rest of the period, during which time you can confer with writers or teach small groups. There is never enough time for either of the latter in secondary schedules, and so you'll see we've made some suggestions for days when you don't teach a lesson and instead teach micro lessons or small groups. It's also fine to have a day when you don't teach a lesson, and your kids work on their writing while you confer. Those kinds of days work best after you've done some mentor text work or taught a few lessons that writers can capitalize on, so students have enough to do.

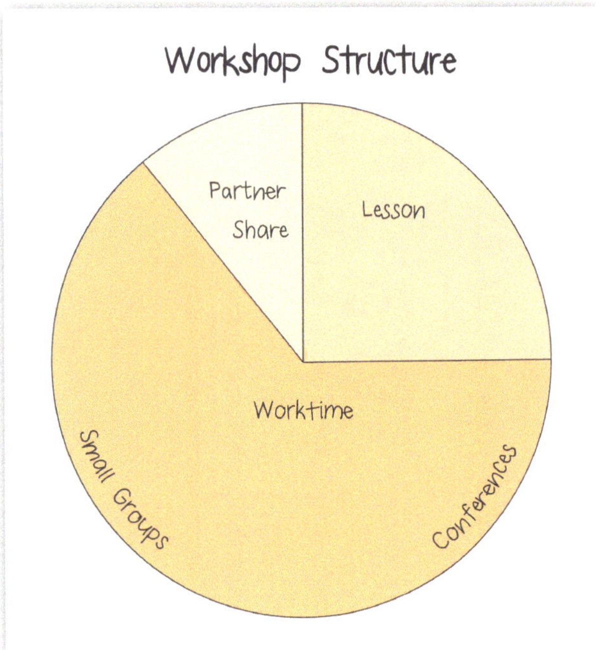

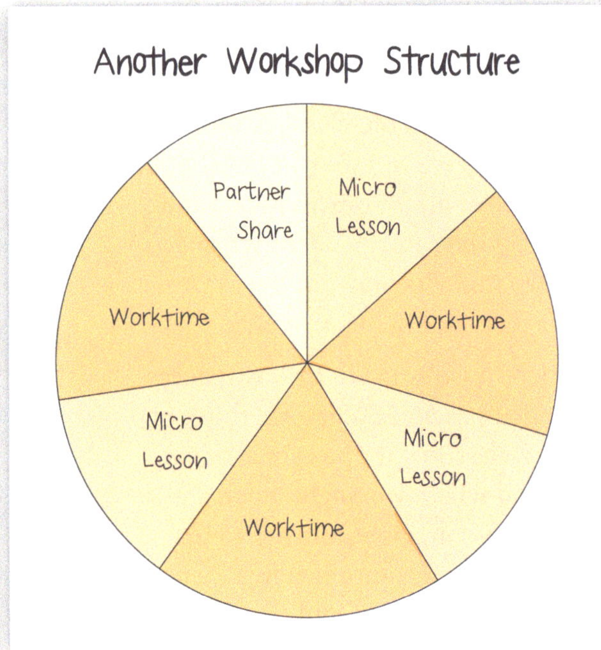

Independent Work Time

One of the goals of writing workshop structure (where you demonstrate or lead an inquiry, then kids have time to work on their writing) is for kids to have time to work on their writing in class, in your presence. With AI becoming so accessible as a writing coach, and if kids are unwise, a pinch-hitter writer, it's all the more important for them to do some drafting in your presence, so you get an idea of how they write on their own. It's also more democratic for all kids to have some time to write in school, where you know they have a quiet environment that is relatively free of distractions (there will also be young writers who write much better outside of school, not because they use AI but because they escape the tumultuous social pressures of high school classrooms).

When we are in a writing unit, spending several days working on writing, we give kids time to write in class, so they build some energy for their writing, and so we can observe and talk to them while they are in the midst of writing.

Conferring and Coaching

Another goal of workshop structure is that while kids work, you have a little time to talk to them about their writing. We tend to structure that time in two ways. Sometimes we confer: We pull up alongside one writer, or a partnership, and we talk to them about their work, listening, giving advice, offering tools. Other times we plan small groups, either as seminars, which any writer can join, or as targeted instruction to support certain writers. In *Write Beside Them* (2008), master teacher Penny Kittle described her sense of joy when she knew she would be teaching writing—that her day would be spent listening to and talking to kids about their writing. Writing workshop is structured to help you have more time to achieve that kind of intimacy.

You'll find, inside each lesson, prompts for conferring, ones that we think will help you coach individual writers or partnerships. They reflect our experience with the predictable ways that some students might benefit from a little support, while others may be ready to extend the work of the lesson. For example, here you see suggestions for supporting kids once you've taught a lesson on setting up quotes:

PROMPTS TO COACH STUDENTS AND PARTNERSHIPS

Set the scene for your audience. Even if they haven't read the book, they should be able to understand. What details do you need to include so the audience can picture this moment in the text?

Watch me read and give feedback on your partner's writing. Pay attention to how I give feedback on the details they include, and how they connect this moment to other parts in the text.

Now that you've introduced one moment, how can you explain other parts of the text in relation to this? For example, does your next piece of evidence occur shortly after this, much later, or before?

Chart and Tools

This book is full of charts, all available for download on our website. Grant Wiggins, who published many articles and books about the challenges of transfer, often referred to charts and tools as cueing systems for transfer (2008, 2024). Kids need reminders of their learning that they can refer to as they work.

The charts and tools included here are intended for you to share with students, post, remake alongside students during lessons, or use during conferences and small groups. If you share them with kids, pass them off as yours. If you share them with colleagues, we'd appreciate it if you'd reference Lauren; while we collaborated on content, Lauren is the artist who created these jewels.

One of the things we miss most from elementary classrooms (besides the beautiful bulletin boards and robust classroom libraries) are the writing centers that kids can freely use. They house charts and sticky notes and pens and mentor texts for kids to grab as they brainstorm, draft, and revise. Because elementary teachers don't share classrooms, they can create robust writing environments. Chances are you do share a room, or you move around, or you work from a cart. We've taught in all of those modes, and it is annoying. Still, look at the classrooms where you do teach, and consider setting up a writing center, knowing that kids can then grab charts as needed. Or you might upload these charts to Padlet or other digital site, as a reference for your students.

Setting Up Writing Partnerships

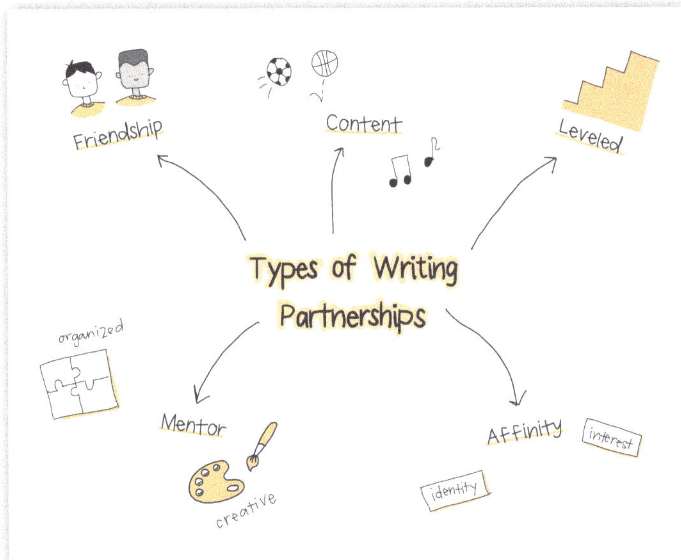

In literary essay, it's important to get students into stable writing partnerships. Teens are going to do braver, better work in the company of peers who they trust. Tyrone Howard often calls these partnerships *learning alliances*, which captures the sense of students as interdependent beings, joined in a learning coalition (Howard, Milner-McCall, Howard 2020). In general, we love our students to have some voice over their partnerships, while we also recognize the need to do some social engineering. You might have kids fill out a form indicating who they'd like to be partnered with, then do some negotiating and reworking, or they could partner with whomever they sit near (their own form of social engineering), or you can negotiate with students. You can study these partnerships and adjust them so they are supportive and productive.

It will be important that you don't simply use these partners to "peer-review" each other's work. Instead, you want them to be more of a thought partner throughout the process, talking through ideas, asking questions, reading sections their partner wants feedback on. As you might imagine, kids won't do this naturally, so you'll have to set things up, model, and coach partners toward this work. In our experience, it's usually best if kids hold their own writing, read together, and talk aloud. It matters, too, that writers are in a stable partnership across the whole writing process, so that each day, their writing partner is already caught up on their topic, where they are in their draft, and so on.

Your Role as a Mentor Writer

Whenever you enter a writing unit of study, we recommend experimenting with the genre yourself first. It always helps to revisit your process as a writer, track the decisions you made, name what was challenging. This is also a great time to break free from the typical literary essay structure and try your hand at something a little different. Whatever you choose to write, show the product and, more importantly, your process to students. Showing your writing process is like opening the hood of a car and showing how the engine works and what makes the car run.

When you show your writing to students, you have a few choices. You could show a small chunk of it and explain your process as a writer. You might do an inquiry and invite students to notice and name the moves and decisions you made as a writer. Above all, it's best to write in front of students in real time. This doesn't necessarily mean you have to "wing" it. Often, we know what we're going to write, or how we're going to revise, but we show the thinking in real time. Writing in front of your students allows them to see you grapple with the same processes they will encounter. Sometimes when we show young writers only our polished pieces, things can seem unattainable. You can also invite kids to write along with you, asking them to try out context for a piece of evidence or asking them to brainstorm different ways to word your thesis statement.

Your students would love to see your writing, but sometimes we are pressed as teachers and would prefer to borrow someone's demonstration text. You can, of course, share any of the essays that we share here. You might simply say, "One of my friends, Coley, wrote …" or "One of my colleagues, Mary, wrote this essay," or "A writer I know, Lauren, for example." Or pass one of our essays off as yours. We're fine with that! Borrow away—everything we wrote here, we wrote for you and your students.

Inculcating Writing Process and Mentor Text Immersion

One of the most important aspects of this work is that your writers internalize a writing process that they can bring to every task and every genre. Ultimately, because they have you as a writing teacher, your students will be confident tackling any writing task, knowing that they will spend a little time on each stage: researching/collecting; planning and drafting; revising/raising the level; publishing. In these two visuals, you can see a flow chart of the writing process overall, and one writer's personal writing process.

We want students to grow familiar with the components of this process but also recognize that their writing process is their own and might deviate slightly from the recursive cycle of this one. Coaching students to figure out how they like to develop ideas or when in the process they like to

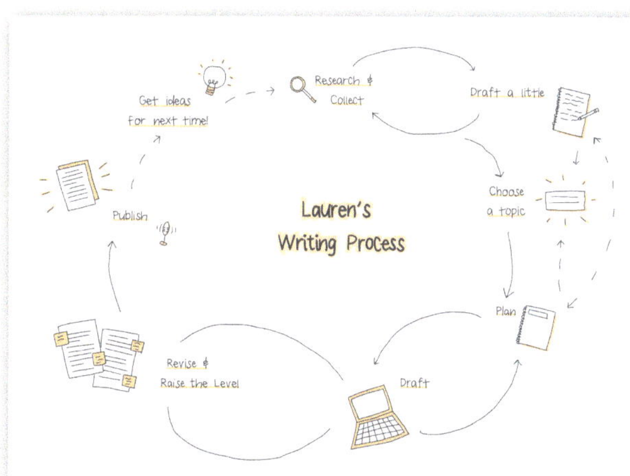

begin revision is work that transcends the genre and is ultimately helpful to writers in everything from crafting literary essays to drafting important emails. We want writers to own their process and continue to refine it.

When we talk to students about the writing process, we always emphasize the importance of revision. The problem, though, is that they usually don't share our enthusiasm for this part of the writing process. If this is what we value, we can't leave it up to students to engage in this process intrinsically. The conditions we put in place are what set students up for revision work. To get students to revise their writing, beyond just editing, it's important that we move at a quick pace, encouraging students to get a draft down in one or two sittings. If we move paragraph by paragraph or part by part when we ask them to go back and revise, they'll tweak a few commas and be done with it. If we ask them to draft at a quicker pace, it means their initial quote integration and analysis might be kind of limited. That's good! Then we can offer them tools to radically raise the level of their work.

We want students to come out of their drafts like you'd come up for air after swimming laps in a pool. It often gives them renewed energy, more clarity, and a willingness to make changes. We've also found it helpful for students to have a paper notebook, large sticky note, or a document other than their draft, where they can experiment with revision. They'll tend to be more innovative, and write more, outside of their draft, than when they simply tinker inside of it.

Inside of this work you'll want to emphasize how writers turn to mentor texts across the writing process, so that your writers, no matter what genre they are working on and where they are in the writing process, know they can seek mentor texts to help them raise the level of their writing. In this book you'll see that we include mentor text lessons to help students get to know the genre and to study how writers structure their writing, what kind of evidence writers use in their essays, and how they weave analytical thinking.

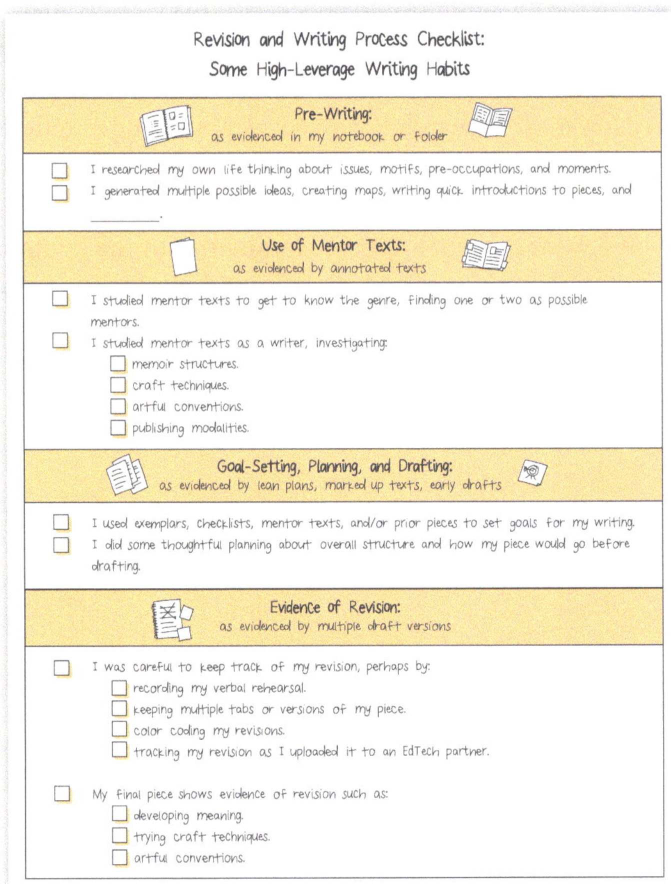
Revision and Writing Process Checklist:
Some High-Leverage Writing Habits

Pre-Writing: as evidenced in my notebook or folder

- ☐ I researched my own life thinking about issues, motifs, pre-occupations, and moments.
- ☐ I generated multiple possible ideas, creating maps, writing quick introductions to pieces, and ________.

Use of Mentor Texts: as evidenced by annotated texts

- ☐ I studied mentor texts to get to know the genre, finding one or two as possible mentors.
- ☐ I studied mentor texts as a writer, investigating:
  - ☐ memoir structures.
  - ☐ craft techniques.
  - ☐ artful conventions.
  - ☐ publishing modalities.

Goal-Setting, Planning, and Drafting: as evidenced by lean plans, marked up texts, early drafts

- ☐ I used exemplars, checklists, mentor texts, and/or prior pieces to set goals for my writing.
- ☐ I did some thoughtful planning about overall structure and how my piece would go before drafting.

Evidence of Revision: as evidenced by multiple draft versions

- ☐ I was careful to keep track of my revision, perhaps by:
  - ☐ recording my verbal rehearsal.
  - ☐ keeping multiple tabs or versions of my piece.
  - ☐ color coding my revisions.
  - ☐ tracking my revision as I uploaded it to an EdTech partner.
- ☐ My final piece shows evidence of revision such as:
  - ☐ developing meaning.
  - ☐ trying craft techniques.
  - ☐ artful conventions.

With literary analysis, we suggest showing students examples of all different types of literary analysis, including student exemplars from previous years, published mentor texts from sources like the *New York Times* and NPR, academic literary criticism, and even mentor texts in other modalities, like podcasts, video essays, and books. This can feel a little outside the box if you're used to showing

Wise Use of Technology & AI:
as evidenced through self-reporting, references and/or chat records

- ☐ I used appropriate technology to publish my piece.
- ☐ If I used an AI partner, I may have trained my partner by:
  - ☐ explaining my goals and content.
  - ☐ uploading mentor texts.
  - ☐ uploading other tools such as checklists or rubrics.
  - ☐ insisting that my partner explain its suggestions.
  - ☐ asking my partner not to draft for me.
- ☐ If I used AI, I referenced it, for instance:
  - ☐ in a footnote.
  - ☐ in an endnote.
  - ☐ in acknowledgements.

Reflection
as evidenced by freewriting, conversation, or process pages

- ☐ I reflected on my identity and what I learned about myself through writing.
- ☐ I reflected on my progress as a writer.

Access the full Writing Process Checklist at hs-guidetoteaching.org.

students traditional essays as samples, but often all these different analytical works have the components we care about most, the ones linked to our state standards: thesis statements, evidence, commentary, structural choices, background information, and craft. Our website houses tons of sample mentor texts for you to use with your young writers.

Turning to Mentor Texts Across the Writing Process

Researching & Collecting	Planning & Drafting	Revising & Raising the Level	Getting Ready to Publish
• Getting to know the genre • Gathering ideas for content • Envisioning ways to publish	• Imagining possible structures • Deconstructing 'parts' inside this genre • Studying beginnings and endings	• Finding ideas for craft techniques • Mirror writing at the sentence level • Studying authorial voice and how it is achieved	• Revisiting conventions • Envisioning modalities • Considering specific audiences

Access a collection of mentor literary analysis at hs-guidetoteaching.org.

It's also important to collect mentor texts of unfinished work: reading notebook entries, revised thesis statements, outlines, categorized lists of evidence, rough drafts, and so on. Our goal in this book is to showcase these kinds of artifacts, so you can see what student work looked like during each of these lessons. Across the lessons, we showcase the work of several young writers, which will likely resonate with your students. If you want to try this yourself, you could ask a few students to document and reflect on their process across a whole unit. It is powerful for the teen writer and a powerful teaching tool.

Becoming Adept and Ethical with AI

You'll see that we include several lessons on wise ways to turn to AI. OpenAI, and most EdTech AI, can give remarkably expert, insightful feedback to writers, in a kind and affirming tone that high school writers need. And young writers need to learn why *not* to turn the work of drafting over to AI—for ethical reasons and also so that AI trains them to become more powerful writers, rather than replacing them. In these lessons, we emphasize how to train an AI partner: how to give it a lot of information, so that its feedback and suggestions are personalized to that writer. We also continually teach students how to reference AI support, in a footnote, an endnote, or an acknowledgment.

We believe we have an ethical responsibility to teach students about the ways writers use AI, in learning environments that allow students to play in the AI sandbox. For the lessons in this book, you can set up EdTech AI chat partners, such as MagicSchool or Flint, or you can teach students how adults use OpenAI, depending on your school policies. Your students will benefit from an AI partner as readers, as well, as they develop their interpretations. If you want to think more deeply about the future role of AI and writing, we encourage you to read *AI-Enhanced Literacy: Practical Steps for Deepening Reading and Writing Instruction* (Ehrenworth and Seyfried 2025) and *Co-Intelligence: Living and Working with AI* (Mollick 2024). We do recommend that students have EdTech AI partners, as otherwise they will seek Open AI, and you won't be able to advise them or shape those interactions.

Supporting and Celebrating Multilingual Students and Newcomers

We teach and coach in bilingual classrooms, in classrooms full of newcomers, in international classrooms where every student is multilingual, in classrooms where the teacher is monolingual and the students have a dozen languages between them, in classrooms where only a few students are learning English, or the classroom language, and everything in between. What we know for sure is that we want to create communities of care and belonging, and we want to institute structures that will both reveal and extend students' linguistic competencies.

In their gorgeous book, *En Comunidad: Lessons for Centering the Voices and Experiences of Bilingual Latinx Students,* Carla España and Luz Yadira Herrera describe a primary pedagogical goal when teaching multilingual students: "to embrace their full linguistic repertoire" (2020, xvii). For us, part of that work lies in making strategic decisions about curriculum and texts—choosing texts that mirror the identities and experiences of our students, making sure there is rich representation in the mentor texts and authors students encounter. But there is more. We also try to focus on our interactions and our structures. In our interactions, we follow Ofelia García's advice to embrace translanguaging as a) a natural part of linguistic development and b) a way for students to express themselves with more nuance (García and Kleyn 2016; García et al. 2017).

We add in using AI, a newer development, as a tool for students to translate text. With this tool, we can read a memoir written by a student who has come from Ukraine yesterday, and we can respond as well, crossing language differences to know our students and communicate with them and their families more deeply. Our multilingual students, even as they learn a new language, can express their thinking in the language they are most powerful in, so their learning continues at multiple levels and they show their full competencies (Ehrenworth and Seyfried 2025).

Literary Analysis in a New Paradigm

Literary analysis is a genre of writing that students spend a lot of time learning, from elementary school all the way until senior year of high school. Because of this, kids usually take one of two paths. Either they get really good at the "formula" for this type of writing, so they can write one of these essays without much thought. Or, alternatively, students find the genre slow and painful, each sentence feeling like an entire essay. We don't love either of these realities for you or for writers. Instead, we want our students to fall in love with words and stories and writing the same way we have. We want them to be part of book clubs and write down lines that haunt them in their notes app and write reviews on Goodreads. We want them to see the literary analysis as part of this love affair, as a way for their voice and their ideas to be heard.

Part I
Writing about Reading and Interpretation

Chapter One: Collecting Engaging Ideas

Finding ideas for what to write about is always the hardest part of the writing process, in any genre. For literary analysis, though, the process starts long before the blank writing page of the essay plan or draft—it starts with the annotating and jotting, the scribbling of arcane marginalia, the inserting of colored sticky notes, the overly copious underlining and highlighting that show a mind grappling with a story.

It also starts in those moments when, as you were reading, your heart shifted, when you were surprised or horrified or intrigued. Louise Rosenblatt (1994), in her gorgeous descriptions of transactional reading response, suggests that every time a reader feels a strong emotional response to the text, they should mark that moment, because something is happening in the text they should pay attention to. Stories that stir our emotions are the ones we want to talk about. To prepare for those talks, we'll want to gather our interpretations as we read, organizing them in a way that works for us, so we can return to them later.

All readers respond more to texts when they have some choice over what they read, and so we encourage you to foster choice, ideally by creating opportunities for students to read a few novels or short stories, so they can choose which ones they want to write about. Writers also write best about topics they know and understand and care about. We realize that sometimes the curriculum doesn't offer much choice—students may all be required to write about the same novel, for example. In such instances, it's all the more important that they have strategies for finding the *parts* of the story and the ideas that intrigue them, so when called to do so, they can write with voice and insight.

The first couple of lessons in this chapter teach students to read with tools (sticky notes, pens to annotate, etc.) at hand, so that they are not waiting until the end to trace ideas and explore language. We'll also teach students how to find the stories and characters they care about and ideas they'll find pleasure in exploring. Then we share several strategies for how readers can explore their lives, including issues they care about as they respond to a text, from identity maps to issue walls to emotional timelines. The strategies in these early lessons linger in the connections readers see in a text and often lead to intriguing ideas that are meaningful to the reader as well as significant in the text. Then we shift to more traditionally academic strategies for reading with critical lenses, lingering in narrative moments, and developing ideas through partner discussion—in this case, with an AI partner as a possibility. If you haven't yet created EdTech AI thought partners for your students (like SchoolAI or Flint, etc.), you'll find that these platforms can really support students in developing their thinking in a safe intellectual space.

You'll notice that, in most of the lessons that follow, students aren't working off a prompt. That's intentional. In a genre that tends to stifle, we want kids to have freedom to write in a way that's true to their voice and perspective, to find a topic that resonates with their identity, to write authentically and unapologetically. If you are used to prompts and aren't quite ready to let them go, try offering multiple prompt options or allowing students to develop their own. If you are looking for a certain kind of writing, based on theme or symbols, for example, try offering multiple pathways students might use to collect their thoughts for those kinds of work, rather than restricting student creativity with a prompt. Letting students develop their literary analyses without a prompt might be uncomfortable at first, for both you and your students, but doing so will often lead them to deeper and more interesting writing.

Figuring out what you want to say about a text you loved (or loathed) is a worthwhile endeavor. We usually find that most students need to explore at least three strategies to help them find ideas they care about. You can self-select ones included here that you find intriguing, or offer several across multiple micro-lessons and see which ones different writers respond to. The lessons in this chapter should feel fun and playful and expectant.

These lessons are really interpretation lessons. They lead students to jot and annotate, to consider ideas, and to reread the text. We do suggest you also invite students to freewrite for a few minutes each day as well, so they capture their emerging thinking, which might become an idea for their whole essay or part of whatever kind of writing work they're doing.

Lesson 1

The Magic of Annotating

STRATEGY

Research shows that any form of writing about reading increases understanding of a text. Literary analysts, then, begin with annotating. Ways to do this include flagging with small sticky notes to mark pages you want to return to, annotating in the margins and inside the text, and jotting thoughts in a notebook.

Visit hs-guidetoteaching.org to access a teacher chart.

USE THIS STRATEGY... to support students with the art of flagging, annotating, and jotting as integral to interpretation. You can also use this strategy to introduce a few different models or systems, so students can find a mode they'll sustain for themselves.

TEACH THE STRATEGY

- Suggest to students that any kind of writing about reading deepens readers' understanding and interpretation. Show students how, when readers are reading for a book club, practicing deep interpretation, or collecting ideas for a literary analysis, they often:
  - flag parts of the text they want to return to,
  - annotate, sometimes with systems and colored pens or with digital tools, to trace different characters, themes, techniques, or ideas,
  - keep a reading notebook where they can sketch, jot, and synthesize their ideas across many pages of text they've read.
- Briefly model different note-taking options on a familiar text, with a rapid, light demonstration that emphasizes purpose and choice. See the student artifacts for examples.
- Invite students to flag and annotate for a few minutes and then share their work with a partner.

- Suggest that students end by jotting down some new ideas they've developed from annotating across the text.

PROMPTS TO COACH STUDENTS AND PARTNERSHIPS

You'll have to figure out what system works best for you in terms of flagging. Some readers prefer small colored sticky notes. Some like to put a bookmark in their digital text. The main point is, flagging helps you mark pages you want to come back to, without slowing down your reading. You can also develop colors that indicate what you're flagging, like purple for character and green for themes.

At the start of the story, you don't really know yet what's important, so pause anytime your emotions are stirred up, then go back to the text and mark up what stirred you. It might be …

- *an interesting craft move or gorgeous language,*
- *a scene that reveals something new about a character,*
- *a twist that feels surprising or unexpected,*
- *some part of the story relates to something in your life.*

You have so many good ideas! Now that you've captured some notes, try some freewriting. What idea have you found that you could develop?

CLASSROOM ARTIFACTS

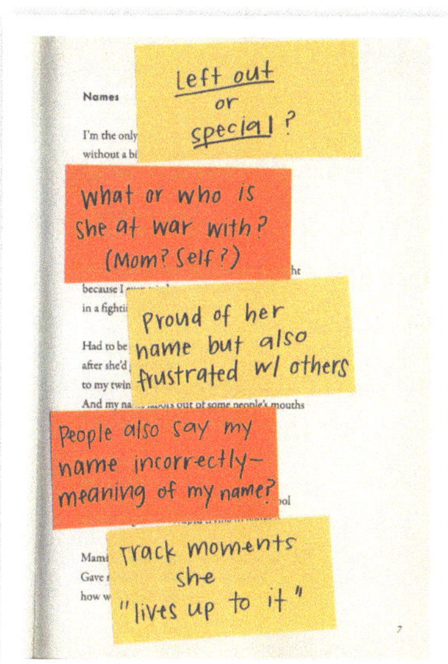

Idea collection in The Poet X.

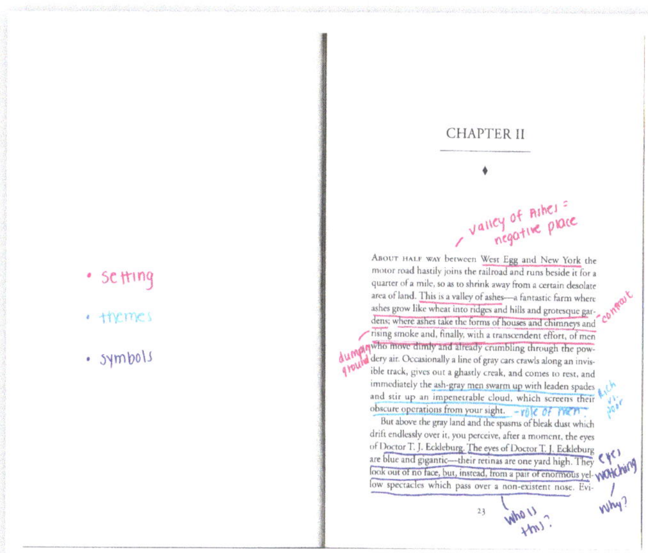

A color-coding system for annotations while reading The Great Gatsby.

Lesson 2

Identity Maps to Illuminate Connections

STRATEGY

When analyzing literature, writers know that they come to the book in front of them with the text of their own lives as well. Often, thinking about the intersection of their own stories with the story they are reading leads to interesting connections and ideas. One way to explore these intersections is to begin with an identity map, representing important facets of the writer's life.

Visit hs-guidetoteaching.org to access a sample identity map.

USE THIS STRATEGY... when you'd love your writers to feel more engaged, personally connected, and confident that their experiences are important to their interpretations.

TEACH THE STRATEGY

- Remind students of Louise Rosenblatt's famous work on transactional reading, where she argued that the reader's emotions as they read are a road map to moments in the story worth attending to.
- Show students your identity map, or, even better, create one in front of them. Be sure to lean into experiences from when you were in high school to parallel the age group you teach.
- Model how you can find ideas for a literary analysis hiding in your identity map by excavating an issue that feels related to events or tensions in the text.
- Jot your thinking, connecting the part of your identity map with the text.

When Lauren sketched an identity map in her class, she modeled how two issues came up in *The Poet X* and in her map. One is her mixed feelings about her teen experiences with a Christian youth group. Another is the tension in high school between wanting to be invisible and wanting to stand out.

- Invite students to sketch identity maps and discuss with a partner how they connect with the text they are reading.

PROMPTS TO COACH STUDENTS AND PARTNERSHIPS

You have so many parts of your identity that are complicated and fascinating. Let's think about a couple that are important to you. Now let's capture these!

Let's think about how your experiences give you unique perspectives on this story.

It can help to try explorative language with your partner. You can say to each other: "Maybe … what about … it could be …"

CLASSROOM ARTIFACTS

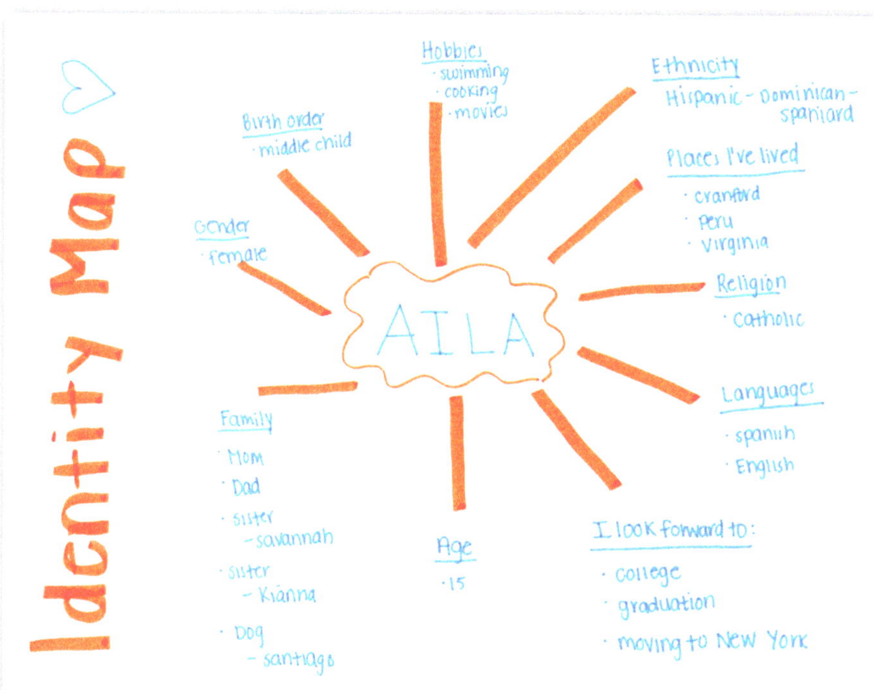

Student creates an identity map to represent her life and connect with text.

Lesson 2
(Continued)

Writers can use identity maps to develop ideas about text and free write.

Issues Hide in the Text and Our Lives

Lesson 3

STRATEGY

Writers investigate issues that are hiding in the text. One way to do this work is to create issue walls focusing on topics that are important in their lives and the texts they are reading. Issue walls are quick, easy-access displays created individually or together that collect issues that a community cares about. Often these lead to meaningful topics for literary analyses.

USE THIS STRATEGY... when your writers' young lives are probably full of common experiences and insights into some of the issues that arise in the stories they are reading. Turn to this strategy as well to support writers in building confidence that their perspectives matter.

TEACH THE STRATEGY

- Suggest that often there are issues hiding in texts that students might like to explore. Invite students to coauthor an issue wall that documents issues that have come up in what they're reading, what they're writing, and the lives they are living.
- Look over the issue wall, modeling thinking about how these issues intersect with issues in your own life.
- Show how you might select a topic you care about, and jot your thinking.

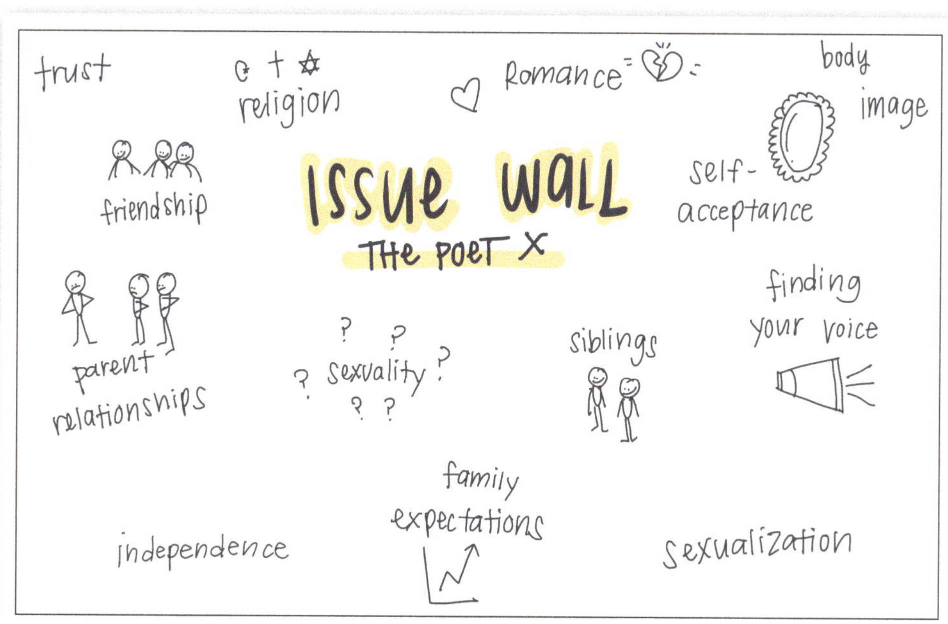

When Lauren created issue walls with writers, she discussed how navigating childhood friendships was an issue she faced in her own life. She also spoke about how, just like Xiomara, Lauren had a childhood friend whose family was quite religious. Their families' different values created tensions at times, but just like Xiomara and Caridad, Lauren and her childhood friend, Laura, always felt at home together. Lauren's conversation modeled how you can find intersections in the book in front of you and the text of your own life.

- Invite students to do this same work, of looking for issues in the text that also matter to them, as ones worth exploring across the text, and later, in an essay. Suggest that they do some freewriting about some of these issues.

PROMPTS TO COACH STUDENTS AND PARTNERSHIPS

What issues are resonating with you? How are you connecting with your character as they experience these conflicts?

I wonder if there are issues that secondary and tertiary characters are facing?

How do you want to track the moments or pages where those issues come up? You might try … or … Which feels like the best way for you?

CLASSROOM ARTIFACTS

Jealousy in *A Separate Peace* is complicated.

Gene acts like he and Finny are best friends and everything is fine but really he's jealous of Finny the whole time. It's like he can't even admit it to himself. Finny is so good at everything, like sports and talking to adults and even getting out of trouble. And Gene tries to pretend he doesn't care but you can tell he does. I think it's weird because he also admires Finny a lot. Sometimes you can be jealous of someone you actually like. Maybe that's why Gene gets so mad and shakes the tree and Finny falls. He doesn't even mean to, or maybe he kind of does but doesn't realize it?? I don't know. It's confusing.

Also it's not just about sports and being popular. I think Gene is jealous that Finny is just so confident and free. Gene thinks too much and Finny just does things. Gene is always worrying about grades and competition, but Finny doesn't even care about that stuff and still somehow wins all the time. I feel like Gene wants to be Finny, but since he can't, he just gets more and more jealous until he ruins everything. I guess jealousy makes you do things you don't even realize, like it sneaks up on you.

Charlie from *Perks of Being a Wallflower* is insecure. This is an issue across the book.

1. Charlie's fear that something is "wrong" with him
2. Charlie's insecurity about his friendships with Sam and Patrick. Hard time approaching them at first?!
3. Charlie's discomfort with romantic relationships- how to be a good boyfriend? Insecurity/doubt about not wanting to be with her.
4. Charlie's insecurity about his own value- feels like a burden to his family

Questions:

- Where does this come from?
  - Does this stem from his family?
  - His traumatic past?
- What steps does he take toward confidence?
  - Who helps him get there?

Writers try out different ways to freewrite, using the issue wall as inspiration for their ideas.

Timelines Spur Thinking

Lesson 4

STRATEGY

Writers try to visualize connections, trace development, and generate ideas as they revisit a text they want to write about. One way they explore this work is to create timelines around topics from the text that include important moments and quotes.

USE THIS STRATEGY... when writers are considering ideas that develop across a text, such as character change, themes or motifs that develop across a narrative, or literary techniques that are significant in several scenes.

TEACH THE STRATEGY

- Suggest to students that it's always interesting to think across a text, and that sometimes jotting timelines helps you create connections. As a class, share possible topics from the text for which students might organize a timeline.
- Choose one of the topics you discussed as a class. With students' help, make a brief timeline of this topic as it comes up in the book. Summarize important moments, use short quotes/text evidence, and include page numbers.

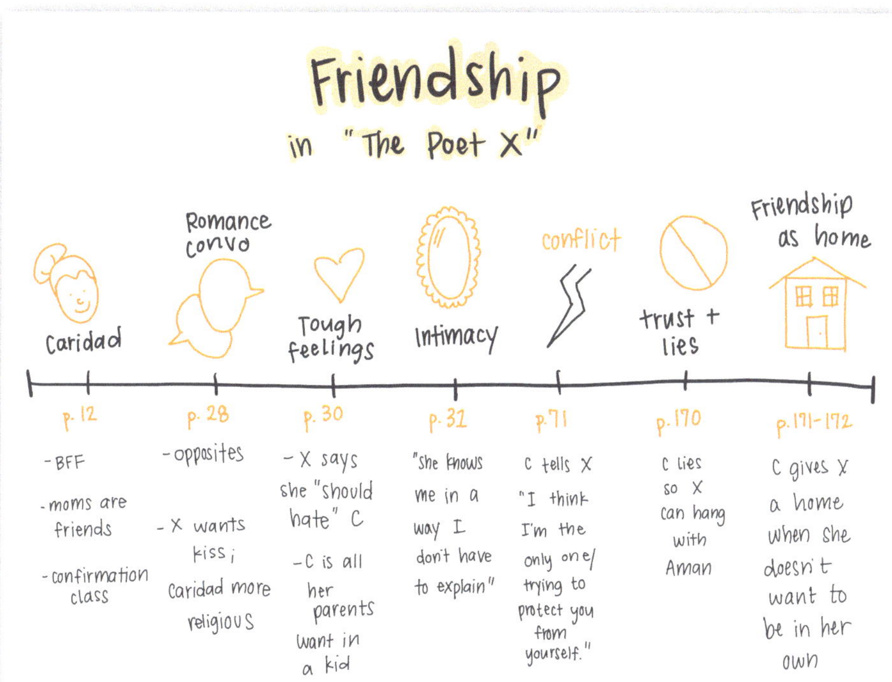

Lesson 4 (Continued)

When Mary taught this lesson, she first invited students to share ideas and possible topics from *The Poet X*. These included topics like religion, friendship, writing, relationships, sexuality, and beauty, as well as more specific ideas like Xiomara's sense of secrecy or the complications of her relationship with her mother's protectiveness, modeled with the topic of friendship. She invited students to help her mine the text to find key moments in the text related to Caridad's and Xiomara's friendship.

- Suggest that students try this work out with their own novels and ideas, choosing a couple to timeline, and then to talk to a partner about. You might invite students to work in groups on chart paper, or they can work individually, on paper or digitally.
- End by having students do some freewriting about new thinking they've come to as they thought about an idea across the narrative they are studying.

PROMPTS TO COACH STUDENTS AND PARTNERSHIPS

Including page numbers will help you more easily find these moments again later!

Brilliant work. You're ready to think about the emotions of the character during each of these moments. When does her emotional state change? Stay the same?

Now that you've created a timeline, consider what ideas come out of it. How does this part connect to the big ideas in the text? How do these two moments connect?

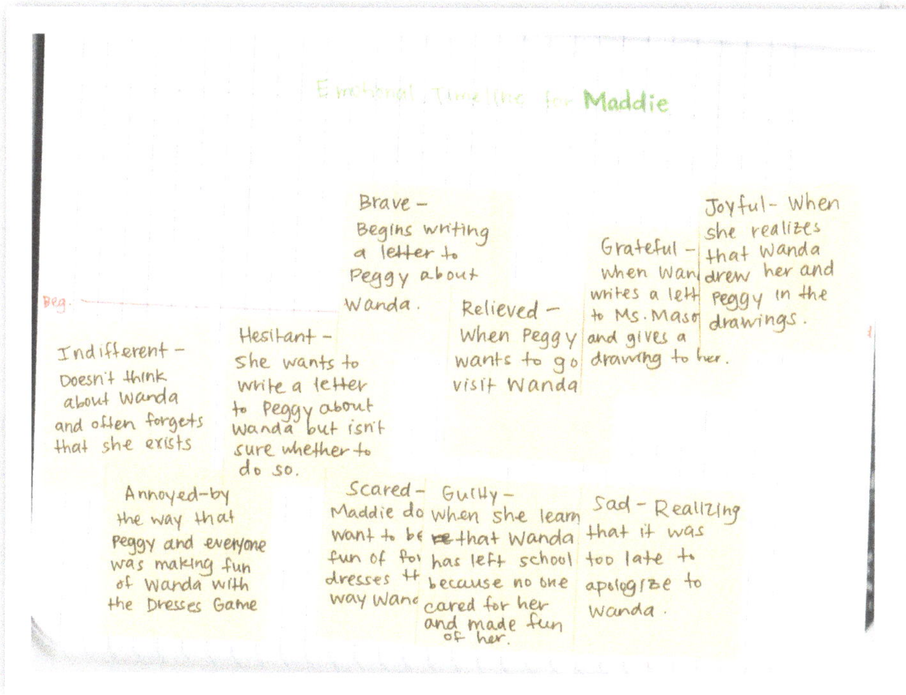

The writer creates timeline focused on emotion in A Hundred Dresses.

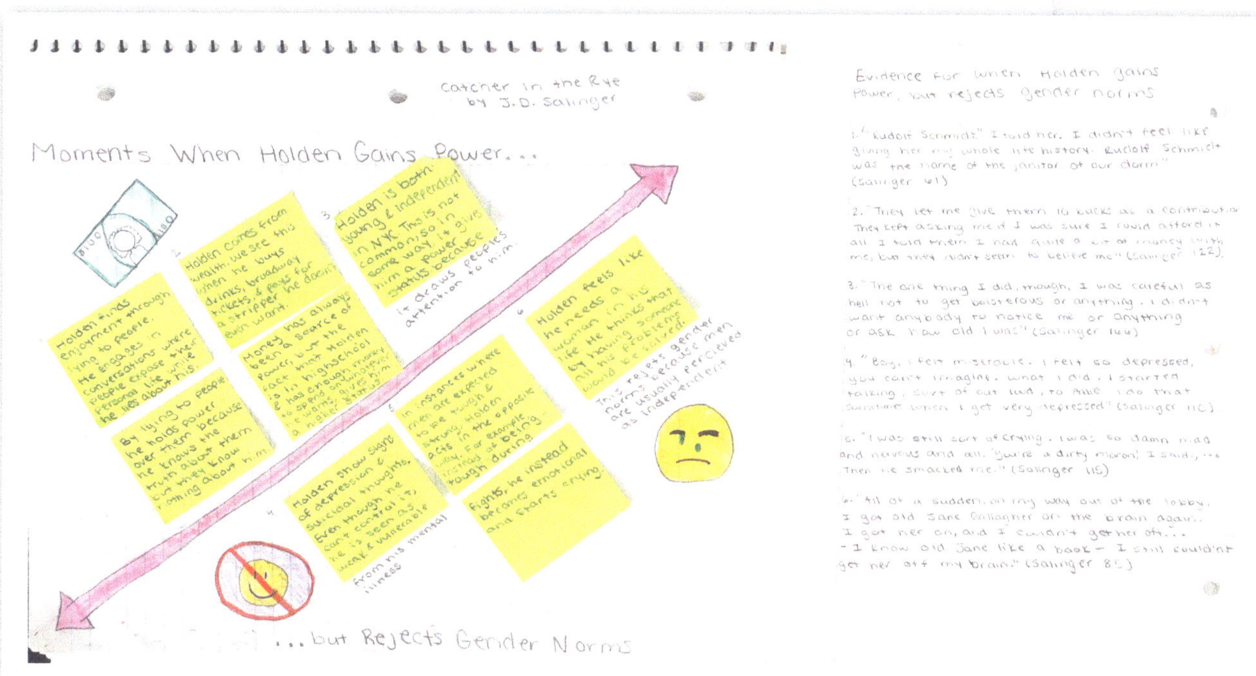

Another writer creates a timeline on power in The Catcher in the Rye *and provides specific quotes from the text to support her thinking.*

Lesson 5

Focusing on What Stirs You Up

STRATEGY

Writers thrive when they can choose what they want to write about. For literary analysis, they think about which stories, which characters, or which parts of stories they loved the most or found disturbing, and they focus on those (even if they have to align it to a specific writing assignment on a given text). They can freewrite why they care about that text/character/part, or they can sketch to develop new thinking.

USE THIS STRATEGY... when writers can choose a text they have a lot to say about. Also use this strategy when the writing assignment allows for limited choice, and you want to help students identify the parts of the text or characters they do love—or have strong feelings about—and focus on those, which will give their writing more authenticity and vibrancy.

Visit hs-guidetoteaching.org to watch a video of this lesson.

TEACH THE STRATEGY

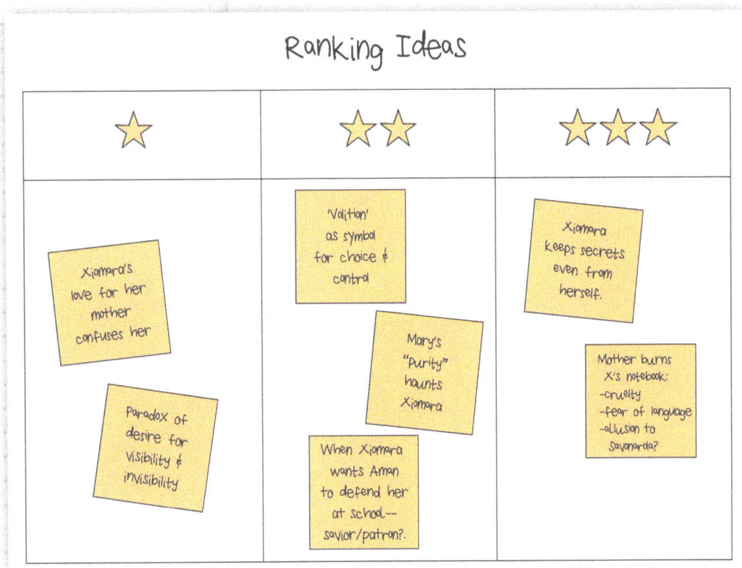

- Explain how important it is for writers to write about what they know and feel strongly about.
- Demonstrate how you might think about which stories have been most meaningful to you. You might return to your identity map or issue wall to revisit connections.
  - If your students have a narrower choice of text, show how you consider which characters you'd most like to explore and why, or which parts of the text you found most fascinating. Revisiting those parts can help you also notice literary techniques, structure, and so on.

Mary models collecting the ideas that are most interesting to her and ranking the ones she's most drawn to. Then, she does some freewriting off one of those ideas.

- Invite students to do some ranking of texts/characters/parts of texts they find most intriguing, and to explain to a partner what they're drawn to, as a way to rehearse their ideas. Use the below chart, or one like it, as a way for students to prompt their thinking!
- Finish with students doing some freewriting about why they chose this text/character/idea/part.

Focus on What Stirs You Up

To collect engaging ideas...	Try asking...
Zoom in on what excites or unsettles you.	What moment disturbed or thrilled you? What's a scene you can't stop thinking about?
Notice inner conflict.	Where does a character struggle internally? Where do their desires clash?
Track haunting symbols or themes.	What images or ideas show up again and again? What feels symbolic?
Identify what's hidden or unspoken.	What do characters hide—from others or from themselves? What's beneath the surface?
Follow relationships and roles.	What relationships feel tense, complicated, or powerful? Who's trying to protect, save, or silence whom?

PROMPTS TO COACH STUDENTS AND PARTNERSHIPS

Imagine you were telling someone about this story. What would you most want to tell them about?

It can help to go back to your annotations or notebook work to see what resonated with you or what parts you seemed to have the most to say about.

When you have to write to a prompt, it's even more important to figure out what part of the text you find most interesting—a character, or a scene, that you can return to and study. Oftentimes, parts we're drawn to can fit with all types of prompts.

Lesson 5 (Continued)

CLASSROOM ARTIFACTS

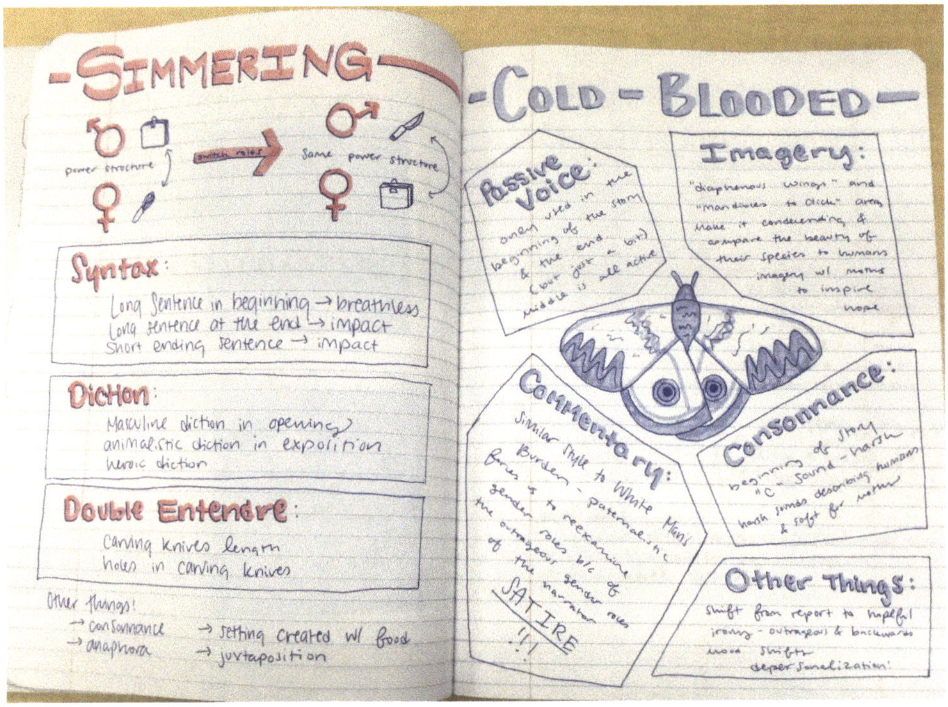

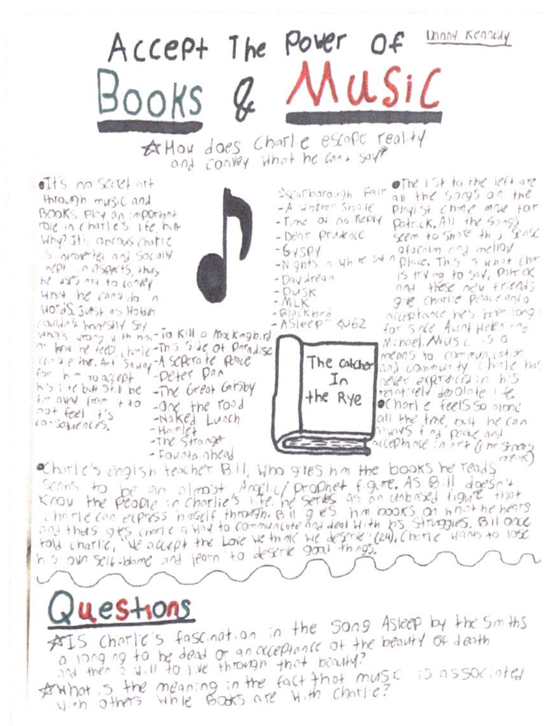

These writers return to their notebooks to explore what parts of the text they found most fascinating from The Perks of Being a Wallflower *and* In Cold Blood.

Engaging with Story Elements

Lesson 6

STRATEGY

Writers engage with story elements to practice interpretation and develop thinking for literary analyses.

USE THIS STRATEGY... to help writers (and readers) attach more significance to story elements across a text. Thinking about story elements is also often an accessible entry point for beginning to analyze literary craft.

Visit hs-guidetoteaching.org to download the teaching charts.

TEACH THE STRATEGY

- Suggest to students that rereading with lenses focused on story elements often leads writers to find new ideas. Collect or display a series of story elements such as conflict, character, setting, theme, symbolism, or time shifts.
  - You can keep these lenses simple or, if students are ready for more complexity, layer in more specificity such as internal conflict, character motivation, the role of minor characters, settings as systems, and psychological settings.

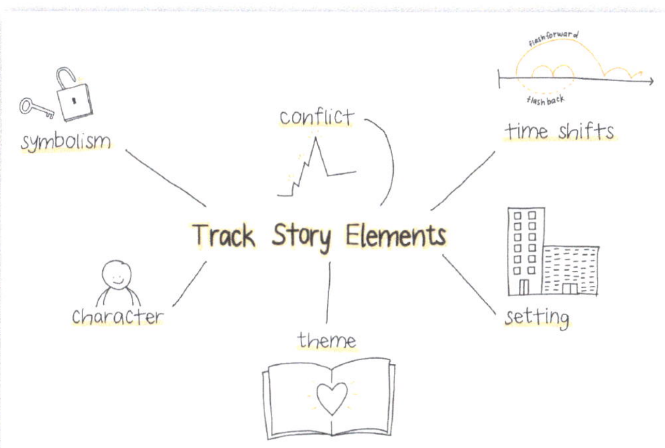

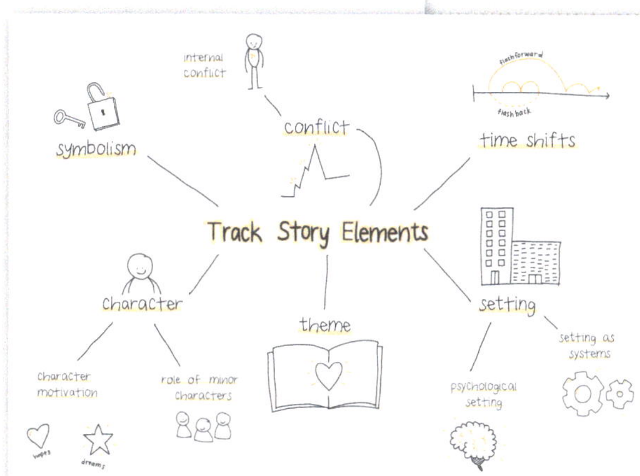

- Choose one lens to work with, such as setting.
- Model thinking about a few parts of the text that align with the lens you selected.
  - For example, with setting, it might just be a list of places that come up again and again in the text: school, home, church, and so forth. Or you

might mark how the psychology of a place feels in different moments—when does the character feel safe/unsafe, who feels differently in those spaces, does it change across the narrative?

- Scan the text with that lens in mind, looking for more specific moments.
- Analyze patterns in the specific moments you're connecting, inviting students to add to your thinking. You might look for character emotions, behaviors, or conflicts characters face.

As Coley collected moments here, she noticed that Xiomara writes consistently about school and church. She modeled thinking about these places in front of students, noting how church and school can be intimidating places, but also places of self-discovery. Coley asked aloud: "What kind of places are these for Xiomara?" Then she generated deeper ideas around the settings of church and school. She explored the idea that both these settings don't allow Xiomara to be her true self and developed this by naming that even though Xiomara externally acts similarly in both situations, internally, she's curious about school but shut down about church.

- Channel students to choose a lens, collect moments, and think about these moments to practice interpretation.
- End with students freewriting about their ideas.

PROMPTS TO COACH STUDENTS AND PARTNERSHIPS

Let's think together about how these moments are connected. What are you noticing?

See what comes up for you with a different lens, using these same moments. Try that.

You might try applying the lens to less obvious parts of the text—that could be a powerful experiment!

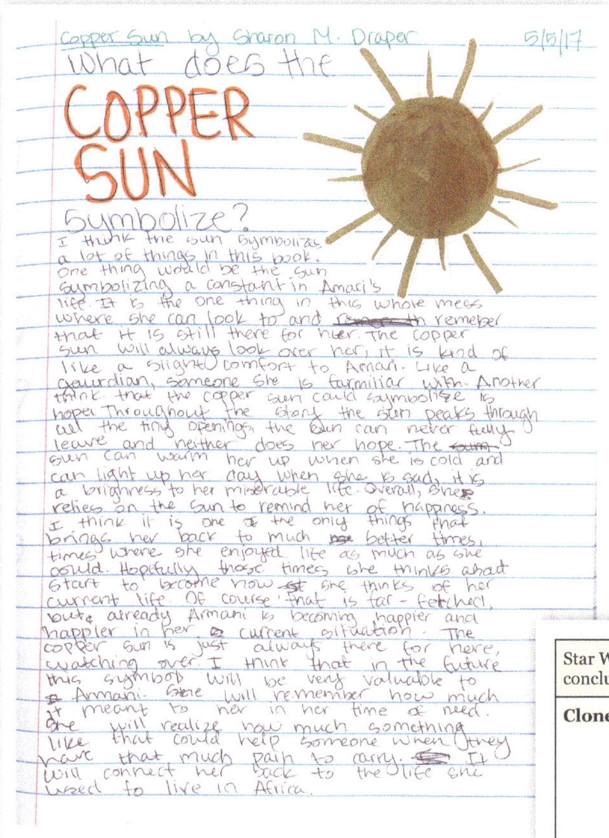

Copper Sun by Sharon M. Draper 5/5/17

What does the COPPER SUN symbolize?

I think the sun symbolizes a lot of things in this book. One thing would be the sun symbolizing a constant in Amari's life. It is the one thing in this whole mess where she can look to and remeber that it is still there for her. The copper sun will always look over her, it is kind of like a slight comfort to Amari. Like a gaurdian, someone she is farmiliar with. Another think that the copper sun could symbolize is hope. Throughout the story the sun peaks through all the tiny openings, the sun can never fully leave and neither does her hope. The sun can warm her up when she is cold and can light up her day when she is sad, it is a brighness to her miserable life. Overall, she relies on the sun to remind her of happiness. I think it is one the only things that brings her back to much better times, times where she enjoyed life as much as she could. Hopefully those times she thinks about start to become now she thinks of her current life. Of course that is far-fetched, but already Armani is becoming happier and happier in her current situation. The copper sun is just always there for here, watching over. I think that in the future this symbol will be very valuable to Armani. She will remember how much it meant to her in her time of need. She will realize how much something like that could help someone when they have that much pain to carry. It will connect her back to the life she used to live in Africa.

Star Wars the Clone Wars, seasons 3–7 (mostly 3 and 4, but some moments for season conclude key themes/ideas)

Clones

- How do the clones explore themes of brotherhood?
    - Camaraderie shown on battlefield
        - They always have each other's back
        - Watch out for the weaker clones among them
- What is the toll war takes on a person?
    - Show clone death, nightmares, friendly firing, changing perspectives, etc.
        - The sterile environment they were raised in shatters upon entering the battlefield.
- How do clones represent/struggle with disillusionment?
    - Show cynical outlook
    - Demonstrate progression from optimistic to a more realistic view of war

Character Evolution

- Character evolution
    - Maul
        - His views toward his fellow Sith change
        - Recovers from madness
            - Dathomirian heritage
        - Slowly bond with his brother with whom he initially has one-sided relationship
    - Ahsoka
        - Evolves from bratty teen to accomplished leader
        - Has a unique dynamic with Anakin and its evolution

Political Intrigue

- Political opinion of Jedi slowly transitions against them
- Sith often employ the guise of legitimacy (both Sidious and Dooku operate as heads of state)

The philosophies of the clones (how they treat each other and view the war) and the futility of their sacrifices.

Readers explore story elements from The Copper Sun *and* Star Wars.

Lesson 7

Close Reading with Critical Lenses

STRATEGY

When writers want to see new things in a text, they often return to a text to reread it with critical lenses. This close reading often leads writers to new observations, such as parts that suggest motifs about power, representation, archetypes, stereotypes, and narrative trajectory.

Visit hs-guidetoteaching.org for some suggestions of multimodal texts to practice reading with a critical lens and to download the following chart.

USE THIS STRATEGY... when you'd like students to read more closely and critically. Note that practicing this work on a visual, accessible text makes this complex work more accessible for students.

TEACH THE STRATEGY

Critical Lenses Readers Use to Analyze Text

- Archetypes
  - Victim, Savior, Mentor
  - Hero, Sidekick, Villain
- Stereotypes
  - Gender, Cultural, Social Group
  - Racial, Age Group
- Power
- Resistance
- Marginalization
- Exoticization
- Demonization
- Master narratives
- What's invisible/left out

- Suggest to students that rereading with critical lenses leads readers to think more deeply about subtext—what's percolating under the surface of a text, a kind of hidden curriculum.
- Introduce critical vocabulary, by watching an ad or narrative music video or short animated narrative where it is easy to see some of these motifs. (We study Taylor Swift's music video, *Bad Blood*, available on YouTube, which sixty million people have watched.)
  - ♦ It's okay for the texts to be flawed with stereotypes. That's what makes the critical lens work so visible.
- Display a chart of critical analytical vocabulary students can explore as they analyze a short text together.
- Invite students to talk about what they notice, and what parts of the text become more significant when read through these critical lenses.
- Demonstrate how you might sketch some of your thinking with one of these lenses around a shared text, such as "Bad Blood" by Taylor Swift.

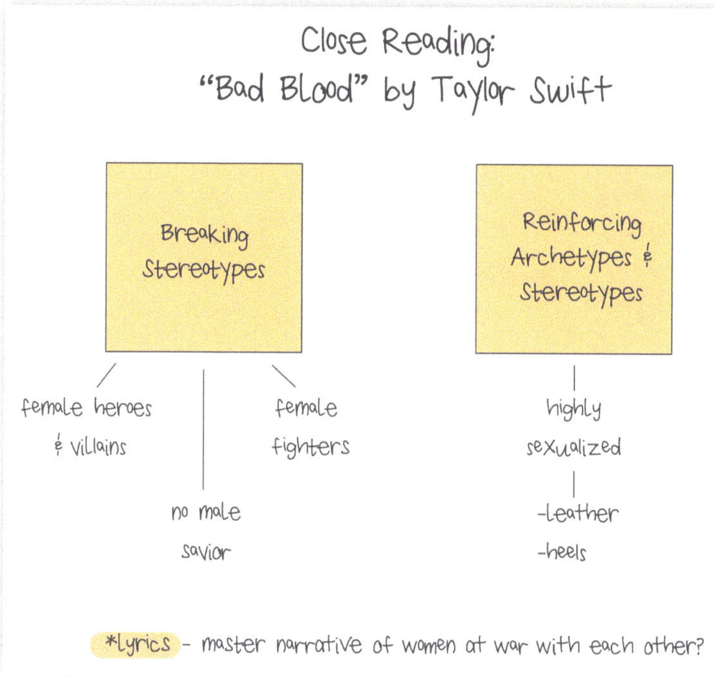

When Coley tried this work with her students, for example, they considered how the depiction of women in "Bad Blood" breaks with and reinforces stereotypes.

- Invite students to pick a critical lens to look through their narratives with. Then, give them a few minutes to flag pages/small chunks of text that are illuminated with that lens, invite them to discuss with a partner, and finish with students doing some freewriting to capture their thinking.

PROMPTS TO COACH STUDENTS AND PARTNERSHIPS

Sometimes a critical lens makes you realize that stories you love also have parts that are problematic. That's okay—most texts operate on more than one level like that.

Often characters don't exactly fit with a single role, and that's interesting. For instance, they may start as a victim but then be repositioned as a hero—but only with another character's intervention. Or there might be a master narrative (such as that girls should be obedient), but the story also offers moments that interrupt that narrative.

Ask: What is it about that lens you find particularly significant? Then ask: What other critical lens could you look at this part with?

CLASSROOM ARTIFACTS

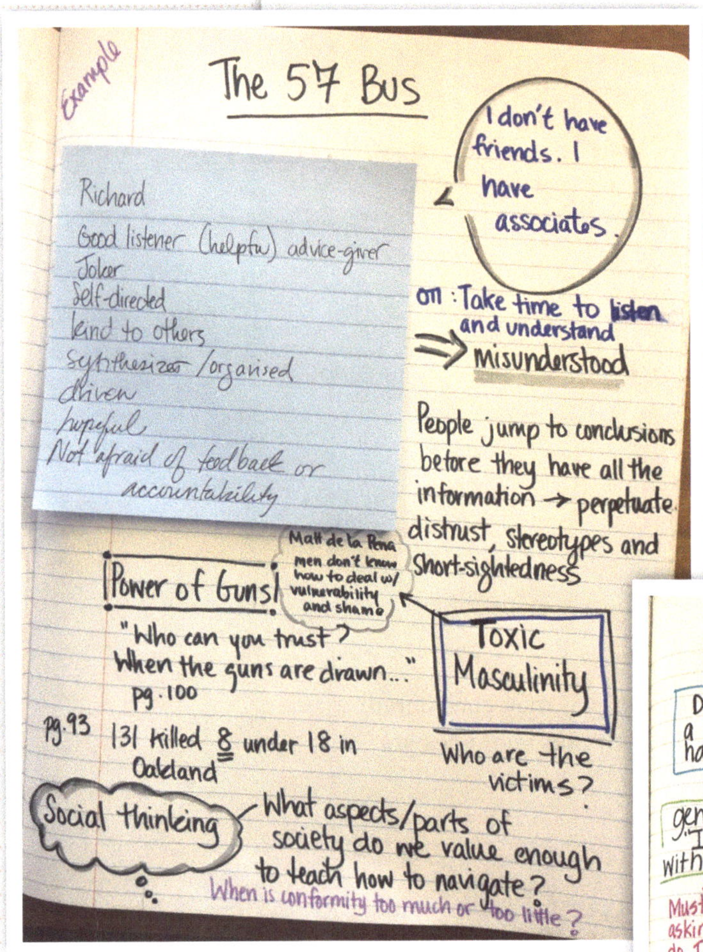

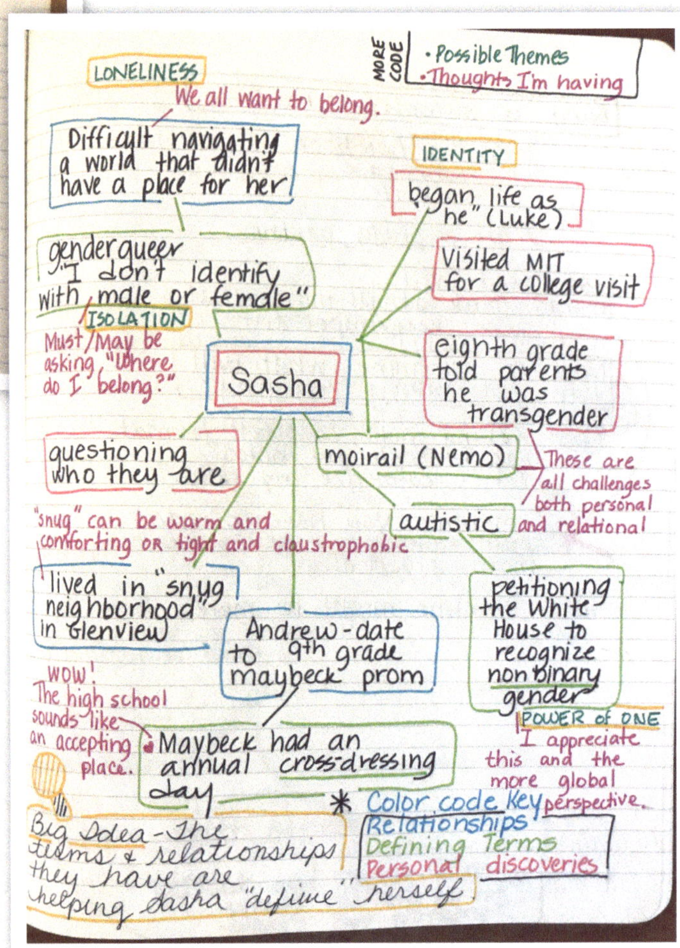

Writers track their thinking and ideas about gender norms in The 57 Bus *and* Sasha Masha.

Exploring Literary Techniques

Lesson 8

STRATEGY

Writers often choose to explore ideas about characters, themes, or issues alongside exploring literary techniques the author uses to develop these. There are two ways to approach this:

- One approach is to return to the parts of the text that support an idea, and ask yourself: What narrative techniques does the author use here?
- Another is to explore literary techniques you noticed in the text, and ask yourself: How does the author especially use some of these techniques to develop the character/a theme/an issue?

USE THIS STRATEGY... to support students in finding academic language to identify, describe, and analyze literary techniques. The visual chart is particularly helpful with this!

Visit hs-guidetoteaching.org to access an illustrated chart of literary techniques.

Inquiry Questions

- What narrative techniques does the author use here?
- How does the author use these techniques to develop a character/theme/issue?

LAUNCH THE INQUIRY

- Suggest to students that writers not only explore characters, themes, and issues, they also pay attention to literary craft. Consider two ways to approach studying craft in a text:
    - Return to key moments and see what craft is present.
    - Choose a technique, try to find it in the text, and investigate the significance of that part.
- Identify and revisit an important passage in the text. Reread it, investigating which literary elements and techniques are present.
- Once you identify the literary techniques the author uses, model thinking aloud about the way the literary technique develops a character/theme/issue.

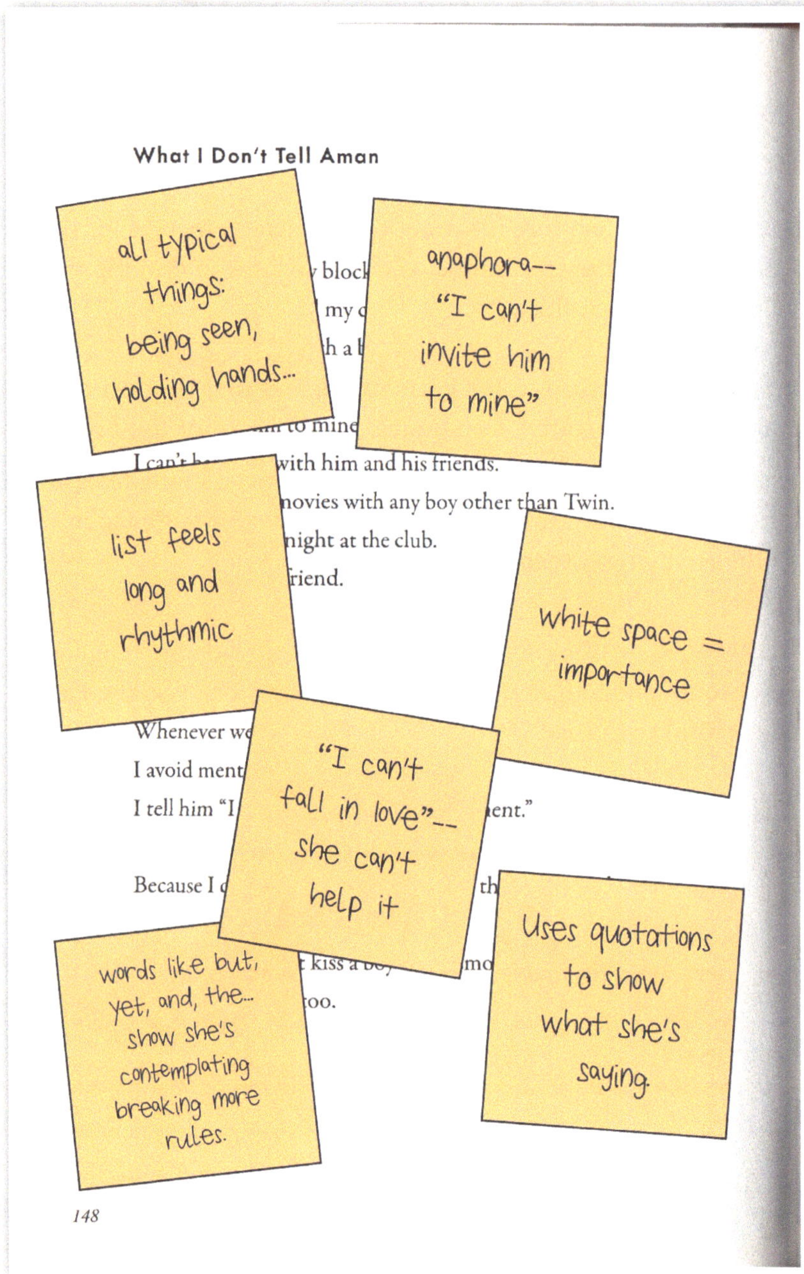

When Mary did this work, she returned to a page she had flagged in the novel that supported the idea that Xiomara is trapped by her secrets, read a bit of it out loud, and engaged her students in looking at their Narrative Literary Devices and Narrative Effects chart, which led them to identify techniques Acevedo uses to develop the idea that Xiomara is trapped by her secrets, such as repetition and white space.

- Try it another way: Suggest a technique, find a place in the story that demonstrates that technique, and invite students to think with you about an idea those parts develop.

Mary, for instance, suggested revisiting poems where Xiomara breaks grammar rules, which led to a discussion of how Xiomara wants to break rules, wants to not be trapped by convention, and her poetry allows her to show that desire.

- Give students copies of the Literary Elements and Techniques chart, and invite them to try this work out with their own stories and their own ideas. Often, it's helpful to work with a partner.
- End with students freewriting to capture their thinking.

PROMPTS TO COACH STUDENTS AND PARTNERSHIPS

Sometimes you can use literary techniques almost like literary Bingo. Put a small sticky note on any technique you find in the story, then look across and ask yourself, which of those do you find most intriguing?

Your author might have used literary techniques that aren't on this chart. Let's look at some of your favorite parts of the text, and see if we find other techniques.

You can turn to your AI partner to ask about literary techniques as well. If you describe your favorite parts of the text, AI might make some suggestions about possible techniques.

CLASSROOM ARTIFACTS

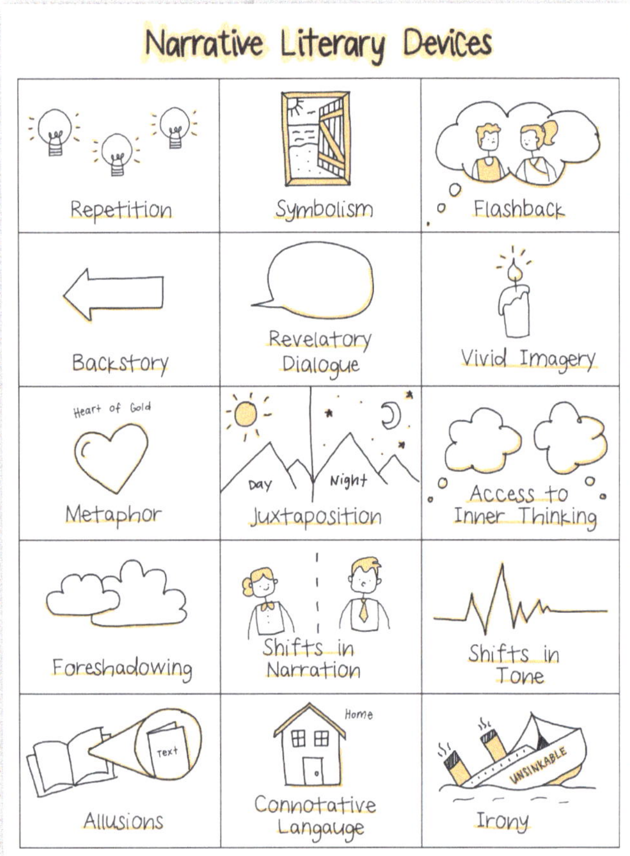

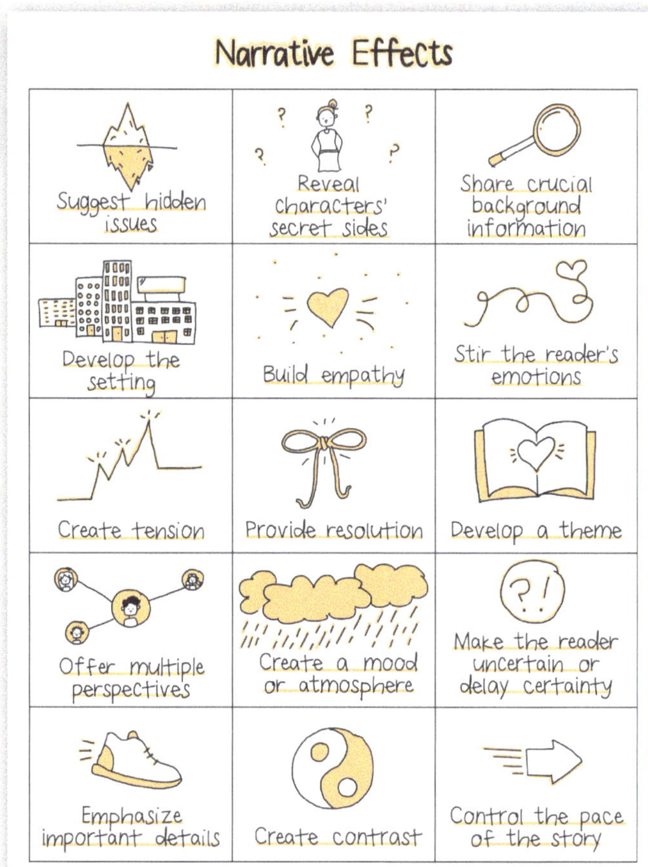

Chapter Two: Crafting Artful Thesis Statements

When teens analyze texts that they understand and find intriguing, they can craft interesting thesis statements. Ask them to nominate some ideas, for instance, about their favorite music, sports team, show, or novel, and they'll often surprise you with their insightful ideas. Some of your students will do the same with literary texts: they'll develop an idea or theory that is elegant and provocative. A lot of students, though, need support and, even more importantly, practice developing thesis statements.

The biggest challenges students often contend with as they develop thesis statements for a literary analysis include when they:

- craft a thesis statement that is so extensive and narrow that it limits the parts of the text they can use,
- craft a thesis statement that has so many parts that it becomes burdensome to support,
- are asked to support a thesis they are not passionate about or did not develop themselves,
- have a complex idea but they need more sophisticated language to express this idea.

Our first goal, then, is to teach students the art of developing ideas for literary analyses that *they* find intriguing and want to explore. You'll get better content out of the kids, their writing will have more voice, and you won't have to read a hundred essays on the same subject. Felicia Rose Chavez (2021) suggests that we support students in fulfilling their vision for their writing, not ours. One way to do that is to allow students—and teach them—to figure out what, within a narrative, they are most interested in. And you'll have taught your writers a valuable skill: the art of figuring out what you want to write about, which is often the hardest part of the writing process. If your students need support with annotation and interpretation, go back to Chapter 1 and revisit those lessons, which help students develop thinking as they read. All of that work will support students in coming up with quirky, original, personal, and, yes, academic theses.

This chapter builds on skills suggested in Chapter 1 and offers a variety of strategies for students to help them develop a thesis they'll be able to support. Visit hs-guidetoteaching.org to access a full chart of common thesis statement language. For a lot of young writers, seeing what theses can look like helps them figure out their own thesis, both their idea and the academic language they might reach for. It can be helpful to sort thesis statements by content, as in statements that develop ideas about characters, ones that develop ideas about themes or social issues, and so on. One quick and playful way for students to become more familiar with academic language stems is to cut up a collection of theses and have partners quickly sort which theses might fit under which type, simply because any kind of sorting compels analytic thinking.

While we love to teach students to develop their own theses, we also recognize that sometimes your writers will find themselves responding to prompts. As writing teachers who teach in universities as well as in high schools, we encourage you to teach your young writers how to *personalize and adapt* a prompt. Our strongest student writers, we notice in high school and in university, are the ones who ask if they may modify a prompt to follow their interests—a powerful move showing academic capital. Even in assessment situations, where the prompt is mandatory, your writers will be empowered if they know how to adjust their response to a prompt so they can best write about the parts of a narrative they know well and have a lot to say about.

If you're thinking of prompts as a way to guide students, you might...

Suggest students modify or adapt a prompt to lean into the parts of the text they know well.	Share several possible prompts on a topic and let students choose among them.	Offer thesis statement suggestions as possible starters, allowing students to personalize these to their interests.
Provide students a set of inquiry questions that will lead to thesis statements through answering these questions.	Share a word or phrase and ask students to brainstorm a thesis that includes that word or topic.	Offer students prompts as a scaffold instead of a default.

Inside of this work, you can actively support kids' writing process. There's a natural tendency to want students to progress methodically. We've found this is rarely how writing works. Expect, therefore, that some students may be tinkering with a thesis, others might be outlining or mapping their drafts, and others collecting evidence. If you can allow this messiness (and we strongly encourage you to!), it means that while you support your students in writing deep and complex literary analyses, equally importantly, you're supporting your young writers in internalizing the writing process.

As you teach some of these lessons, remember the value of writing partnerships. Writers who can test their ideas on other writers are less alone in this process. Partners who have read the same narratives, especially, can help each other develop, test, and refine their theses. An AI partner can also help young writers develop their thesis. It's just important for students to come to this partnership having looked over their notes, and with some ideas, so their AI partner supports their thinking, rather than supplanting it.

You may turn several of these lessons into micro-lessons, offering them on the same day, as options. You may choose a few that you think are well matched to your writers. You may offer some as conferring or small-group options. Students' theses don't have to be utterly perfected at this stage of the writing process. Expect, as they collect evidence, outline, and draft, that your writers will come to a more nuanced understanding of their original thesis, revising their thesis statements or providing a more developed one toward the end, in the conclusion.

Academic Language for Thesis Statements
When exploring ideas about characters...
One aspect of Xiomara's **character that is especially significant** is her lack of confidence in herself. **This trait, which reveals itself across the novel,** keeps her from expressing her true self.
Xiomara's secrecy protects her, **but also** keeps her from **growing across the novel.**
Xiomara **is unusual among literary heroines for her** self-doubt, which disempowers her. Ultimately it is poetry that helps Xiomara **overcome this emotion.**
Xiomara **evolves from** a silenced daughter **into** a self-empowered young woman **who finds** her voice despite cultural and familial resistance.
Xiomara's anger **is not just** rebellion **but a** necessary force **that** propels her toward self-discovery and agency.
Xiomara's rebelliousness **is deeply shaped** by her strict upbringing and religious expectations.
Like Xiomara, **I too** find it difficult to talk to my mother about topics we disagree on. Xiomara's journey to express herself **taught me about the importance of** learning to speak up.
When exploring ideas about themes and social issues...
Across the novel, Xiomara **faces challenges that shape** her resistance, **including** expectations about religious participation, about beauty, and about sexuality.
Xiomara's **inability to** express her emotions openly **reveals how** repression can lead to loneliness and self-destruction.
Xiomara's **struggle between** family expectations and personal beliefs **highlights the tension between** cultural heritage and individual identity.
The Poet X **explores how** rigid cultural and religious expectations can silence young women, **but also how** reclaiming one's voice can lead to empowerment.

An issue that haunts Xiomara in The Poet X **is one that haunts many teens.** That is how love—whether romantic, familial, or self-love—requires honesty and vulnerability, but societal pressures often make these difficult to achieve.

In The Poet X, poetry **becomes** a tool for Xiomara to process the pain of being unheard, **illustrating that** art can be a form of healing and reclaiming power.

When exploring ideas about literary techniques...

The novel's free verse **structure mirrors Xiomara's fragmented yet evolving sense of self, reinforcing her journey toward** confidence and self-acceptance.

Xiomara's poetic narration **blurs the line between** truth and self-deception, **highlighting** her deep-seated struggles with identity and vulnerability.

Acevedo's **use of** vivid metaphors **captures the tension between** empowerment and objectification that Xiomara experiences as a young woman.

The fluid, stream-of-consciousness **style of** Xiomara's poetry **allows readers to experience** her emotions intimately, making her growth feel raw and immediate.

Lesson 1

Revisiting Our Reading to Get Ready to Write

STRATEGY

Writers often get ready to draft preliminary theses by reviewing what they were most interested in as they read. They do this reflective work by reviewing their notes, their annotations, and their conversations, and asking themselves: In all this material, what ideas am I most intrigued by?

USE THIS STRATEGY... to help writers use all the thinking they did as they read to develop a thesis they can likely support and that they find personally interesting.

TEACH THE STRATEGY

- Suggest to students that when seeking a thesis to write about, writers often revisit their notes and texts, asking themselves: What am I most intrigued by?
- Gather your annotated text, with its markups, any flagging, and any jotting you did in a notebook. Model skimming to find a part you find interesting, and show how you annotate your own notes with insights.

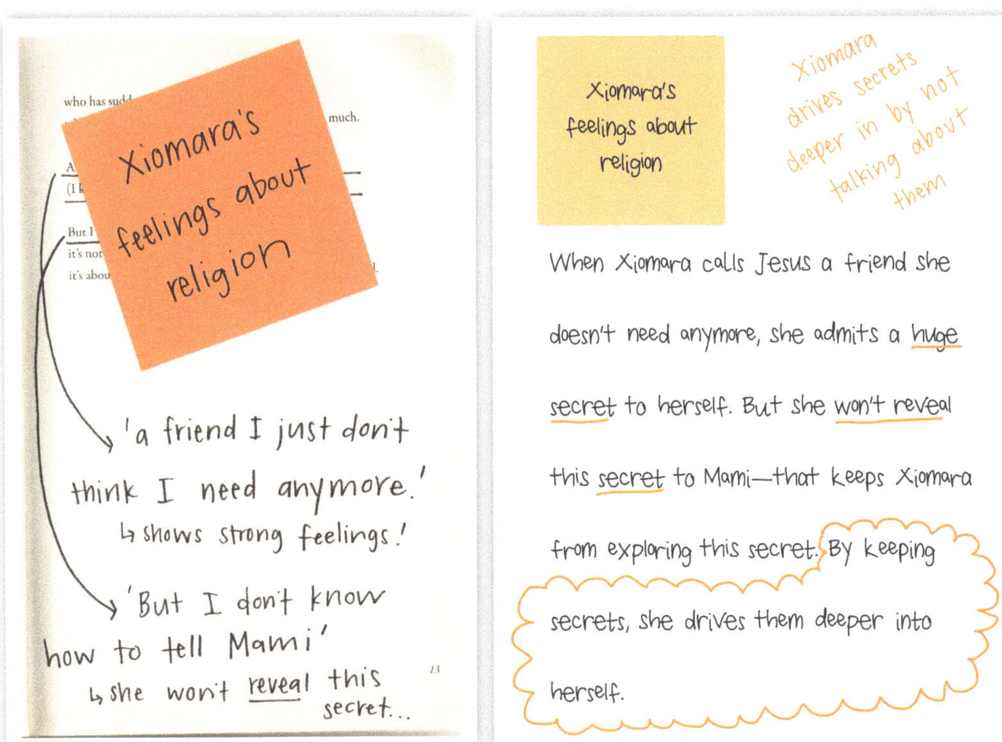

Mary demonstrated by skimming to a page of annotations from her book, where she had noted a couple of important lines that suggest Xiomara admits a secret to herself but not to her mother. Then, when she goes to her notebook to share the jotting she had done about this part of the text, she adds new thinking that could be a possible thesis—that Xiomara drives secrets farther into herself by not sharing them. What matters here is that Mary shows how her thesis emerged from her jottings, so she's likely to be able to support it.

- Invite students to gather their materials, including their texts, any notes, and colored pens and sticky notes, and revisit their thinking and jot down some possible theses.
- End by having students test out their ideas by telling their partner how their writing might go.

PROMPTS TO COACH STUDENTS AND PARTNERSHIPS

It often helps to go back to a part of the text you had flagged, and ask yourself: What did I find most interesting here?

It can be helpful to use a different-colored pen or a different-colored sticky note to mark that you are jotting an idea, a possible thesis.

You don't have to be able to prove this idea yet; it can be one that you find interesting, that you want to go back and think about by rereading.

CLASSROOM ARTIFACTS

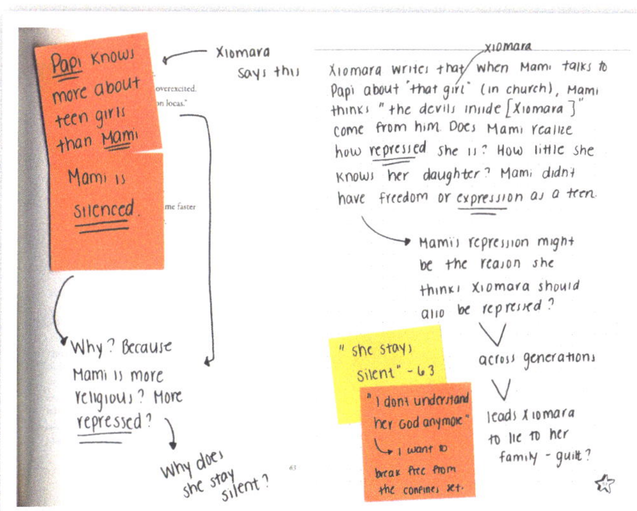

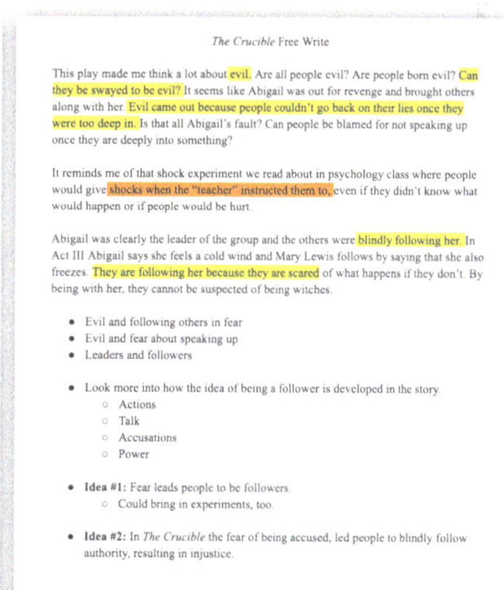

The Crucible Free Write

This play made me think a lot about evil. Are all people evil? Are people born evil? Can they be swayed to be evil? It seems like Abigail was out for revenge and brought others along with her. Evil came out because people couldn't go back on their lies once they were too deep in. Is that all Abigail's fault? Can people be blamed for not speaking up once they are deeply into something?

It reminds me of that shock experiment we read about in psychology class where people would give shocks when the "teacher" instructed them to, even if they didn't know what would happen or if people would be hurt.

Abigail was clearly the leader of the group and the others were blindly following her. In Act III Abigail says she feels a cold wind and Mary Lewis follows by saying that she also freezes. They are following her because they are scared of what happens if they don't. By being with her, they cannot be suspected of being witches.

- Evil and following others in fear
- Evil and fear about speaking up
- Leaders and followers

- Look more into how the idea of being a follower is developed in the story.
    - Actions
    - Talk
    - Accusations
    - Power

- **Idea #1:** Fear leads people to be followers.
    - Could bring in experiments, too.

- **Idea #2:** In *The Crucible* the fear of being accused, led people to blindly follow authority, resulting in injustice.

These writers revisit their notes and freewrite to develop ideas using The Poet X *and* The Crucible.

Lesson 2

Developing Theses by Rehearsing Your Evidence

STRATEGY

One way that writers test a thesis is by verbally rehearsing how their essay might go, focusing on the evidence that supports their thesis. By trying this work with more than one thesis, writers can figure out which one is easiest to support or most interesting to them.

USE THIS STRATEGY... to help writers test their thesis and review their preliminary evidence. Use it, as well, to help students who say a lot more than they write develop more fluency with their ideas.

TEACH THE STRATEGY

- Suggest to students that often talking through how a piece of writing will go is the best form of rehearsal, allowing the author to develop a logical sequence, test their ideas, and begin to organize evidence to support their ideas.
- Model how you look over your notes and jottings and gather some possible thesis ideas. Jot these on sticky notes if you haven't done so before.

Xiomara is secretive.

Xiomara keeps different kinds of secrets.

Secrecy runs through Xiomara's life like a river she can't control.

Mary experiments with ideas about secrecy. The first version allows students who would benefit from a character-trait thesis to see a simple model. These often allow students to write essays that focus on "times when" a character is a certain way, one of the most accessible (and still interesting!) forms of literary essay. In the third iteration, you see the kind of more developed and narrower thesis statement that can be fascinating, but harder to support, as each bit of evidence has to be about secrecy *and* loss of control.

- Demonstrate rehearsing (sometimes you can call it "talking in essay") by jotting a quick plan and then trying to say some of your evidence out loud as you point to each bullet. You might try more than one, and have students give you feedback on which you supported with more fluency.
- Invite students to do the same work—to look over their notes and to jot some preliminary theses and to test their ideas by "talking in essay" with a partner. Some writers may choose to video-record their rehearsal, as it can be helpful later in the writing process.

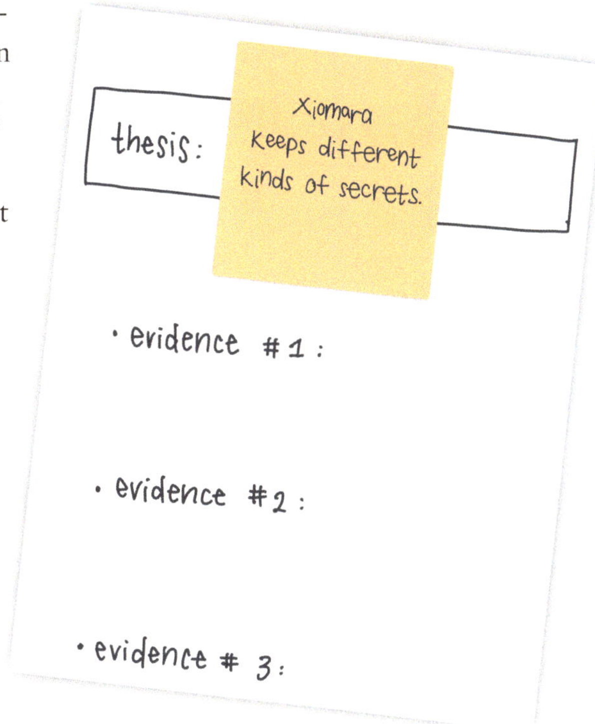

PROMPTS TO COACH STUDENTS AND PARTNERSHIPS

Sometimes you can try different versions of a thesis. An open thesis, like "Xiomara is secretive," or "Secrecy is an important force in The Poet X, *" allows you to explore a lot of different places in the book. Then, if you come to any more specific, more nuanced thinking, you can share that in your conclusion.*

Some theses have two parts, like, "Xiomara is secretive, and her secrets hurt her." Then you have to decide if each part of the text you analyze will be about secrecy and damage, or if the first part of your essay will look at secrecy, and the second part will look at how her secrets hurt her.

If you try one thesis and, when you talk in essay, it doesn't turn out well, go back to your jottings. There is probably something else there that you have better support for.

CLASSROOM ARTIFACTS

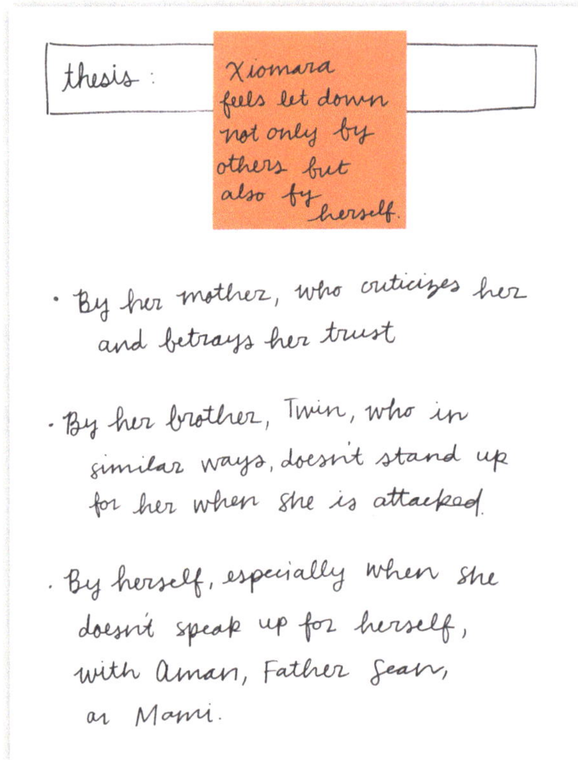

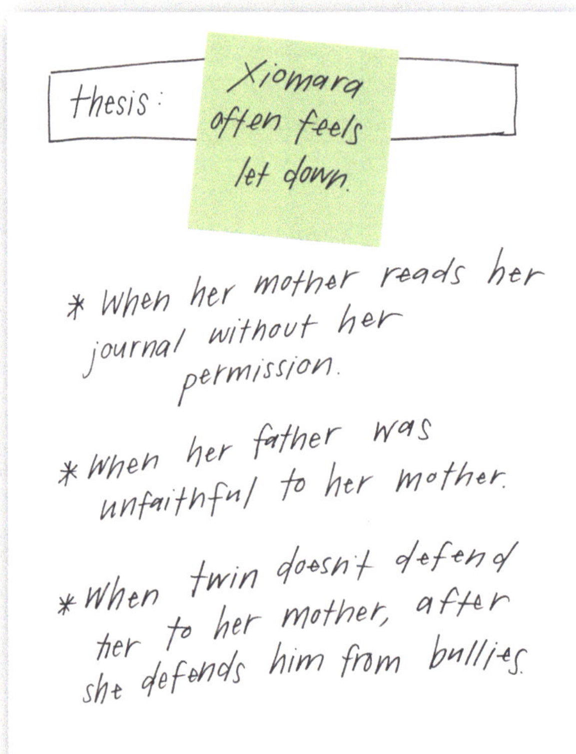

Lean jotting to support verbal rehearsal for essays on The Poet X.

Thesis Statements Can Look More Than One Way

Lesson 3

STRATEGY

Writers often study different types of theses to be inspired to try new forms. They do this by collecting examples or definitions and then envisioning how their own thesis might match one of these.

USE THIS STRATEGY... when writers are ready to revise their thesis statements for specificity and voice or when writers are used to using one type of thesis statement and are ready for exposure to different ways they might go.

Visit hs-guidetoteaching.org to download the chart of thesis statement types.

Inquiry Questions

How can different types of theses help writers effectively communicate their ideas about a text?

LAUNCH THE INQUIRY

- Suggest to writers that there are a lot of different kinds of theses, and these different theses generally launch different kinds of writing.
- Post the inquiry question.
- Distribute the Thesis Types chart, cut up as boxes, in an envelope.
- Guide students to work with a partner to match the thesis type with the definition and example. If needed, you can match one together, as a class, to demonstrate the process of reading a thesis statement, reading the definitions, and considering which best match.
- Coach students to rank the thesis statements, in terms of which they feel are most compelling for their own ideas.
    - There is no one right answer for this, but look for students to justify their ideas.
- Encourage students to compare their thesis to the different thesis types. Then, invite them to revise, using the examples as inspiration. If there is time, students can rehearse, verbally, how their drafts might go.

Thesis Types

Thesis Type	Definition & Example
Open	An open thesis makes a broad, overarching claim without listing specific supporting points. <u>Example</u>: Xiomara keeps secrets from her mother.
List	A list thesis outlines multiple specific points that support the main argument. <u>Example</u>: Xiomara's relationship with her mom shapes Xiomara's relationship with God, with Aman, and Xiomara's relationship with herself.
Personal	A personal thesis makes a connection between the writer and the text. <u>Example</u>: Like Xiomara, I often struggle to explain myself to my mother. <u>Example</u>: Xiomara learns many lessons, and in doing so, teaches the reader. The most important lesson for this reader was to be true to herself.
Question	A question thesis poses an inquiry that the analysis will explore and answer. <u>Example</u>: How does Xiomara's relationship with her mom impact her identity?
Counterclaim	A counterclaim thesis introduces an opposing viewpoint before asserting a stronger primary argument. <u>Example</u>: Although Xiomara gains significant self-awareness through the structures that shape her life, such as church and school, her relationship with her mother proves to be the most transformative in her journey of self-discovery.
Compare and Contrast	A compare and contrast thesis examines the similarities and differences between two or more elements. <u>Example</u>: Xiomara and her mother present differently, but are similar in personality and their commitment to the people and causes they love.
Hypothetical Thesis	A hypothetical thesis speculates about an alternative scenario to explore its implications. <u>Example</u>: If Xiomara's mother had embraced her passion for poetry, Xiomara's journey toward self-acceptance might have been less fraught with rebellion and conflict.

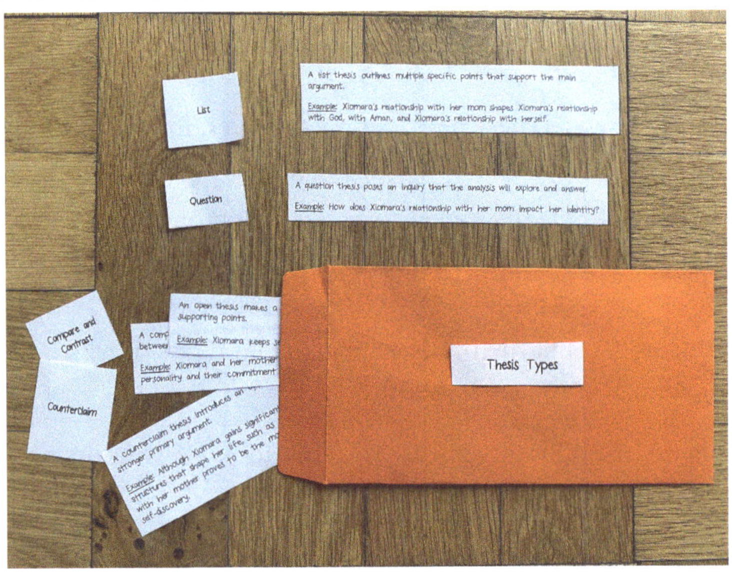

Students pair the example with the type of thesis, thinking through the qualities of each type.

PROMPTS TO COACH STUDENTS AND PARTNERSHIPS

You can collaborate with your partner. Try reading the definition and example out loud.

I see you've sorted these. Now you can try to mirror-write a mentor thesis. Try out the same structure with your ideas. Think about which one feels best to you.

Now that you've tried out your thesis a different way, ask yourself: Is there one here that feels like the best fit for your argument, or one that feels new and different?

CLASSROOM ARTIFACTS

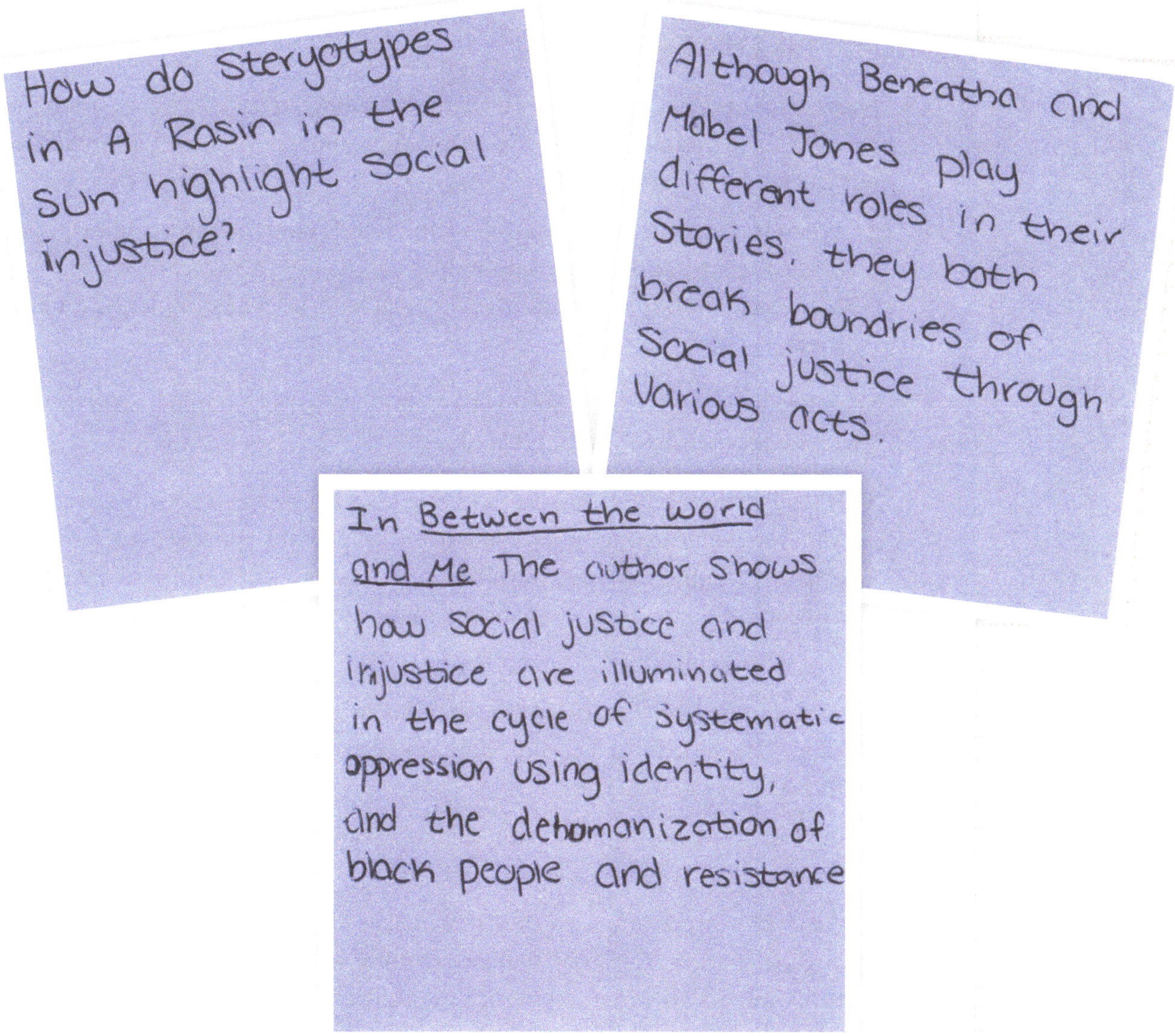

This writer experiments with different thesis statements for an essay on A Raisin in the Sun *and* Between the World and Me.

Lesson 4

Pairing Tangibles and Intangibles

STRATEGY

One way that writers can generate theses about texts is to pair concrete parts of the text with abstract ideas. They do this by studying relationships and connections between tangible things in the text and intangible ideas suggested in the text.

Visit hs-guidetoteaching.org to download the chart of tangibles and intangibles.

USE THIS STRATEGY... to support students in getting started forging a thesis statement, especially when you want students to try out multiple ideas.

TEACH THE STRATEGY

- Suggest to students that one way writers find new ideas is to think about tangibles and intangibles in a text. Quickly define *tangible* and *intangible* to students.
    - When it comes to texts, tangibles can include concrete aspects like people, places, events, and things. Intangibles can include abstract ideas like concepts, emotions, and motifs. Give students a few examples of each of these.
- Set students up to work in groups to create one list of tangible parts of the text and another list of intangible ideas.
    - If students are all writing on the same text, break them up into groups and have some groups generate a list of important people, places, events, and other tangible things from the story. Ask another group to generate abstract ideas that come out of the text.
- Collect ideas onto a chart of tangibles and intangibles in a familiar text. Use the chart to build the start of a thesis. Choose one or more ideas from each column. Combine tangibles and intangibles to explore how different parts of the novel impact each other.
- Briefly list a few key moments and details from the text that support the thesis to make sure it's possible to defend.
- Invite students to compose a thesis, using the chart, or to first jot a tangible/intangible chart on the story they are reading with a partner. Coach students to turn and talk to verbally practice the thesis first and then jot it in their notebooks. If there is time, students can try out a few different theses.

Tangibles	Intangibles
• Xiomara • Writing/Poetry • Church • School • Parents • Twin brother • Caridad • Subway/Train • Father Sean • Aman • Apples • Essays • Cell phones • Neighborhood	• Voice • Community • Love • Friendship • Loss • Growing up • Maturity • Beauty Standards • Race • Language • Music • Names • Childhood • God • Faith • Sexuality

Tangibles and Intangibles in *The Poet X*

Xiomara's use of both **Spanish and English, demonstrates...** how she is caught between two lives: the confined one her **parents** want for her and the life of freedom she wants for herself.

The juxtaposition between **Xiomara's and Twin's romantic relationships and sexuality highlights...** the contrasting ways they navigate familial and societal expectations.

When Coley tried this work with a 10th grade class reading *The Poet X*, they generated a chart like the one shown here. From these ideas, Coley generated a few theses.

Lesson 4
(Continued)

PROMPTS TO COACH STUDENTS AND PARTNERSHIPS

You've already been doing so much reflecting about these elements of the text. Talk about a couple you can't stop thinking about. Try those out in a thesis!

Let's think about some of these intangibles together. If you were to name a few that feel interesting to you to write about, which would you pick? How might you look at some of the tangibles and turn that into a thesis?

It can help to try out a few theses. Once you have one, try another!

CLASSROOM ARTIFACTS

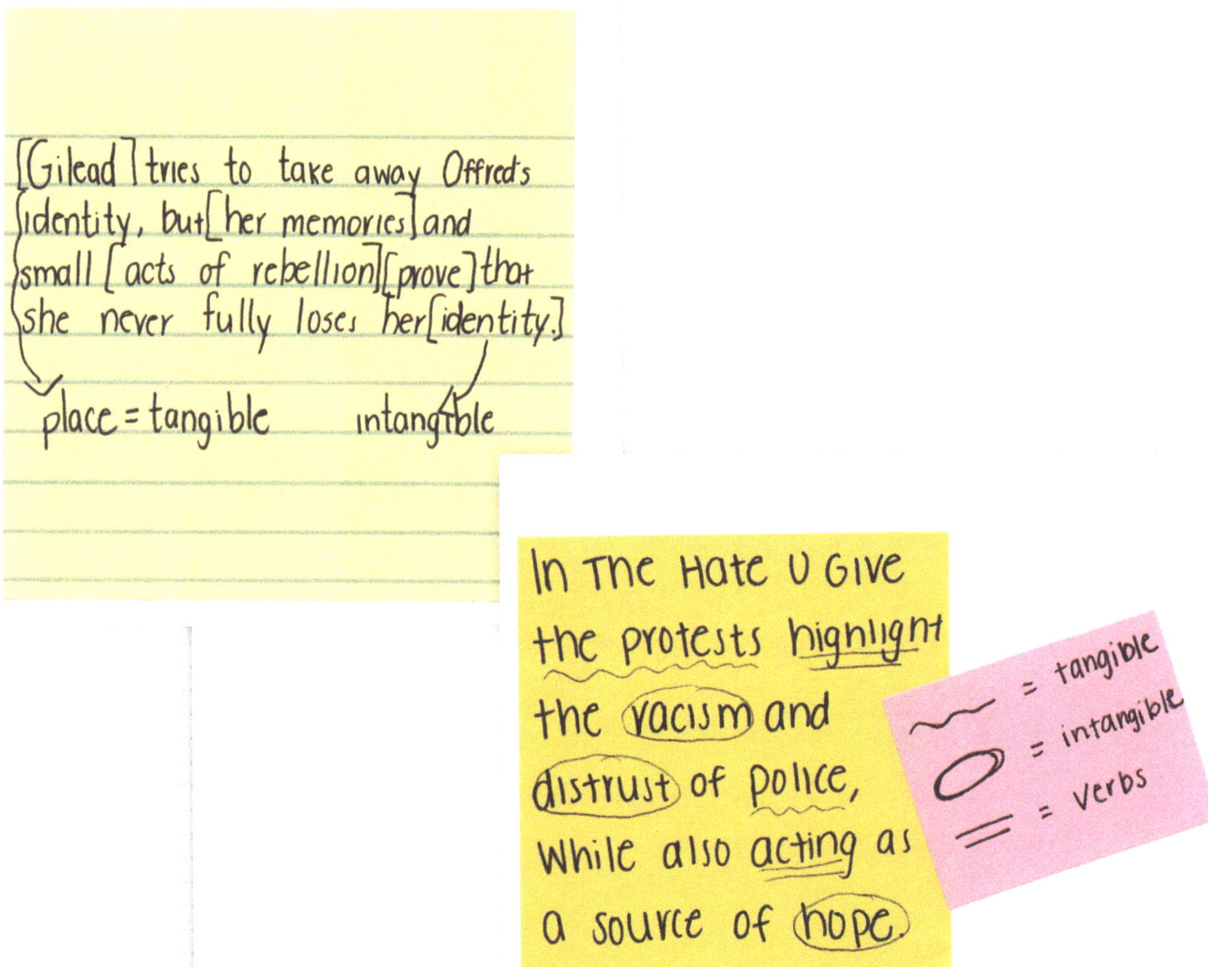

Students experiment with tangibles and intangibles in The Handmaid's Tale *and* The Hate U Give.

Moving Beyond and Around a Prompt

Lesson 5

STRATEGY

When writers have to respond to a prompt, they can learn to use a prompt as a springboard to develop a thesis that they are invested in and can support well. Options (depending on the context for the prompt) include restating a prompt, modifying it, or adding to it.

USE THIS STRATEGY... when students have prompts as a guide, when the prompts might be inhibiting them from developing their ideas, or students want to explore ideas that go beyond the prompt. This strategy is also useful when students need to adjust a prompt so that they can write about the parts of a text about which they have a lot to say.

Visit hs-guidetoteaching.org to download the chart of ways to go beyond a prompt.

TEACH THE STRATEGY

- Explain to students that while most of the meaningful writing they do in their life will reflect their own ideas, sometimes they have to respond to a prompt, and that when that happens, there is an art to figuring out how to respond to a prompt so it brings out your strongest writing and thinking.
- Display a prompt (or prompts) for students.

> Poetry plays a powerful symbolic role in Xiomara's life. Analyze how Acevedo uses poetry as a symbol of freedom, identity, and resistance throughout the novel.

- Demonstrate restating the prompt as a thesis, originally keeping it intact.

> Keeping the prompt intact and restating it as a thesis
>
> In the novel *The Poet X*, Acevedo uses poetry as a symbol of freedom, identity, and resistance throughout the novel.

- Model a few ways writers can go beyond the prompt, or modify it, to generate new ideas:
  - Rewrite the question to fit your own ideas.
  - Pick a word or phrase that stands out to you.
  - Add in another layer or lens to shift the prompt closer to your own thinking.

Go Beyond the Prompt

Prompt: Poetry plays a powerful symbolic role in Xiomara's life. Analyze how Acevedo uses poetry as a symbol of freedom, identity, and resistance. throughout the novel.

Rewrite the prompt to fit your own ideas.

Analyze how Acevedo uses Xiomara's body as a symbol of objectification, especially through her poetry.

Pick a word or phrase to brainstorm with.

Xiomara resists typical beauty standards and societal expectations placed on her as a young woman, using her freedom and identity as a form of resistance.

Add in another layer or lens.

Xiomara's poetry is a symbol of feminist freedom, identity, and resistance.

Coley experimented with a prompt focused on *The Poet X*. You'll want to do the same, using a text that is very familiar to your students.

- Invite students to play with a prompt that you want them to write about as it's written or to make it their own using one of these strategies.
- Coach students to use the new prompt as a springboard for honing their own thesis statements. Once they've jotted their thesis, they can do some verbal rehearsal to think about how their writing will go.

PROMPTS TO COACH STUDENTS AND PARTNERSHIPS

When you're ready, use the question you created or the idea you grew to do some longer freewriting and brainstorming.

If the prompt is feeling a bit wordy or overwhelming, try picking out important words or phrases you can use as a jumping-off point.

It's always important to find out from whoever gave you a prompt how much leeway you have in adjusting it. One way is to write to a teacher or professor. Another is to speak with them directly. A third is to include the parts of the prompt you don't address in the body of your essay in your conclusion or introduction.

CLASSROOM ARTIFACTS

The Things They Carried – essay

Choose **ONE** of the following essay prompts. Respond to the prompt in essay format. Remember to provide textual evidence and original analysis in each body paragraph.

Compare to IR BOOK

also one without a traditional enemy

1) *The Things They Carried* is a war story without traditional heroic characters. How do you think O'Brien defines heroism? Choose TWO characters from the text that are not traditional heroes but who demonstrate heroic qualities according to the author. Be sure to explain what makes each character a "hero."

→ They called us enemy

Hero vs. Villain

Loss changes people

2) War changes people causing a ~~loss of innocence~~ in the novel. How do the ravages and horrors of the Vietnam War cause the characters to move from innocence to experience? Choose TWO characters that experience a loss. Be sure to discuss the catalyst for each character's change.

and loss

compare

3) O'Brien uses many examples of both horrific and beautiful images and events in the novel. Choose TWO horrific images/events **OR** TWO beautiful images/events in the novel. Discuss what O'Brien is saying about war and the human condition.

How does O'Brien juxtapose beauty and horror?

This writer experiments with ways to revise writing prompts for an essay on The Things They Carried.

Lesson 6

Shifting from Motifs to Thesis Statements

STRATEGY

One way writers develop academic thesis statements can be to start with a motif, such as loneliness or secrecy or poetry. Then they ask: What does the novel/author suggest about this motif? They can also ask: What does the character learn about this motif? The answer will often generate a more nuanced, academic thesis.

USE THIS STRATEGY... to support students with an easy strategy for developing thematic statements and theses. This strategy also helps students develop academic theses that they are likely to be able to support, because they have traced the original motif in their reading.

TEACH THE STRATEGY

- Suggest to students that often, a motif runs through a story, and asking what the author/story suggests about that motif leads to interesting thesis statements about themes.
- Display a motif that runs through a familiar text. Demonstrate asking yourself: What does the novel/author suggest about this motif, or what does the character learn?

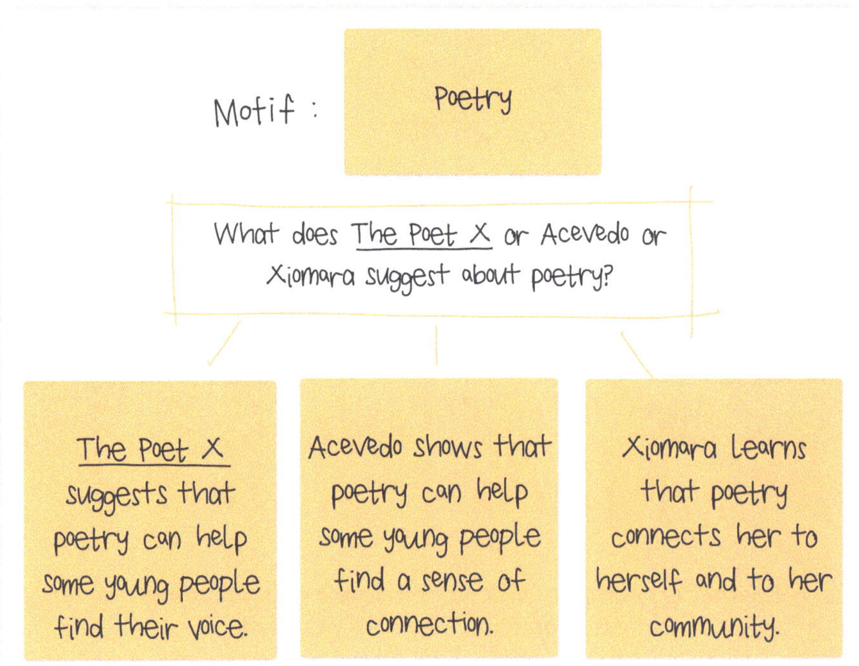

When Lauren demonstrated, she jotted the simple motif, "poetry," and then she asked: What does *The Poet X* or Acevedo or Xiomara suggest about poetry? Then she tried out several answers with her students.

- Jot some more motifs for students to practice with, and invite them to try asking and answering questions like: What does the author suggest about this motif? How does the character connect to this motif? What's its purpose in the story?
- Suggest students write their answers as more developed thesis statements.

PROMPTS TO COACH STUDENTS AND PARTNERSHIPS

It's often interesting to start with what seem like simple motifs—one word for something that runs through the story, like courage or secrecy or abandonment. First, ask yourself where you see this motif in the story and in what parts.

Sometimes it's interesting to ask what the story teaches about a motif. Other times, it's interesting to ask what the character learns.

You can focus on motifs you find personally interesting that run through your life as well—then you'll have more to say about that idea.

CLASSROOM ARTIFACTS

The novel *Thirteen Reasons Why* tells the tale of a teen, Hannah, who commits suicide, arranging for cassette tapes of her reasons to be delivered to each of the students she wants to know her story. The show has generated a lot of controversy about whether it glorifies suicide. This article isn't about that controversy. It's about the subtexts of alternative music, tragedy, and the outsider that operate through the score of the show.

There are musical references throughout the novel. The narrator, Clay, is interested in music, in a way that sets him apart from other characters. But it's in the Netflix series that music emerges as a force in the narrative, weaving thematic parallels, symbolic allusions, and a subtext of the outsider.

This writer expands the motif of music into an examination of theme, symbolism, and subtext in Thirteen Reasons Why.

Sacrifice in *The Hunger Games*

Ideas:

Katniss's sacrifices = caught between personal survival and the well-being of others.

Katniss demonstrates how sacrifice is a strength and a burden/disadvantage (word?)

We learn through Katniss that sacrifice means you are fighting for something bigger than yourself.

Exploring lessons characters learn in The Hunger Games *helps this young writer develop interesting thesis statements.*

Crafting Personal Thesis Statements

Lesson 7

STRATEGY

Some of the most powerful published forms of literary analysis blend the personal and the analytical. Writers who want to try this work often craft thesis statements that bridge the personal and literary by exploring connections with characters. Often they do this by exploring character traits, issues characters struggle with, or lessons characters learn.

USE THIS STRATEGY... if you are open to students writing hybrid literary essays, that bridge the personal and literary. These essays are especially moving, in how they highlight the connections students have made with literary characters.

TEACH THE STRATEGY

- Explain to your writers that when readers immerse themselves in a story, they are in a kind of positive or negative apprenticeship with the characters in that story, and that can be interesting to write about. Often, they find themselves connecting with experiences and emotions that the character feels, because they have felt the same.
    - For students to develop connections between their books and their own lives, turn to the lessons centered around identity maps and issue walls in Chapter 1.
- Curate a few personal and text connections and practice turning the connections into thesis statements. Try this a few ways, noting that there are different ways to structure a personal thesis.

Secrets

Xiomara	Me	Both
• Secrets hurt relationship with her family • Religion and culture are sometimes reason for secrets • Holds in from everyone	• Protecting people in my family from secrets • Trust teachers and other adults with secrets- X doesn't trust any adults	• Wouldn't need to keep secrets if parents were more open to teenage life • Writes to share secrets

- Just like Xiomara, I often wrestle with keeping secrets from my mother. For both Xiomara and me, these lies become destructive forces in our relationship.
- How does keeping secrets from family members shape relationships? Examining the secrets Xiomara keeps in her life, and those I keep in my life, reveals patterns.
- It's not just that Xiomara and I both keep secrets, it's that it's also hard to find confidants because issues of trust can run through relationships, even with people you love.

Lesson 7 (Continued)

When Lauren tried this, she made a chart to compare her experiences with secrets with that of Xiomara's. Then, she pulled ideas from the chart to try out a few different personal thesis statements that could anchor a hybrid personal-literary essay.

- Identify the differences between these theses, noting that one focuses on similarities, another focuses on differences, and one is written more broadly, so both personal and literary experiences can be included later.
- Suggest that students try this work out, first finding points of connection and then trying out different theses to see which one works best.

PROMPTS TO COACH STUDENTS AND PARTNERSHIPS

It can be helpful to think about what part of the story you most connected with, and why. Is there a character trait that you really admire that you'd like to develop as well? Or is there a trait that you also embody that you could write about?

Sometimes the character experiences these very strong emotions, and you feel this sense of sympathy, because you've felt those emotions too—that's always interesting to write about.

Your thesis might sound like …

CLASSROOM ARTIFACTS

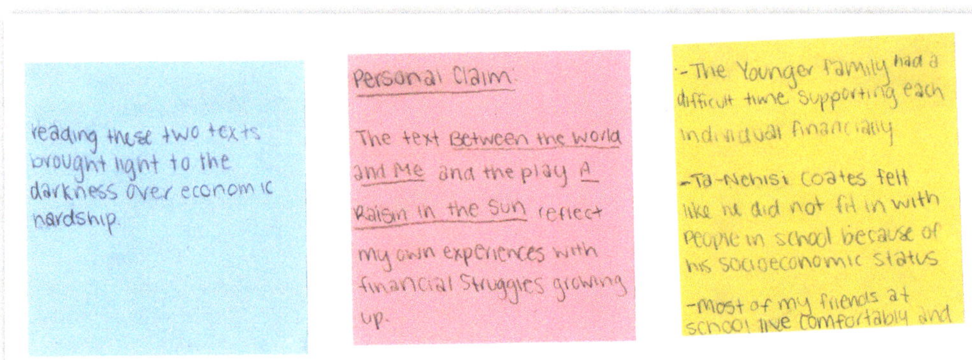

A writer's progression in experimenting with a more personal thesis analyzing A Raisin in the Sun *and* Between the World and Me.

Lesson 8

Using AI to Hone Nuanced, Academic Thesis Statements

STRATEGY

Writers can turn to an AI partner to help them develop more nuanced academic thesis statements. They can do this by prompting their AI partner to ask probing questions, suggest multiple versions of a thesis statement the student has drafted, or explore alternative angles to their thesis statement.

USE THIS STRATEGY... once writers have jotted some preliminary thesis statements. It's important that students come to AI with some ideas. Otherwise, their AI partner will make suggestions that students don't necessarily understand and can't support. An AI partner can help novice writers envision multiple possible ideas as starting points. An AI partner can also help a proficient writer see new possible angles to develop.

Visit hs-guidetoteaching.org to download the chart.

TEACH THE STRATEGY

- Suggest to students that AI can be a very helpful partner when developing thesis statements. Remind students how easily AI will offer many suggestions, and, therefore, how important it is to come to AI with your own ideas as a starting point so that your AI partner supports your thinking.
- Share a teaching chart with some sample prompts for an AI partner.
- Demonstrate one of the strategies, such as prompting your AI partner to ask the writer some questions.
    - Show the messy thinking work of brainstorming answers to these questions, adding on to the thesis, rewriting it all together, and so on.
- Set up students to try this work with their own thesis, having partners check that each student has a preliminary thesis to bring to their AI partner.

Use AI as a Thought Partner to Develop a Thesis

Prompt the AI:

I'm reading... by.... My preliminary thesis is....

Then, ask it to push your thinking by prompting...

- Please suggest some questions that might help me make this thesis more complex.
- Please suggest 5 versions of this thesis, so I can play with the wording.
- Are there some angles on this thesis that might be interesting to explore, that will make it more complicated?

Lesson 8 (Continued)

PROMPTS TO COACH STUDENTS AND PARTNERSHIPS

Remember that AI can easily replace your thinking—you want to use it to make your ideas more powerful. So, first, come to it with an idea. And second, watch for when it might be leading you away from your idea, and tell it to be more careful in helping you strengthen ideas you care about, not ones it cares about.

Once you've reworded your thesis, try rehearsing your ideas again, to take your thesis for a test run. That will ensure you can support this more nuanced thesis.

Sometimes the suggestions your AI partner makes will lead you back to the text. You can reread parts, and perhaps explore new angles, that your AI partner suggested.

CLASSROOM ARTIFACTS

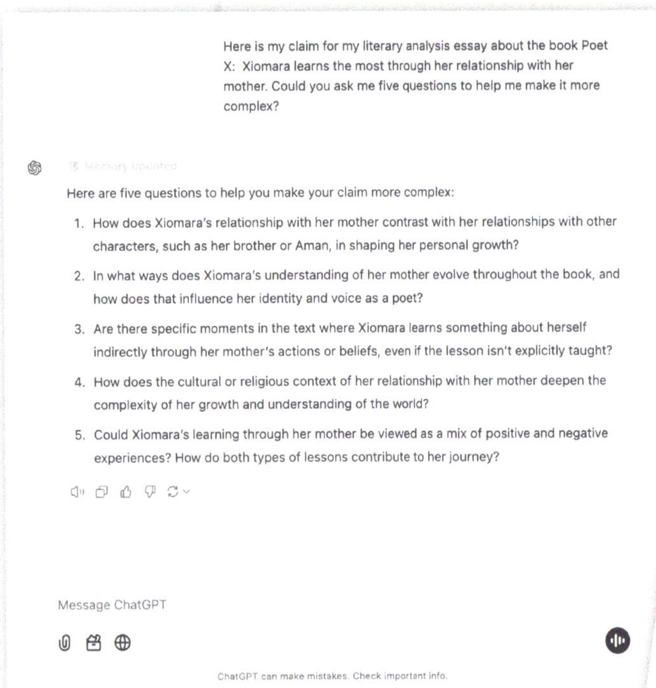

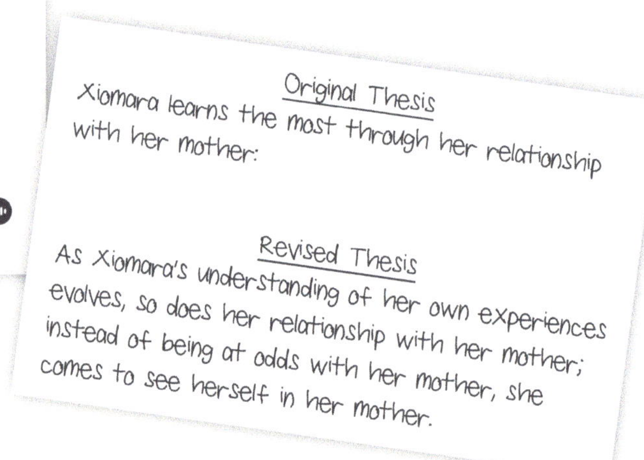

Coley models sharing her thesis and prompting her AI partner to ask her questions. Then she talks over possible answers, ultimately revising her thesis to be more complex.

Here is my thesis: In Pride Remix, American Street, and Punching the Air, Ibi Zoboi uses different writing and storytelling techniques to explore belonging. Could you try writing this five different ways? I'm trying to play with the wording. Keep my ideas in tact.

1. In *Pride Remix*, *American Street*, and *Punching the Air*, Ibi Zoboi uses a variety of writing and storytelling methods to explore the theme of belonging.
2. Ibi Zoboi explores belonging in *Pride Remix*, *American Street*, and *Punching the Air* through different writing styles and storytelling techniques.
3. Through distinct writing and storytelling techniques, Ibi Zoboi examines the theme of belonging in *Pride Remix*, *American Street*, and *Punching the Air*.
4. In *Pride Remix*, *American Street*, and *Punching the Air*, Ibi Zoboi employs various writing and storytelling approaches to explore the idea of belonging.
5. Ibi Zoboi uses different writing and storytelling methods to delve into the theme of belonging in *Pride Remix*, *American Street*, and *Punching the Air*.

Here is my thesis: In Pride Remix, American Street, and Punching the Air, Ibi Zoboi uses different writing and storytelling techniques to explore belonging. What could I replace belonging with?

Here are some options for replacing "belonging" in your thesis:

1. **Identity**
2. **Self-acceptance**
3. **Community**
4. **Connection**
5. **Cultural identity**
6. **Place**
7. **Home**
8. **Inclusion**
9. **Understanding**
10. **Empowerment**

A writer asks her AI partner to wordsmith her thesis but keep her ideas intact.

I'm reading The Catcher in the Rye, and am interested in the idea that the only true love Holden really shows is for his sister, Phoebe, even though he's never with her in the novel. Can you suggest some angles on this thesis, that I could explore?

That's a fantastic thesis! Holden's relationship with Phoebe is one of the few sources of genuine love and connection in *The Catcher in the Rye*, and it reveals a lot about his character. Here are some angles you could explore:

Phoebe as a Symbol of Innocence

- Holden idealizes childhood innocence, and Phoebe embodies that for him.
- His dream of being "the catcher in the rye" reflects his desire to protect children, especially Phoebe, from the corruption of adulthood.
- His interactions with Phoebe contrast with his distrust of adults and older peers, highlighting his fear of growing up.

The Absence of Phoebe and Its Impact on Holden

- Although Holden constantly thinks about Phoebe, he doesn't actually see her until late in the novel.
- His loneliness and downward spiral might be linked to his physical and emotional distance from her.
- When he finally reconnects with her, it marks a turning point—his love for Phoebe may be what keeps him from completely giving up.

An AI partner offers some sophisticated angles.

Chapter Three: Gathering and Organizing Evidence

Reviewing and evaluating evidence in anticipation of drafting is an important step in the writing process for literary essayists. It's a time when writers might revise their thesis to better match their evidence, sift evidence and collect more as needed, and begin to think about the parts of the essay. Hopefully this work doesn't feel surprising for your writers. If they've been building thesis statements and mining for evidence since elementary school (most state ELA tests assess these skills), they've likely spent time considering evidence to support their theses. But, it *is* important to remind them that, as experienced writers, they'll want to consider and *reconsider* both their evidence *and* their ideas as they collect supports for their thinking. Often, reviewing evidence leads writers to deepen and extend their ideas.

The lessons in this chapter assume that students have spent some time collecting ideas and evidence about their reading. If your students still need to spend some time annotating, developing ideas, and generally thinking about the text, we suggest you return to Chapter 1, for some lessons that will help them with that important reading work. It's worth it to invest in kids' reading work as, ultimately, literary essays are only as strong as the thinking students have done about a text.

You'll find in this chapter different angles on collecting, sorting, and evaluating evidence. The first lesson speaks to the fact that writers usually refine their thesis based on the evidence they collect. This lesson responds to a challenge we often see with young writers: where their evidence begins to lead in a slightly different direction, but they don't adjust their thesis statement to match that direction. Teach students that writing is an exploration and that their thinking needs to be open to revision across the writing process.

If you notice some kids are still struggling to match their evidence to their thesis, that might be an indicator that either the text is too hard for them or their thesis is too complex. If it's the former, you might talk to them more about the book, or set them up with an audiobook or different version of the text. If their thesis is overly complex, suggest scaling back to a simpler one that they'll be more successful in supporting. With literary essays, all too often, what looks like writing trouble is really reading trouble.

You'll also find that many of these lessons begin by helping writers review their evidence, and then lead to writers categorizing evidence, so that they become more proficient in deciding which parts of the text best support their ideas. As students categorize their evidence, structures for their essay will often start to emerge.

Similar to earlier chapters, here, we suggest that AI can act as a thought partner, offering writers suggestions for where to find evidence inside the text. Think especially about ways to prompt AI to guide students *toward* evidence but not pick the evidence out for them. In this way, AI does some powerful time-saving work without outsourcing the thinking. You can set these kinds of guardrails if you are using EdTech AI, directing your chatbot to lead students to reread parts of the text, or to consider certain scenes, rather than supply direct quotes. Know that your students, though, can turn to ChatGPT at home, so you'll still want to teach them both how to work with evidence confidently and how to work with AI in ways that preserve their intent and authorship.

Toward the end of the chapter, there's a lesson focused on reading outside the text—turning to reviews, literary criticism, nonfiction, or related narratives as deeper material to explore in a literary essay. A powerful way to make a literary essay more sophisticated is to introduce thinking from outside sources. To make it easy for students to dive into this work, you might provide a "starter set" (we usually provide a Padlet) with some related texts. Students, then, can access and consider ideas from book reviews, or mine literary criticism for lenses, or consider what else was written in this period or this literary tradition. Sometimes we've used the metaphor of a literary family tree, asking what this text grew from, what fertilized it, and what are some of the parallel branches or the fruit that came from it.

The following chart serves as a nice introduction for students to think about how they want to collect evidence. More than anything, the overarching idea of this chapter is for writers to become familiar with a variety of approaches to gathering, sorting, weighing, and evaluating evidence to support and extend their ideas about a text.

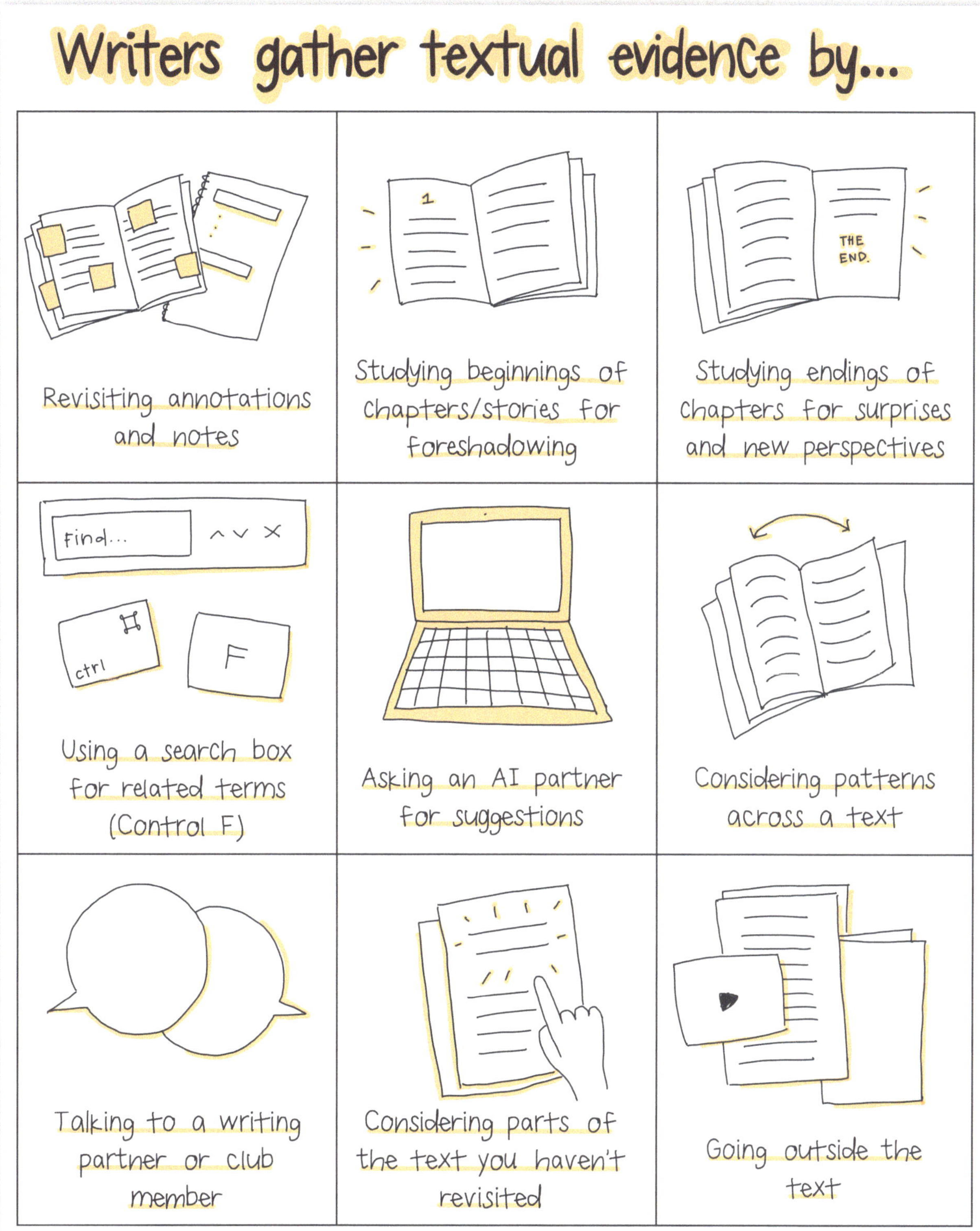
Writers gather textual evidence by...
Revisiting annotations and notes
Studying beginnings of chapters/stories for foreshadowing
1
Studying endings of chapters for surprises and new perspectives
THE END.
Find...
ctrl
F
Using a search box for related terms (Control F)
Asking an AI partner for suggestions
Considering patterns across a text
Talking to a writing partner or club member
Considering parts of the text you haven't revisited
Going outside the text

Lesson 1

Revisiting Evidence Leads to Thesis Refinement

STRATEGY

Writers often revise their theses as they revisit evidence. As writers gather evidence, they can ask themselves:

- How does this evidence connect to my thesis?
- What new thinking does this evidence lead me toward?
- Should I make any revisions to my thesis?

USE THIS STRATEGY... when writers are collecting evidence but aren't fully committed to their thesis statements. This strategy is also helpful in prompting essayists to recognize that some of their evidence doesn't quite match their theses, or the evidence leads the writer in a new direction.

TEACH THE STRATEGY

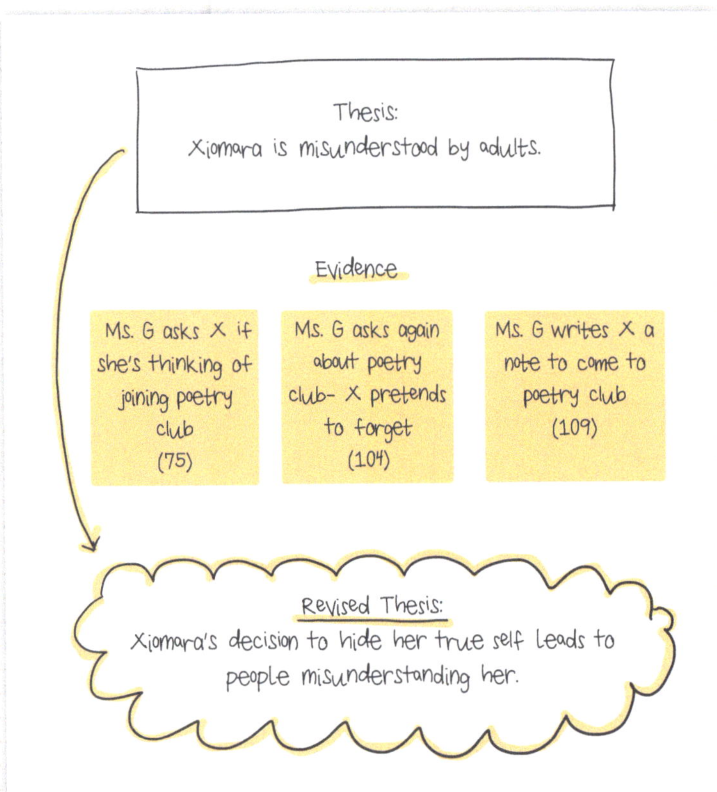

- Remind students that our brains are wired for new information, and that often new information leads to new beliefs. Just as we refine our worldviews all the time, we can revise our theses as we reexamine a text.
- Offer a thesis, ideally one that's open to revision.
- Make a plan for how you'll mine the text for evidence that's related to your thesis. You might revisit relevant plot points, character relationships, or powerful quotes you've noted.
- Flip through the text and your notes to find these moments and mine them for two or three pieces of evidence to support your thesis. Flag these parts of the text with sticky notes or mark them in another way.

- Invite students to join you in considering how this evidence might suggest refining your thesis, asking yourself questions to potentially get to a new version:
  - How does this evidence connect to my thesis?
  - What new thinking does this evidence lead me toward?
  - Should I make any revisions to my thesis?

Lauren, for instance, shared her original thesis about *The Poet X* with the class. As she mined for evidence, Lauren looked for interactions between Xiomara and adults, ultimately finding moments of interaction between Xiomara and her teacher, Ms. Giliano. Using a think-aloud, she talked about how these pieces of evidence led her to changing her thesis, realizing that Xiomara was actually *leading* adults to misunderstand her.

- Encourage students to try this work out, gathering and considering their evidence and asking themselves these questions to revise their theses as needed. Students might then do some freewriting with that new thesis.

PROMPTS TO COACH STUDENTS AND PARTNERSHIPS

So, you're saying this evidence could change your thesis a bit. Let's think about how. You could ask yourself: Is this evidence making my thesis more specific? Is this evidence contradicting something? Could it be that my thesis has to get broader?

Sometimes your evidence will lead to a two-part thesis. Listen to this thesis: Xiomara is misunderstood, and this misunderstanding stems from the secrets she keeps. Do you hear two parts?

It's totally okay if your evidence doesn't change your thesis—sometimes it matches up well! Great work! When you begin doing deeper analysis work, it might change. You just want to make sure you check in at each step of the process.

CLASSROOM ARTIFACTS

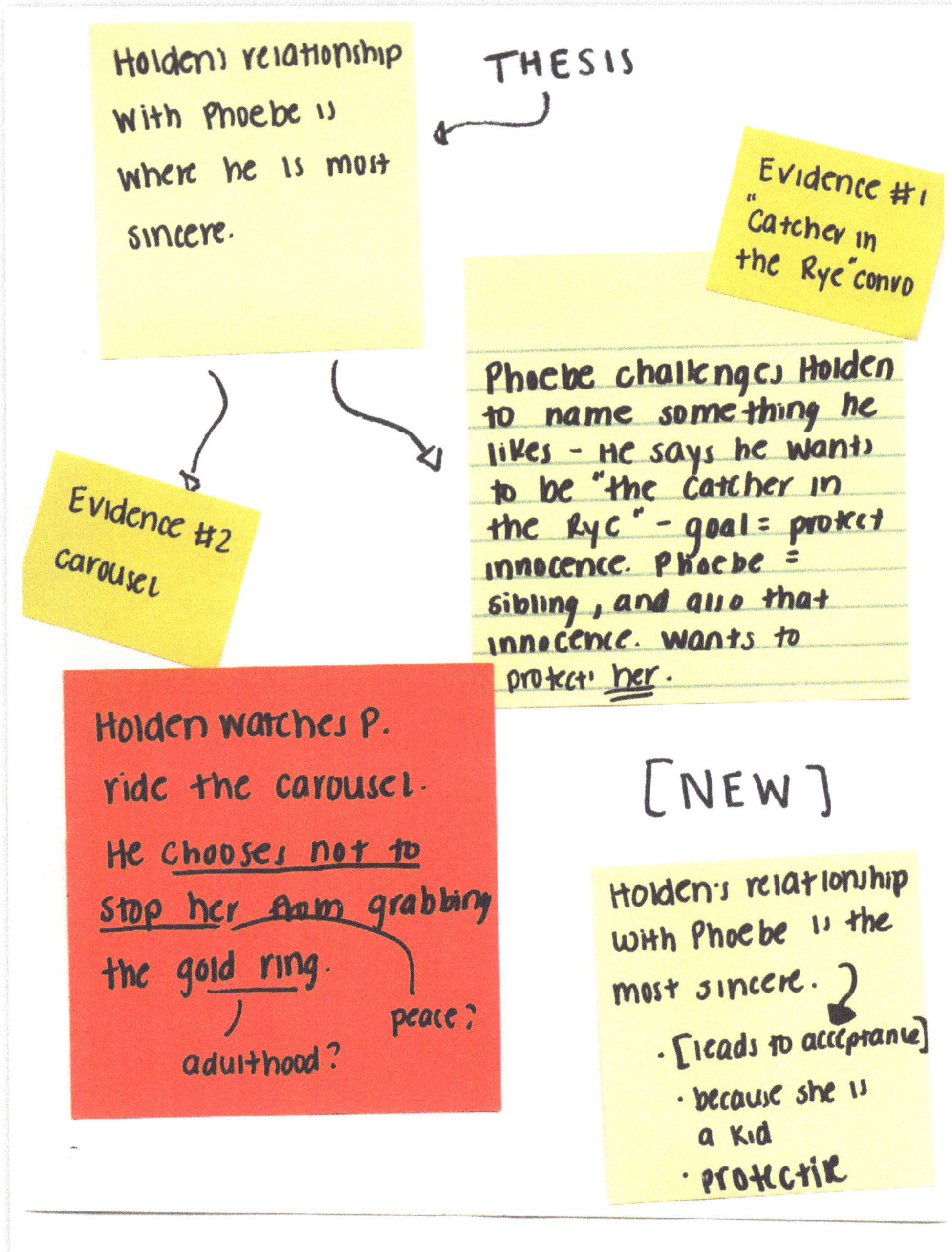

Thinking deeply about evidence leads to thesis revision in this essay on The Catcher in the Rye.

Using Story Elements to Identify Evidence

Lesson 2

STRATEGY

Writers often find that returning to story elements leads them to more easily find text evidence and offers them ways to categorize that text evidence. They might, then, think about things like characterization, setting, conflict, and so on.

USE THIS STRATEGY... when writers have a lot of evidence from one part or chapter of the text and they might need a push to consider different parts of the text in a new light.

- Note that there is a lesson in Chapter 1, Lesson 6, Engaging with Story Elements, to develop new thinking about a text, which would be a good precursor to this lesson.

Visit hs-guidetoteaching.org to download the following chart.

TEACH THE STRATEGY

- Suggest to students that just as writers think about story elements when they are reading, they can return to these elements to both categorize evidence and seek more evidence for their ideas.
- Display your thesis to remind students of the essay you are drafting. Introduce students to a chart listing story elements they might explore.
- Make a chart underneath your thesis with story elements such as setting, character, and conflict (or others you've been exploring).

Thesis:
Xiomara is highly secretive, but the way in which she keeps and reveals secrets changes across the novel.

Setting	Character	Internal Conflict-Desires & Fear of Desires
Science Class - Xiomara is forced to talk with Aman--Lab partners (81)	Xiomara's hesitancy to share - Xiomara doesn't mention Aman to Caridad in Confirmation, but she wanted to (107)	Xiomara memorizes a poem; wants her body to take up all the space, but too scared to share (79)
Smoke Park - Xiomara and Aman only place to spend time together (95)		Xiomara dreamt about Aman and now feels uncomfortable; keeps to self, thoughts swirling. (87)

- Jot down the evidence you already have in each of these categories.

When Lauren modeled this work with her class, she realized she could bolster her evidence in setting and character. She thought aloud about how the evidence across these categories—setting and character—might intersect.

Lesson 2 (Continued)

- Look over the story elements, inviting students to join you in noticing areas where you have a lot of evidence and areas where you have little evidence. Generate more evidence in this category that could support your thesis, or look at some evidence from other parts of the chart with a new lens.
- Set up students to try this work independently. Display your notebook pages as references students can use as they identify and categorize evidence, and make sure students have a chart of story elements.
- Encourage students to share new evidence, or ways they are categorizing, with a partner and to talk through implications for how their essay might go.

PROMPTS TO COACH STUDENTS AND PARTNERSHIPS

You could also use this strategy to figure out what kind of essay you want to write. Your essay about ______ might work best as an essay centered on one story element, for instance.

Know that you can insert your own story elements. Which story elements feel important for your essay?

Could you use that evidence in more than one category? Sometimes how we angle our evidence depends on the lens we use to look at it. Could you look at that moment with the lens of setting? Or maybe look at it with the lens of conflict.

CLASSROOM ARTIFACTS

Story elements writers might explore and use to gather evidence.

Using Motifs to Collect and Sort Evidence

Lesson 3

STRATEGY

Literary essayists know that focusing on parts of a story that demonstrate an overall motif casts a wider net for collecting evidence than a narrower thesis statement. Sometimes, therefore, writers consider motifs connected to their theses and use those motifs to find and categorize evidence.

USE THIS STRATEGY... when essayists could use more evidence for certain parts of their thesis or when a student's thesis feels too narrow to lead to several parts of a text (which may prompt them to revise their thesis). You can also use it when students have lots of evidence and are thinking about ways to categorize it.

- For a lesson on growing ideas about motifs, see Shifting from Motifs to Thesis Statements in Chapter 2.

Visit hs-guidetoteaching.org to download the chart of common literary motifs.

TEACH THE STRATEGY

- Suggest to students that just as readers investigate motifs in stories, writers can return to motifs to find and categorize evidence.
- Review the definition of motif, explaining that motifs can be repeated images, objects, symbols, or ideas. Share a chart of literary motifs that often appear in novels.
- Display your thesis for students. Invite students to join you in asking: What are some motifs that show up in the text that can relate to this thesis? Demonstrate how you use these motifs to guide your search for evidence. Skim through the text, finding a section to reread, asking yourself: Are any of my motifs present here?

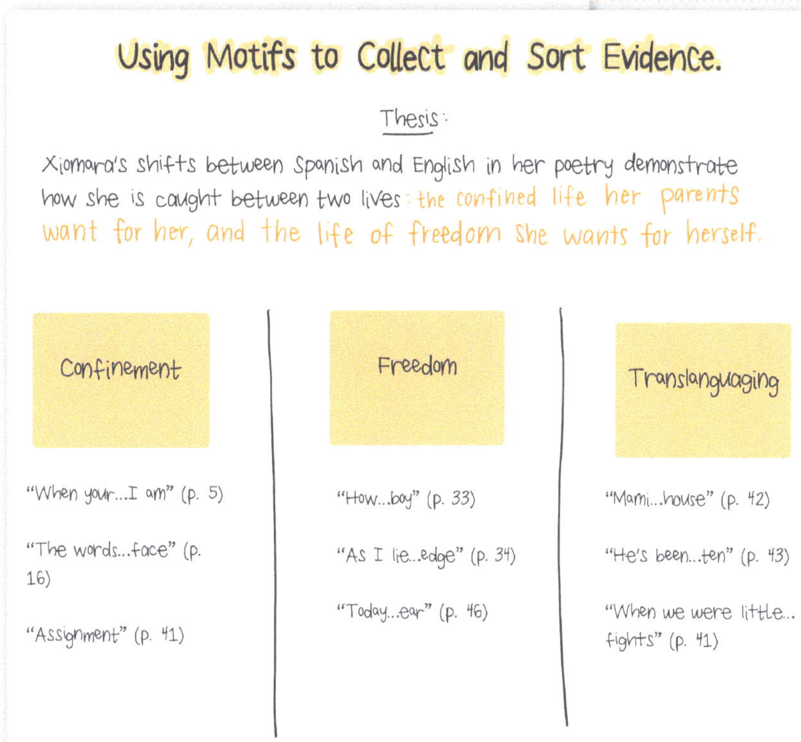

When Coley demonstrated with her class, she generated a chart with several motifs and moved some evidence from her notes in the book into the chart. Coley then thought aloud about how she could add to her thesis and revised it in orange.

- Invite writers to try this work out with their own theses, offering it as a way to search for more evidence and to categorize evidence.

PROMPTS TO COACH STUDENTS AND PARTNERSHIPS

A lot of motifs are shared across narratives. It can help to start by considering some common motifs, asking if these run through your story—and which might relate to your thesis.

Could you organize your essay around these motifs? Does this work as the starting point of an outline?

Sometimes, you find more evidence for a motif that fascinates you than for your original thesis. If this is the case, you may want to revise your thesis.

CLASSROOM ARTIFACTS

Literary Motifs that Appear Often in Novels

Lonliness	Isolation	Regret
Liberation	Transformation	Self-doubt
Oppression	Desire	Resilience
Abandonment	Betrayal	Forgiveness
Entrapment	Sacrifice	Free will
Love	Power	Resistance

Turning to AI to Develop Your Evidence

Lesson 4

STRATEGY

In this digital age, writers can turn to AI as a thought partner to help them develop their thinking, especially about text evidence and parts of the story they want to discuss. When engaging with an AI partner, it helps to be firm in guiding the conversation, to make sure your AI partner helps develop, rather than replace, the writer's thinking.

USE THIS STRATEGY... when essayists have some preliminary thinking and they're ready to develop that thinking by talking through ideas and considering parts of the text that seem important.

Visit hs-guidetoteaching.org to download the following chart.

TEACH THE STRATEGY

- Advise students that AI can be a very helpful thought partner and that it helps to initiate your conversation with an AI partner by explaining what you are most interested in, in detail, to control the conversation.
- Demonstrate, using an EdTech AI that students can use in your class, how you review your notes and use those to share your preliminary ideas (see Classroom Artifacts for a sample).
- Share a sample of the feedback an AI partner might give and invite students to unpack what's helpful about it (see Classroom Artifacts for a sample).

Partnering with AI to Develop Evidence

- Come with ideas to share and describe those ideas in detail
- Tell your AI partner what parts of the text you're already interested in
- Notice how your AI partner often summarizes what you say and inserts new suggestions
- Ask for suggestions of parts you might revisit for more evidence
- Don't let your AI partner take over! Notice if it is veering off into an idea it likes, and bring it back to be your assistant!

Lesson 4 (Continued)

- Share a chart that will support students in this work. Set up students with EdTech AI to practice this work (you can define parameters beforehand), and then jot notes on new thinking they might want to develop in their essays.

PROMPTS TO COACH STUDENTS AND PARTNERSHIPS

It helps to take a moment to prepare for your AI partner talk. Look over your notes, so you can start by sharing what you are already thinking.

Notice when your AI partner summarizes what you said. Often, your AI partner will also tuck in some new thinking that you can consider.

Check that your AI partner isn't becoming overwhelming. If it's giving you too much feedback, or is leading you away from your idea, tell it! Give your AI partner feedback!

CLASSROOM ARTIFACTS

I want to think about evidence for the first part of my essay – how Xiomara is secretive even with admitting things to herself. When I reread my notes, I'm really interested in two parts of the story. One is the part where she admits she maybe has doubts about the church. That's in the poem called "Confirmation Class." Xiomara says that "Jesus feels like a friend/I've had my whole childhood/who has suddenly become brand-new:/who invites himself over too often, who texts me too much./". Then she adds: "A friend I just don't think I need anymore./ (I know, I know...even writing that is blasphemous.") I think it's interesting that Xiomara is so cautious in writing about her feelings, like she can't admit openly that she no longer trusts the Church or feels comforted by Jesus - the way she says he's like a friend she'd like to abandon. It's also interesting how she describes him as someone who invites himself over too much, or texts too much - so that shows that Jesus for her was someone she did initially feel was a friend, and she's not ready to just reject him openly. And when she says her feelings are blasphemous, that feels like she's at this critical point where she is beginning to say things, but also feel guilty for them at the same time. Does that make sense?

Absolutely—this is a fantastic close reading of the poem! You've uncovered several nuanced layers that reveal Xiomara's internal conflict and her position in a liminal space between denial and acknowledgment of her religious doubts.

1. Your observation about the metaphor of Jesus as a clingy friend is particularly insightful. Rather than rejecting faith outright, Xiomara describes a gradual emotional distancing from something that was once deeply important to her. This metaphor captures both past intimacy and present discomfort, showing that her faith still holds emotional weight even as she begins to pull away from it.
2. The line "(I know, I know... even writing that is blasphemous)" is especially powerful. It reveals how Xiomara is:
   - Catching and correcting her own thoughts in real time
   - Possibly imagining how others—perhaps her mother—would respond
   - Acknowledging the boldness or danger of her feelings while still choosing to express them
3. What's also compelling is how the passage itself progresses—from the safer critique ("Jesus is too clingy") to the riskier emotional truth ("I don't need him"). This movement suggests that Xiomara is slowly building the courage to confront what she really feels, even if she can't fully admit it yet.

You might consider looking for another passage that mirrors this same process—where Xiomara starts by expressing discomfort and gradually edges closer to a fuller self-admission. This kind of evidence works especially well for the first part of your essay, since it highlights how poetry becomes a space for Xiomara to voice what she's not yet ready to say out loud. Even in her private writing, she's still filtering and qualifying her emotions—which tells us a lot about where she is on her journey.

↓

Mary demonstrates using her notes to share her initial thinking with her AI partner. She shares what she found interesting about this part of the text. Then she asks her AI partner for some feedback on her thinking.

Leveraging Endings to Find Significant Quotes

Lesson 5

STRATEGY

Writers seek significant quotes that summarize something important or manifest a big idea. One interesting place to search for these kinds of quotes is endings. The endings of sections, chapters, and books often reveal shifts in character or perspective, turns of events, thematic developments, or quotes that provide intriguing textual evidence.

USE THIS STRATEGY... when writers are searching for key moments in the text to return to, to find evidence. This strategy can be particularly helpful when writers need help gathering more evidence or when writers need to gather evidence from across the text, rather than from just one part.

TEACH THE STRATEGY

- Introduce the strategy, discussing a few important reasons to look at the ends of chapters or sections of text, potentially citing Roy Peter Clark, author and writing teacher, who argues the last sentence of a paragraph is more important than the first (2013, 2016).
- Model skimming chapter and section endings, on the lookout for evidence that can support or expand your thesis.
- Name what you're noticing about the evidence you're seeing, while also weighing whether it will work for your essay. Demonstrate, as well, if your thesis expands.

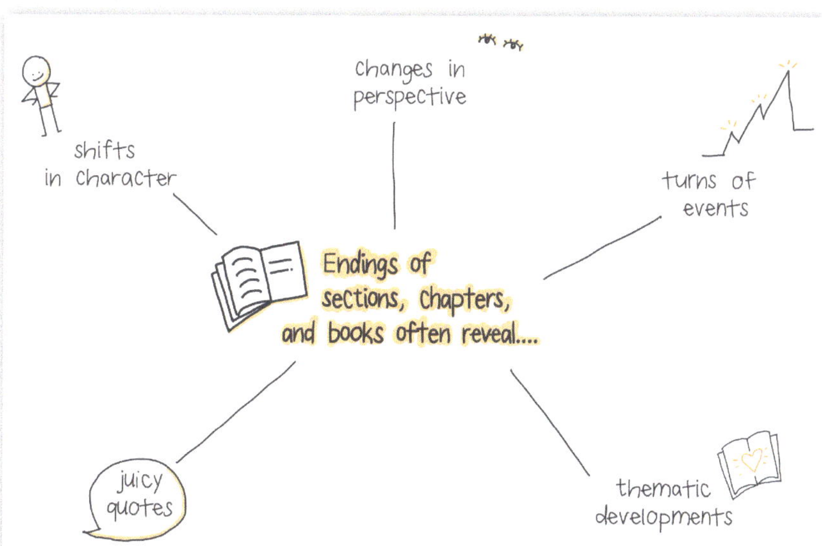

Lesson 5
(Continued)

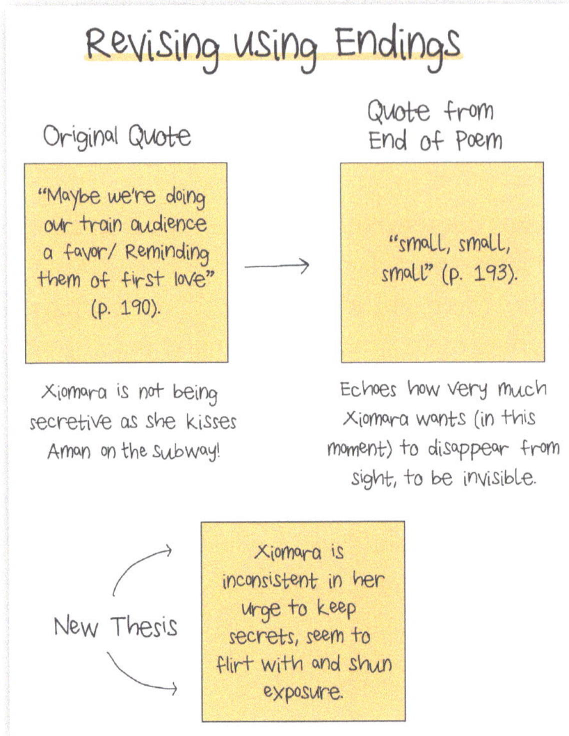

As Mary tried this with a class, she first displayed her thesis—Xiomara is secretive—and started looking for evidence in Part II of the novel. She looked across pages, naming out the last lines of pages, deciding whether they fit with her idea. Soon she read aloud from page 190. Then on page 193, Mary pointed out how Xiomara ends her poem "Together." These parts helped Mary revise her thesis.

- Invite students to try this work by looking more closely at a few endings (of chapters, of parts of text) to see if they might find new evidence that supports/extends their theses.

PROMPTS TO COACH STUDENTS AND PARTNERSHIPS

Sometimes the endings of chapters will also jog your memory of what happened in that part. Endings are a starting point, so remember you can pull evidence from any moment in the text to support your ideas.

Check over your evidence to see which of your ideas you've supported the most and which could benefit from more evidence. Which endings could you turn to in looking for more evidence? Think about sections, chapters, or the end of the book.

Beginnings of the book, chapters, or sections can also be powerful places, as the author is setting up characters and conflict. What beginnings might you want to return to, to support your ideas?

CLASSROOM ARTIFACTS

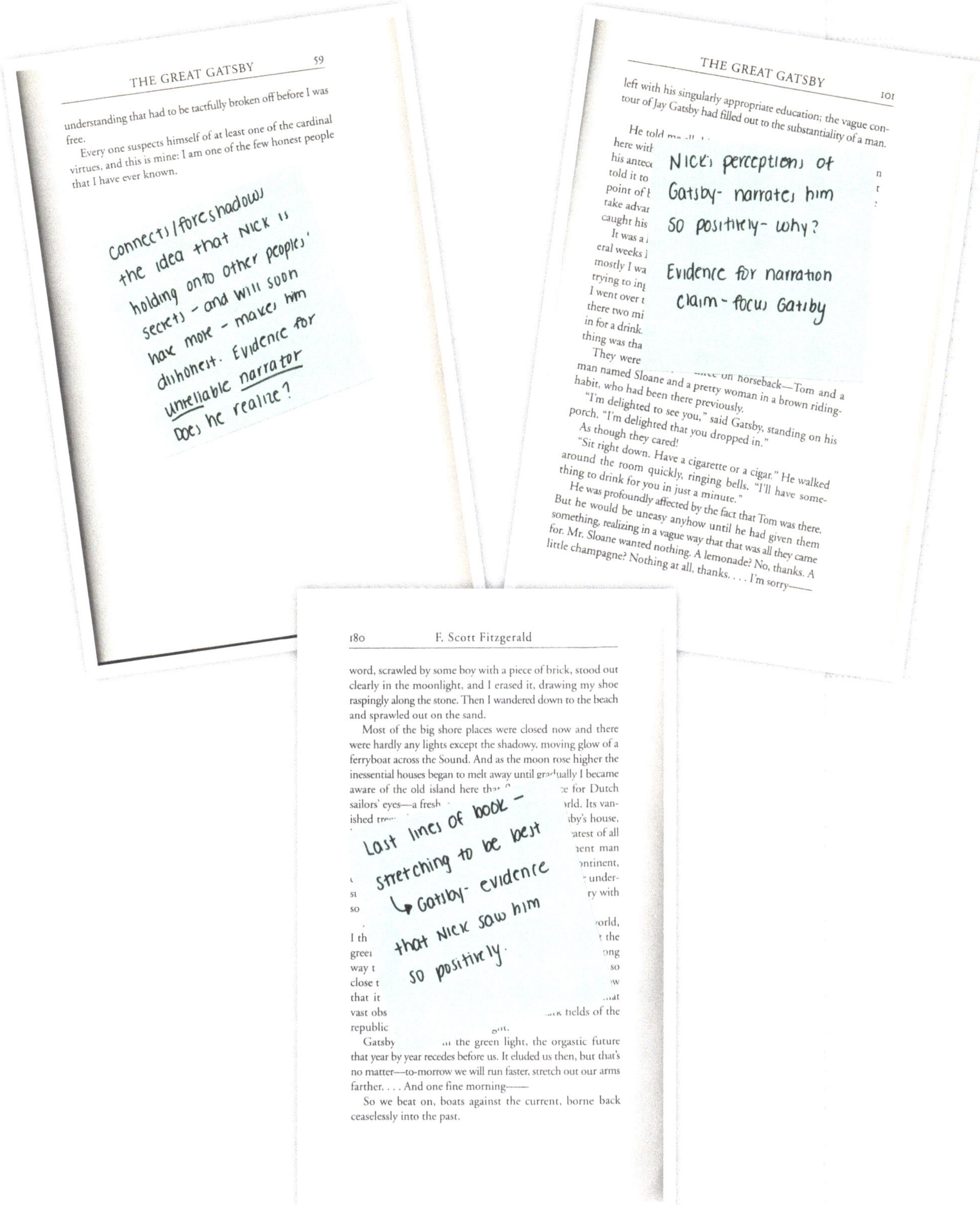

Paying attention to endings in The Great Gatsby.

Lesson 6

Revisiting the Text to Rethink and Revise Evidence

STRATEGY

Often writers end up with more evidence than they will necessarily want to include in their final draft, or they find they have evidence that doesn't perfectly match their thesis. Writers, therefore, often find they need to audit the evidence they've selected. One way to do this is by going back into the text and rereading those parts of the text to see if a different part is a better fit for their thesis.

Visit hs-guidetoteaching.org to download a chart on revisiting evidence.

USE THIS STRATEGY... when writers have collected various pieces of evidence and are ready to home in on which pieces support their theses, they have lots of evidence they need to sort through, or they have sparse evidence they need to develop.

TEACH THE STRATEGY

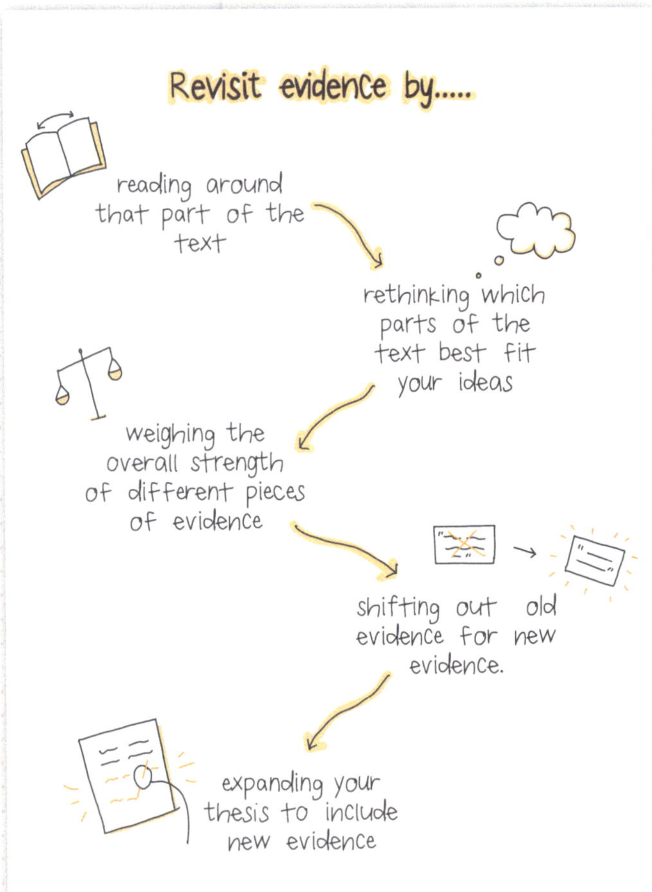

- Suggest to students that as writers get closer to drafting, they often find they have extra evidence, or evidence that may not match their thesis perfectly, or part of their idea that still needs evidence.
- Explain that writers, therefore, often return to the text to consider their evidence. Project the thesis you're using as a model.
- Show a quote from the text as evidence you've selected to support your thesis, one that's loosely connected but isn't quite right.
- Model going back to the page/moments, looking at the text around the quote you selected to find that one that fits best.
- Adjust the quote you're using to support your thesis statement, showing your thinking about what moment you decide to use. Explain your decision making and steps.

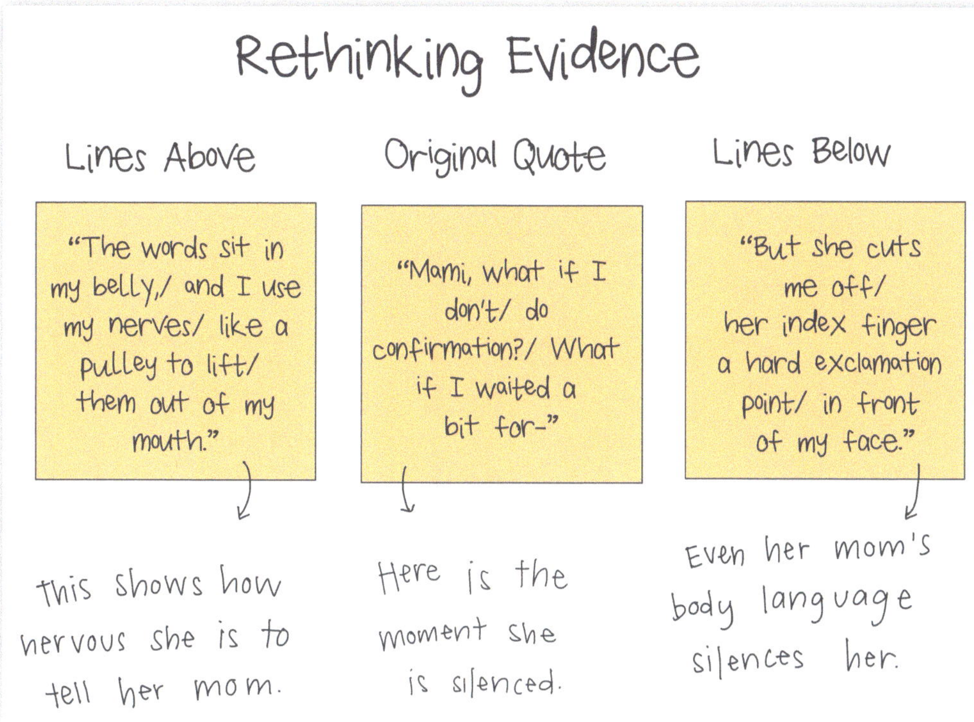

Coley, for instance, modeled this strategy based on one of her body paragraphs focused on the thesis that Xiomara feels silenced by those around her. She showed the quote she picked from page 16 and demonstrated how this quote connects. Coley modeled looking above and below to see if there was a better fit for her argument. She landed on the first stanza on page 16 as her students weighed in on which part of the poem they thought worked better. She also showed how a writer could pair these quotes together.

- Offer students the opportunity to practice these same steps with their own evidence, returning to the text to reread around the parts they've quoted.

PROMPTS TO COACH STUDENTS AND PARTNERSHIPS

Sometimes it's helpful to explain to your partner why a piece of evidence fits your idea. That can help you evaluate how strong that evidence is.

This is a longer quote—can you think about which parts to summarize and which parts to keep? Think about which parts are most important to the thesis.

You could look more than a few lines up and down. You could even go back or forward a few pages. What do you want to try first?

CLASSROOM ARTIFACTS

Thesis:

Xiomara is secretive.

★★ related & obvious	★★★ related & intriguing	★★★★ subtle—comentary explains
"Mrs. Guliano asks me about the Spoken Word Poetry Club/and I try to pretend I forgot about it" (104).	"My brother is no secret, no prophet/but it makes me smile,/this secret hope we share, that we are both good enough/for each other and maybe the world, too" (73).	"I touch my tongue to the world volition,/like it's a fruit I've never tasted/that's already gone sour in my mouth" (26)

Ranking evidence helps writers choose evidence which is best for their argument.

Using Literary Devices to Develop Evidence

Lesson 7

STRATEGY

Writers often find that exploring literary devices leads them to develop new evidence and sometimes new thinking across the text overall.

USE THIS STRATEGY... when writers are ready to explore not only important moments and ideas in the text but how the writer conveys these moments and ideas. Returning to a chart of literary devices also helps writers develop language for techniques they see in the text.

Visit hs-guidetoteaching.org to download the chart of narrative literary devices.

TEACH THE STRATEGY

- Suggest to students that writers often pay attention to *how* parts of the text are written—to literary devices—and that attention often leads to new thinking.
- Display your thesis to remind students of the essay you are drafting and introduce (or remind students of) narrative literary devices, using this chart or one you've created with your class.
- Demonstrate choosing a device and gathering/jotting some of the evidence for that category.
- Set up students to try this work independently. Make sure they have a chart of literary devices to explore. Encourage students to think and jot about the overall effect of these literary devices and how they might relate to ideas the writer has about the text.

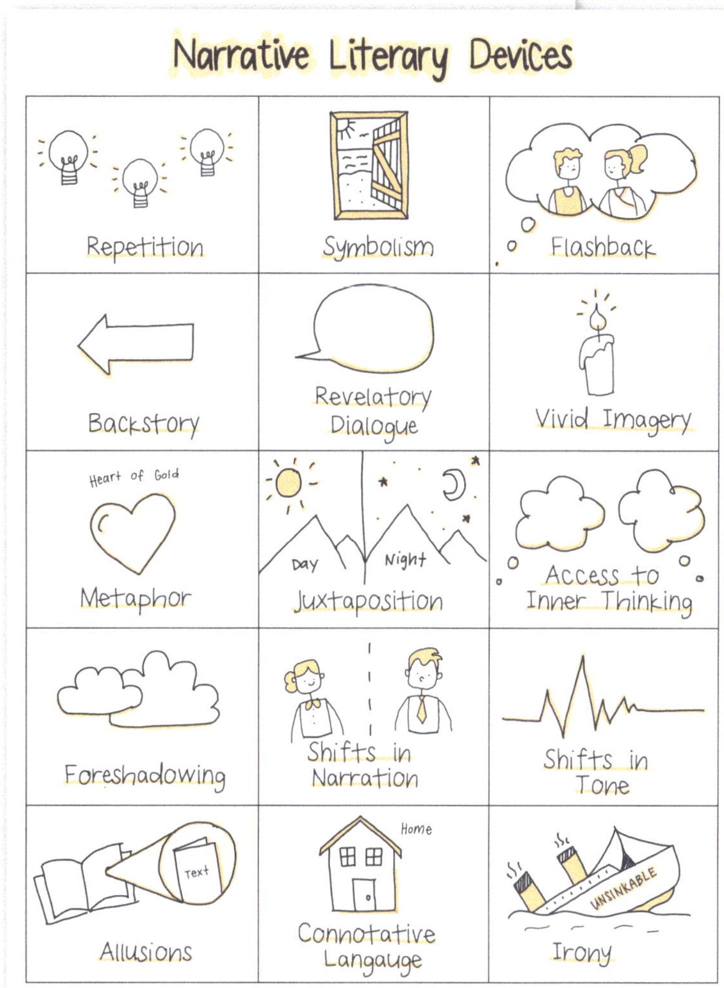

Lesson 6
(Continued)

Thesis:
Xiomara is highly secretive, but the way in which she keeps and reveals secrets changes across the novel.

Repetition

Poem: "What I Don't Tell Aman" (148)

- "I can't...." (date/invite him/be seen with him etc.)
- Then the last line – "I can't fall in love"

Xiomara repeats the line "I can't" and each line feels like one hard thing – then it builds to something impossible, because you can't stop your heart from loving. That idea, that stopping love is impossible, seems to be something Xiomara is hiding from.

When Mary modeled this strategy with her class, she returned to a part of the story where Xiomara's writing strongly reveals the literary technique of repetition, and she thought about what effect that repetition has and how it led her to a new idea to support her thesis.

PROMPTS TO COACH STUDENTS AND PARTNERSHIPS

Sometimes it helps to return to a part of the text you've already noted because it supports your thesis and see what literary devices the author uses there. Then you can ponder the effect of that device and how it helps develop your idea.

You might simply think about the parts of the text that stand out to you for some of these devices. It's almost like playing literary bingo, where you take your chart and look for these devices in the text. See if any of them feel relevant to your thesis.

In some novels, like The Poet X, *the character uses devices as well as the author. For instance, Xiomara's poetry is a feature inside of the novel—the novel is her notebook, so we can talk about devices she uses in her poetry. In other novels, the character may use devices in their dialogue, like Starr in* The Hate U Give *makes allusions, and Holden in* The Catcher in the Rye *sometimes daydreams as flashbacks.*

CLASSROOM ARTIFACTS

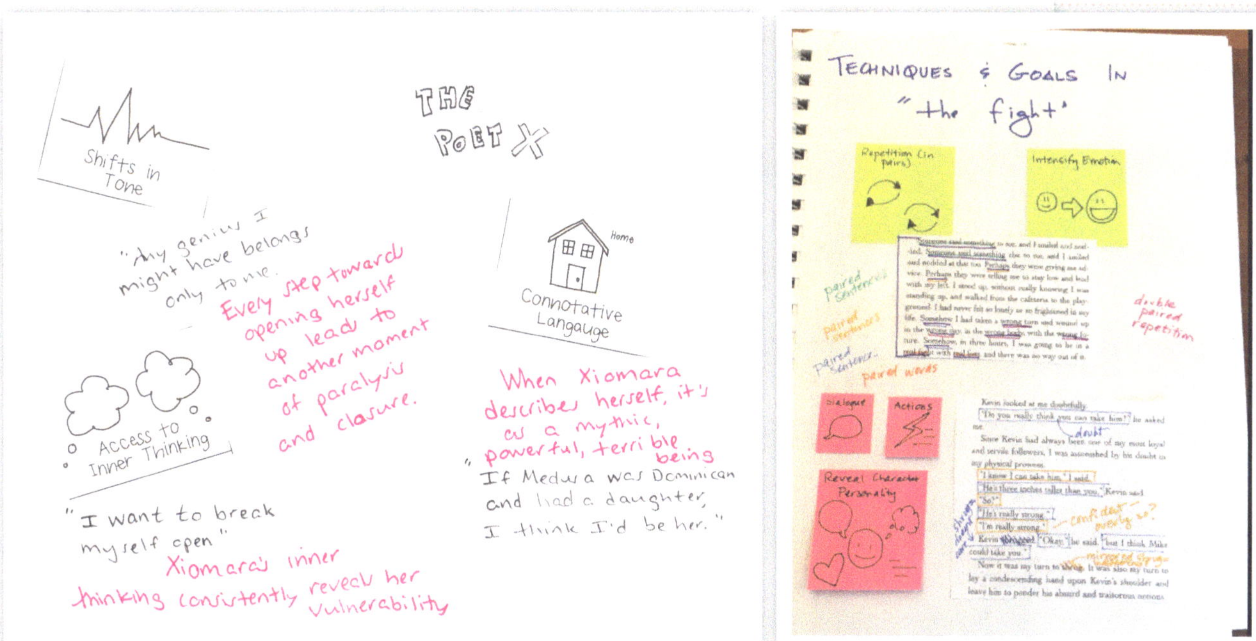

Exploring literary devices leads to close reading in The Poet X *and the short story "The Fight".*

Lesson 8

Reading and Pulling in Evidence Beyond the Text

STRATEGY

Literary essayists often read outside the text to deepen their thinking. They may read to learn more about the literary tradition, the era, or the historical context, or they may read to find out what others have said about the text. All of these options can give essayists more to think about and say.

Visit hs-guidetoteaching.org to access text sets to support reading around the text, including one for The Poet X, as well as other examples.

USE THIS STRATEGY... to help writers deepen their thinking and work with outside sources. This strategy can make a topic more contextualized and can lead to more complex thinking and writing.

TEACH THE STRATEGY

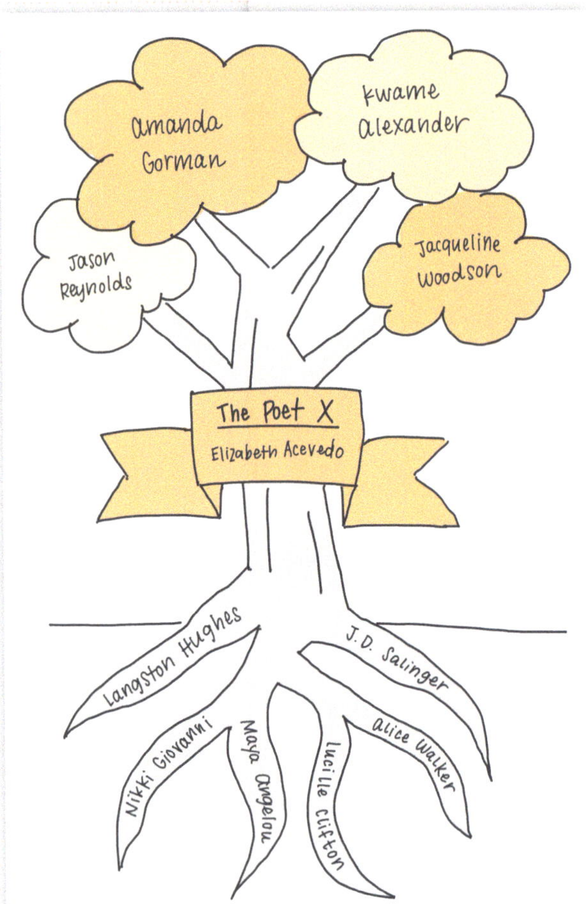

- Introduce the idea that literary essayists often read outside a text to think more deeply about that text.
- You might invite students to think about what might go on a literary family tree for a common text (we use *The Poet X*) and sketch that. To think of a literary tree for a text, think genealogy (antecedents and descendants). The roots are the writers and texts that came before this text and made it possible. The branches are writers and texts that stem from this text, so that altogether the tree helps you envision how this text is part of a literary tradition.
- Suggest that there are common kinds of texts that readers and writers turn to, to extend their thinking, and display a chart with a collection of possible resources. If you've made a text set to support this work, share that as well.
- Invite students to join you in reading a snippet of one of these texts, to consider how it might deepen and extend your thinking.

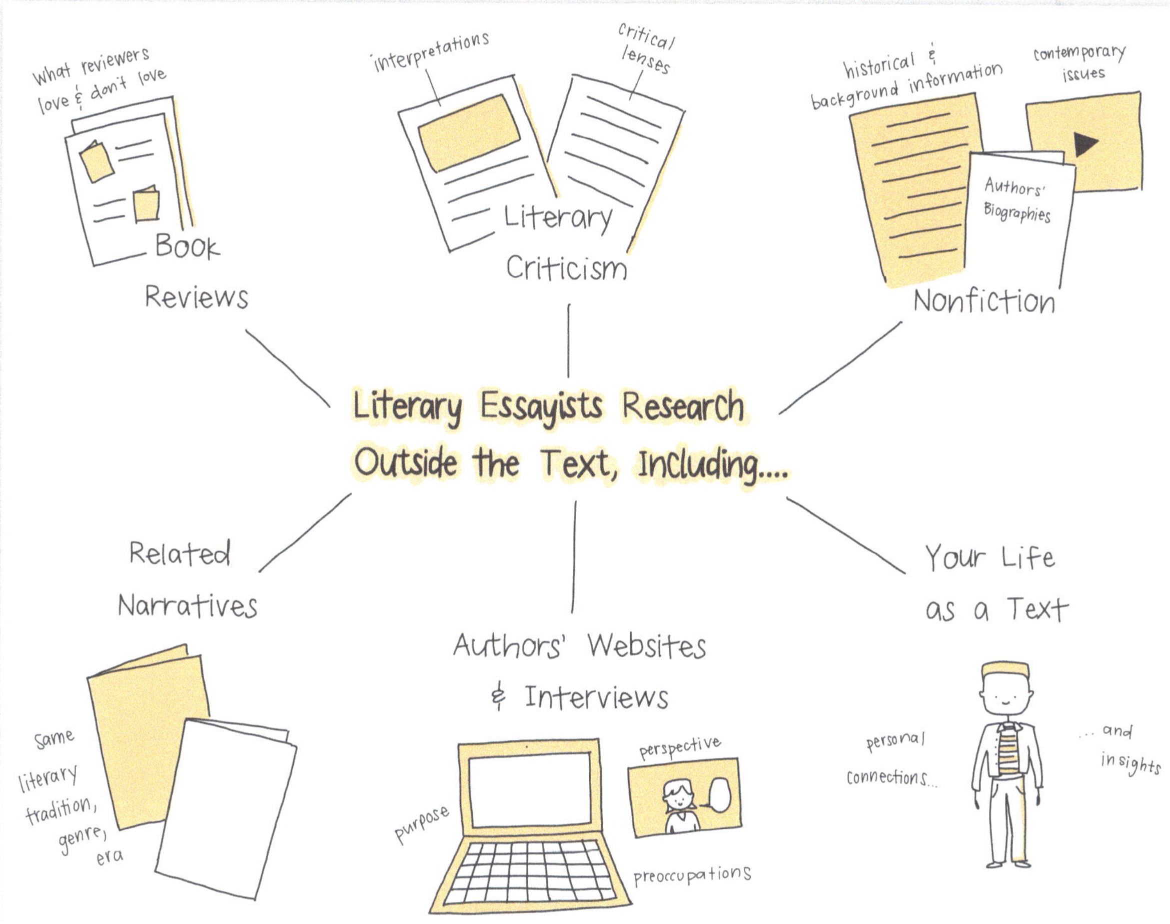

When Lauren tried this out, she first went back to one version of her thesis: Xiomara has parts of herself she keeps secret.

Lauren then invited students to watch a snippet of an interview with Elizabeth Acevedo where she talks about Xiomara's identity as a Morenita, and how strongly she asserts that identity, even while she is so unsure in asserting other parts of herself. Lauren then modeled, adding to her thesis, that Xiomara has parts of herself she keeps secret *and* parts of herself she asserts confidently. She also showed how to add a quote in from Acevedo as evidence.

"As Acevedo explains in her interview with VOX ATL, Xiomara strongly asserts her identity as a Morenita, a light-brown-skinned woman of Dominican heritage."

- Suggest that writers spend some time reading outside their own text, either by sending them to starter sets you've provided or by giving them some easy search terms.
    - Author-title-review
    - Author-title-summary
    - Author-title-literary criticism
    - Author-title-Kirkus/New York Times/ALJ

PROMPTS TO COACH STUDENTS AND PARTNERSHIPS

Sometimes it's really helpful to look at reviews or summaries, to see if there are parts of the text that you haven't considered or ideas you might quote.

Literary criticism often leads to totally new perspectives. If you're inspired, you can reference a critique as a starting point for your own interpretation.

Consider where you want to add this new source into your essay. What other evidence would it pair well with? How will you introduce it?

CLASSROOM ARTIFACTS

The Fragmentation of Male Desire in *The Scarlet Letter*

Nathaniel Hawthorne's *The Scarlet Letter* tells the tale of forbidden and destructive love. The central love focus is ostensibly Hester Prynne, whose histories with the minister Dimmesdale and relations with her own husband, Chillingworth, are shrouded in secrets. The greater intimacy in the story, though, is between Dimmesdale and Chillingworth. This relationship, despite its suppressed, secret, and hidden qualities, is what ultimately subsumes Dimmesdale in a way his relationship with Hester never did. Scott Derrick, author of *Monumental Anxieties,* offers a provocative theoretical framework to analyze *The Scarlet Letter*. He writes that "Hawthorne's *The Scarlet Letter* contains much that we, as contemporary readers, would recognize as the machinery of homophobia." (44). Taking Derrick's framework as a lens, the relationship of Dimmesdale and Chillingworth suggests a world of men as an inchoate world of suppressed desires, incoherent roles, and violent ruptures.

This senior brings critical lenses and outside authors to his reading of The Scarlet Letter.

In episode three, Alex drops into a pool. The Chromatics' cover of Neil Young's "Into the Black" plays while Alex falls into the water. Only it's not actually "Into the Black," but the version of Young's song that the Chromatics cover in an acoustic version that subs in the line "It's better to burn out than to fade away." That line plays behind Alex as he floats upside down in the pool.

Alex comes up for air, but others who knew that line haven't. "It's better to burn out than to fade away," was quoted by Kurt Cobain in his suicide note. There's something else important. Critics of the show fear that it will inspire teen suicide—glamorize it, romanticize it. Neil Young himself was haunted by Cobain's use of his lyric in his suicide note. He wrote and dedicated his 1994 album, *Sleeps with Angels* to Cobain, and inspired a generation of new punk bands, perhaps in the way that Hannah's tapes inspire her listeners.

This writer brings in outside sources to enrich his analysis of the score of Thirteen Reasons Why.

Part II
Drafting and Lifting the Level of Analysis

Chapter Four: Writing with Structure

If your writers are ready to solidify a plan and draft, it's likely that's because they've done a lot of work as *readers*. They have tracked their ideas and thinking throughout the book, refined those ideas and brainstormed thesis statements, and mined the text for evidence. Much of this work can happen as you read a story (best of all in a book club!), or for a few days in a row before students draft. See Chapters 1–3 for many ideas on cultivating students' interpretations and annotation skills.

You'll see this chapter starts with an inquiry that focuses on the structural choices that published writers make. The goal is for young writers to notice that lots of published essays, book reviews, and literary criticism have all the components we're used to: thesis statements, evidence, commentary, background info, and counterarguments. The major difference is how these writers choose to structure their analyses, compared to how we often structure them in school. It can be helpful to shift from thinking of essays or analyses in terms of individual paragraphs and moving toward the idea of sections or parts instead. This approach encourages writers to think about how to best represent each idea and to expand each part across multiple paragraphs when needed.

Experienced writers also know paragraphs can go many different ways—a paragraph might be mostly retelling, an idea fleshed out with evidence and analysis, or it might even be one sentence, with a point that's intended to pack a punch. Across these lessons, the hope is that writers begin to think more intentionally about the *purpose* of each paragraph and the different ways to structure them.

While we are aiming to push the boundaries for students in terms of how they conceptualize literary analysis, we also aim for them to develop their own individualized writing process by learning ways to quickly plan and draft. It can be beneficial to encourage students to ask themselves why they are choosing to plan in a particular way, what's worked for them in the past, and what's been challenging when it comes to writing literary analyses.

Even though it can feel easier for each student to be writing with the same structure, it will be more authentic to let students navigate their own journeys here. Avoid writing one paragraph per day, or having all writers working at the same pace—writers simply don't work that way. In this same vein, we encourage you to teach your students flash drafting, a powerful way for kids to quickly write down the page, writing down their initial ideas in a short burst. Flash drafting often results in a messy first draft, but it leads to a rapid starting place for revision. We find when we move slowly and methodically, paragraph by paragraph, students' writing becomes dull and formulaic, and your writers are burned out by the time you want them to be ready for revision and editing.

Of course, we know getting down the page quickly is challenging for some students. The chart in Lesson 3 hopefully offers a starting point, but we also crafted an If ... Then ... chart to support students in the variety of ways writers might organize their thoughts into parts. You'll find our sample essays in the appendix of the book and a video of us teaching a flash-drafting lesson on our website as well. Feel free to take one of our sample essays and make it into your demonstration text, or, even better, model writing your own. It will be powerful for your writers to see you planning and flash-drafting as a mentor writer.

We hope this chapter serves as an invitation to guide students toward more authentic, flexible, and purposeful writing—where structure serves meaning, and drafting becomes a tool for discovery.

If...	Then...
A student finds organizing a literary analysis overwhelming. . .	You might offer a simple chronological structure: • Intro • For example, early in the narrative. . . • We see this again when. . . • Later in the story. . . • Conclusion
A student wants to adhere to a simple structure but still lead their reader on a journey of thought. . .	You might suggest they start with a question or theory in the introduction and build across a simple chronological structure to a thesis in the conclusion.
A student needs to build fluency with planning what will go in each part of their writing. . .	Return to verbal rehearsal. Invite the student to jot a simple plan of their parts and then rehearse their draft out loud. It's often helpful to record these and invite students to watch the video, so they can make decisions about their sequence or which parts might need more support.
A student is ready to play with structure, breaking free of structures often used for high school assessments. . .	Invite them to study a mentor text with a partner and label the different parts, then imagine which of these parts they might include and in what order. These might include, for example, parts that: • Talk about the author • Give some context for the story • Retell parts of the story • Suggest ideas about characters/themes/issues • Closely read and analyze parts of the text • Explore powerful craft • Make comparisons to other stories/the genre • Criticize parts • Share personal relevance
A student is ready to play with structure, exploring different ways their literary analysis might go. . .	Invite them to draft in parts, and to print each part on a different sheet of paper, then to organize these in different orders, seeing which is most compelling.

Lesson 1

Studying Writers' Structure Choices

STRATEGY

As writers get ready to draft, they often study mentor texts, analyzing these texts for the structural choices they suggest. Then they ask themselves: What structural choices do these writers make that I might also try?

Visit hs-guidetoteaching.org to access a collection of mentor texts for literary analysis.

USE THIS STRATEGY... to encourage students to think more deeply about how structure is connected to content. This strategy is also helpful when your students (and you) are ready to experiment with authentic structures, beyond the "five-paragraph essay."

> **Inquiry Questions**
>
> - What structural choices do writers make to develop ideas across a text?
> - What structural choices do published writers make that I might also try?

LAUNCH THE INQUIRY

- Suggest that writers often look at mentor texts before they draft, to consider what the parts of their writing might be. Introduce the idea that a literary analysis has some predictable parts or components. Share a chart of common components, like the one below.
- Invite students to join you in studying one text, looking for predictable components or parts.

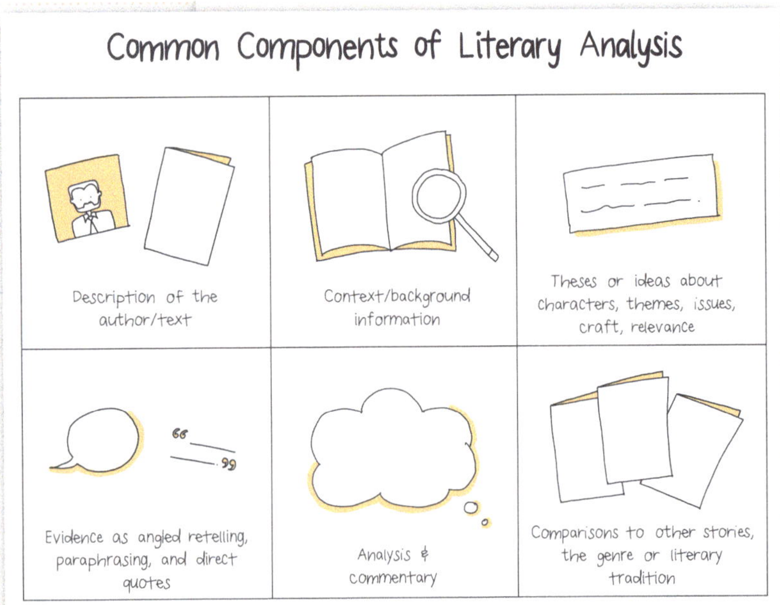

- Ask students to talk with a partner about what they notice about the author's structural choices, especially how it may be similar or different from the ways they've tended to structure in their own essays.
- Offer students a collection of literary analysis mentors, and invite students to study another analytical essay, paying attention to structural choices the author makes that they might also make as writers and the way structure can lead to voice.
- Curate a list of these structure choices as a class.
- Encourage students to think about which of these moves they'd like to try in their literary essays. Give students time to map out their essays.

Writers Make Structural Choices Like...

- Varying the length of paragraphs — some really short, some longer
- Using more than five paragraphs
- Starting with a first paragraph that leans into background information
- Choosing different internal text structures, such as:
  - Chronological order
  - Compare/contrast
  - Cause and effect
- Using an unusual genre or modality (e.g., written as a letter or a list)
- Sometimes including paragraphs of counterargument
- Starting paragraphs with:
  - A topic sentence
  - A piece of evidence
  - A transition
- Listing evidence in quick succession
- Focusing on just one moment or excerpt in some parts
- Discussing multiple moments connected to an idea in other parts

PROMPTS TO COACH STUDENTS AND PARTNERSHIPS

Which moves do you want to try out with your literary analysis? You can mentor yourself to a whole piece, or choose different parts that you liked, across pieces.

If you are crafting a literary analysis that's a different modality, look for mentors in that modality to study the structural moves.

It can be helpful to think about purpose and audience. If you are publishing for a journal, for instance, you can play extensively with structure. If you are writing for a teacher, it makes sense to find out about their structural preferences.

CLASSROOM ARTIFACTS

Coley annotated "Ted Lasso and the Fantasy of Soft Masculinity" (Abdelmahmoud 2023), with her class, marking components such as thesis, evidence, analysis, and background information (see Classroom Artifacts). She invited students to join her in analyzing the parts, paragraph order, and section of the text, thinking about how the structure helped develop ideas.

Trying on More Than One Structure

Lesson 2

STRATEGY

Published writers tend to turn to a few dependable structures as they draft. Encourage writers to try more than one structure, testing out which will be most powerful for their thesis, their audience, and their purpose.

USE THIS STRATEGY… when students are used to writing essays one way, when students are ready to outline, or when students' ideas are complicated enough that they'll benefit from a more complicated structure.

Visit hs-guidetoteaching.org to download the chart below.

TEACH THE STRATEGY

- Suggest to students that there are a few common structures that writers often choose from, matching the structure to their intent and style.
- Show students graphics of a few common structures that essayists often use.

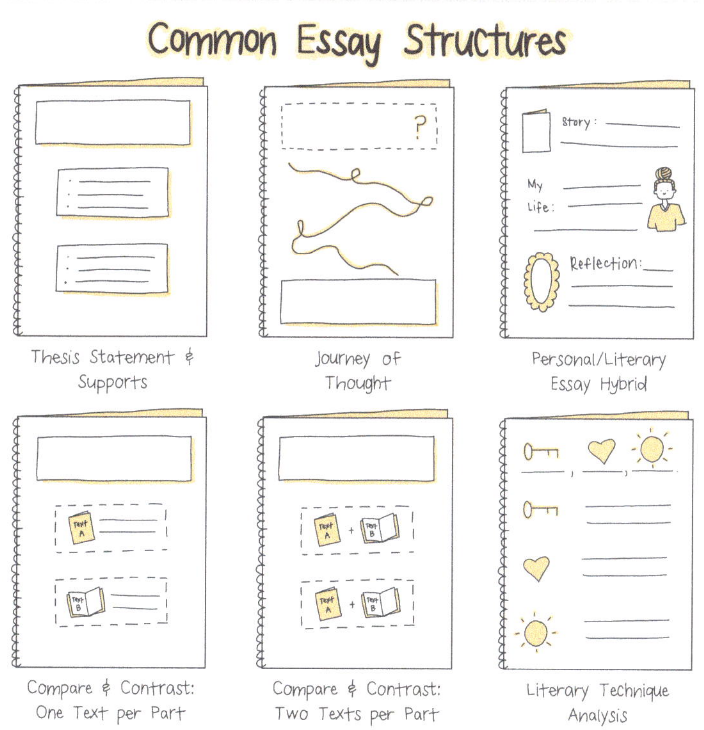

- Demonstrate how you might try out, verbally, a couple of these structures, pointing to the plan and saying parts of your essay out loud.
- Coach writers to work with a partner to try out a couple of structures verbally.
- Have your writers begin to map an essay plan or plans.

Lesson 2 (Continued)

PROMPTS TO COACH STUDENTS AND PARTNERSHIPS

It's often worth it to try "talking out" a couple of structures—literally point to the different parts, and tell your partner what you would write.

When something in the text really strikes you emotionally, the personal/literary hybrid can be beautiful. Journey of thought essays are great when you're interested in a question or theory, and writing will help you explore that idea. Try posing a question or theory, and see where the answer leads you.

If you're thinking of writing in a modality beyond an essay, you can still rely on some of these structures. Consider how they might fit into a video you're making or a podcast script you're writing.

CLASSROOM ARTIFACTS

One of the greatest struggles of high school is feeling like you want to fit in, and you want to stand out. *The Poet X* illustrates this struggle, revealing how Xiomara is caught between wanting to be ordinary and extraordinary at the same time. Ultimately she learns to assert her true self, a lesson I wish I had learned earlier in high school.

From Poet X
Xiomara's relationship with poetry
- Writes poetry but keeps it secret
- Joins poetry club but keeps it secret
- Finally performs on stage

From my life
Uncertainty about desire
- Secret crushes on girls
- Outwardly seeking boys
- Not talking to friends/family about it, similar to X
- Never really achieving transparency, unlike X

Even writing this essay is helpful, for allowing me to think through Xiomara to myself, to learn from characters in stories, and to learn through writing.

Outlining a hybrid personal/literary essay for The Poet X.

Ultimately, Starr can't be her full self until she acknowledges the role race places in her family, her friendships, and her identity.

Times when race shapes Starr's family
- Time when Dad talks to her about police stop
- connection to this after Khalil is killed.

Times when race shapes Starr's friendships
- when Hailey says racist things - Starr notices

Times when race shapes Starr's identity
- when she switches between Garden Heights and Williamson Prep (talks, acts, dresses)

Starr is her true self when she sees race (racism) as part of daily life - speaks out

A lean outline for an essay on The Hate U Give.

Choosing a Drafting Method

Lesson 3

STRATEGY

Writers do some thinking about how they are going to draft. For some writers, a lean plan is best; for others, a detailed plan works well; and for a few writers, it's preferable to draft straight from their head and then create a plan from what comes out.

USE THIS STRATEGY... when writers are about to draft, to coach them to make strategic decisions before they move toward drafting. This strategy also helps writers understand that each writer has to develop their own process, which may be different from other writers'.

Visit hs-guidetoteaching.org to access a chart, Choosing a Drafting Method, as well as charts, checklists, and tools on the writing process.

TEACH THE STRATEGY

- Introduce the idea that there are many ways to go about drafting an essay, or any writing. Let writers know they have to decide what works best for them and the task at hand.
- Invite students to study the chart "Choosing a Drafting" Method and model exploring the chart and deciding which of these strategies will work for their writing.

Choosing a Drafting Method

- Demonstrate choosing one of these plans and thinking how you would start drafting, knowing yourself as a writer.
- Encourage students to talk with a partner about how they expect to draft and then set themselves up to execute that plan, getting out any work they've done around their thesis, evidence, and so on. Then, encourage them to start drafting, whether it's a part of their draft or the whole thing.

PROMPTS TO COACH STUDENTS AND PARTNERSHIPS

If you feel like you just want to write, go for it. Then, after writing, go back and create a quick outline of what you wrote. This will allow you to double-check that your writing is focused and connected to the thesis.

If the blank page is feeling overwhelming, try using a different modality to draft, such as speech to text, recording yourself, or a notes app.

Remember how powerful verbal rehearsal is. Even after you create an outline or a plan, say your draft aloud before you write it. Listen for what parts sound strongest!

CLASSROOM ARTIFACTS

Thesis: In *The Poet X*, Xiomara keeps secrets from her family, from her classmates, and even from herself, revealing how secrecy protects her but also holds her back.

Body Paragraph 1 – Secrets from Family

- She hides her poetry notebook.
- She lies about Confirmation classes and seeing Aman.
- These secrets show how afraid she is of her mother's disapproval.

Body Paragraph 2 – Secrets from Herself

- At first, she denies her own desire to be heard.
- She writes poetry but doesn't call herself a poet.
- She begins to realize what she truly wants: freedom and self-expression.

Conclusion

- Xiomara's secrets show both her fear and her growth.
- As she becomes more honest with herself, she also starts to demand honesty from others.

Thesis: Elizabeth Acevedo's *The Poet X* explores how secrecy shapes Xiomara's identity. She hides her poetry and her relationships from her family, and even hides her true self from herself. These layers of secrecy show how young people may protect themselves from judgment—but also risk losing their voice in the process.

Body Paragraph 1 – Secrets from Family: Survival and Silence

- Topic Sentence: Xiomara keeps secrets from her mother to avoid punishment and protect her own independence.
- Evidence: She hides her relationship with Aman and skips Confirmation class.
  - Quote: "My mother would never let me have a boyfriend. Not that I have one."
- Commentary: Xiomara uses secrecy to carve out space for herself in a home where she feels constantly judged.

Body Paragraph 2 – Secrets from Herself: Internalized Fear

- Topic Sentence: Xiomara also avoids admitting things to herself, especially her need to be heard.
- Evidence: She writes but doesn't share; she minimizes her identity as a poet.
  - Quote: "It almost feels like the more I bruise the page, the quicker something inside me heels."
- Commentary: Her poetry becomes a mirror she can't look into directly—at least at first.

Body Paragraph 3 – Breaking Secrecy as Empowerment

- Topic Sentence: When Xiomara begins to share her secrets, she begins to transform.
- Evidence: She finally reads her poem at the poetry slam.
  - Quote: "And I think about all the things we let go by without being said."
- Commentary: Telling the truth becomes a form of rebellion and healing.

Conclusion

- Restate how Xiomara's secrecy shows both her fear and her growing courage.
- Insight: Acevedo suggests that when we find the courage to speak the truths we've hidden—even from ourselves—we begin to rewrite our lives.

Two different draft plans for The Poet X.

Writing in Parts

Lesson 4

STRATEGY

Writers often draft their essays in sections or parts. As they draft, they make a quick plan for each part, reminding themselves of the purpose of that part. Occasionally writers draft parts out of order, starting with whatever part they are most ready to write.

USE THIS STRATEGY... when writers would benefit from breaking their essay into smaller chunks and drafting it as a series of smaller parts.

TEACH THE STRATEGY

- Remind students that writing large pieces can sometimes feel overwhelming, but that it can help writers to think about their writing as a collection of parts and draft each part, bit by bit.
- Demonstrate this process in front of students, introducing a chart to showcase how writers make decisions as they draft particular parts.

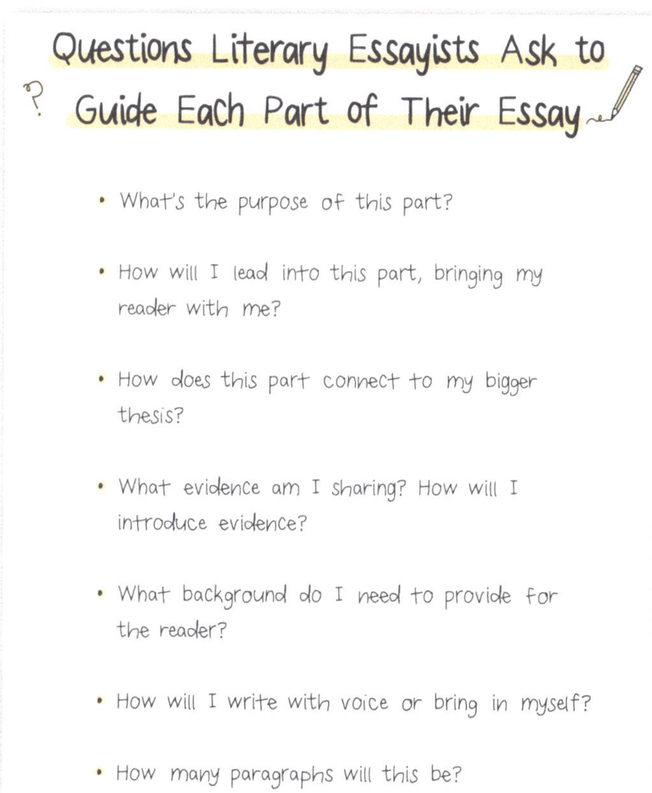

When Lauren drafted in front of her class, she revisited her purpose for a section that would support her thesis: Xiomara stops keeping secrets and finds her voice through poetry.

First, Lauren named the purpose of one part, which was to talk about how Xiomara found her voice. Even though this is toward the end of her essay, she felt it was the easiest place for her to start. She first pulled a compelling piece of evidence. Then, she added analysis. After she read it, she thought about how she could contextualize this—what would the claim of the section be? Finally, she reread it and tweaked the flow of the writing (see Classroom Artifacts).

- Invite students to choose a section to draft. Remind them to use the chart and think about all the work they'll accomplish in each part of their essay. Suggest they move from one part to the next as they draft.

PROMPTS TO COACH STUDENTS AND PARTNERSHIPS

You can start drafting! Get the parts you know down, and build around them.

You can do this work at a sentence level, too. Consider how each sentence connects to the one before and after it. This practice will keep you on track with your purpose.

Once you draft one part, choose the next part to draft. It may be a paragraph that comes before or after, or it may be something in a different part of your writing.

A Progression of Analysis and Framing Inside a Body Paragraph

Xiomara finds her voice on stage. She says, "I let the words fill the room./ I let the words carry me away" (279). She also adds, "I can't wait to do this again" (280).

Xiomara finds her voice on stage when she says, "I let the words fill the room./ I let the words carry me away" (279). When Xiomara describes her words as "filling the room" (279), she shows that she understands her voice matters, a dramatic shift from earlier in the text when she didn't want anyone to read her poetry. When she adds, "I can't wait to do this again," she insinuates this is just the start of Xiomara's journey in finding confidence in her own voice (280).

In a crucial early scene in the novel, Caridad, Xiomara's best friend, and Twin, her brother, take Xiomara to an open mic night, and Xiomara gets on the stage and performs. Afterward she writes, "I let the words fill the room./ I let the words carry me away" (279). Xiomara describes her words as "filling the room," showing that she understands her voice matters, a dramatic shift from earlier in the text when she didn't want anyone to read her poetry. At the end of the event we know something inside Xiomara shifted because as she leaves she thinks to herself, "I can't wait to do this again" (280). These thoughts foreshadow the idea that this is just the start of Xiomara's journey in finding confidence in her own voice.

Xiomara uses the stage as a way to find her voice. Caridad, her best friend, and Twin, her brother, take her to an open mic night, and Xiomara gets on the stage and performs. Afterward she writes, "I let the words fill the room./ I let the words carry me away" (279). By describing her words as "filling the room," Xiomara shows that she understands her voice matters, a dramatic shift from earlier in the text when she didn't want anyone to read her poetry. At the end of the event we know something inside Xiomara shifted because as she leaves she thinks to herself, "I can't wait to do this again" (280). These thoughts foreshadow the idea that this is just the start of Xiomara's journey in finding confidence in her own voice, and that the stage is going to be the place where she grows the most.

Lauren drafts in front of her class, naming the parts of her essay and the purpose of each section.

Lesson 5

Compare and Contrast Structures

STRATEGY

When writers compare and contrast narratives, they often do so by comparing how a theme is developed in similar or different ways, or how characters compare, or how issues develop in different narratives. Occasionally they'll compare and contrast literary techniques as well. Because it's easy for readers to get lost between two stories, writers often keep to simple structures for these analyses.

USE THIS STRATEGY... to help students clarify for their reader when they are analyzing one text or another and to support them in idea development across texts.

TEACH THE STRATEGY

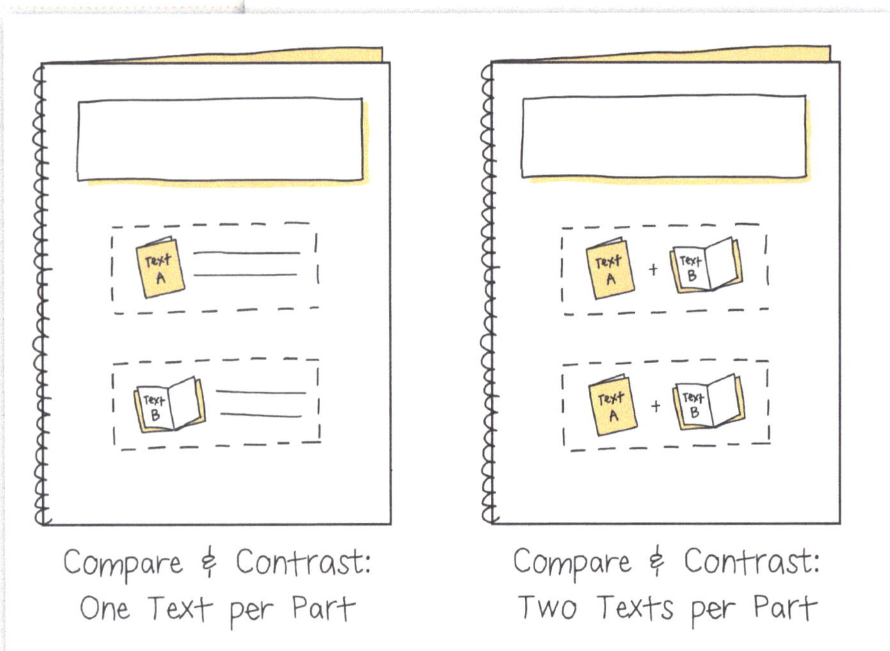

- Suggest to students that when writers are comparing and contrasting narratives, whether they are analyzing themes, or characters, or issues, or techniques, it's often helpful to draft inside a simple, cohesive structure, to help the reader follow lines of thinking across two texts.
- Share a chart that introduces two simple structures: one text per part, or two texts per part.
- Using the chart as a planning tool, say out loud how your writing might go, if you were to use one structure or the other.
- Invite students who are writing about two texts to talk to a partner about which structure they might choose and, therefore, how their draft might go.
- Suggest students jot a plan and then begin writing when ready.

PROMPTS TO COACH STUDENTS AND PARTNERSHIPS

It's definitely easier to write first about one text and then about the second, and then you can use your conclusion to share insights on the differences between them.

When you're entranced by characters, then it's interesting to move back and forth between them, allowing for a lot of nuanced compare-and-contrast work.

Let the type of compare/contrast you're doing inform the structure. If you're reading about how Text A influenced Text B, then it makes sense to start with Text A. If you're comparing a story element, it might make sense to weave the texts together.

CLASSROOM ARTIFACTS

Text A/Text B

Introduction

- While both characters keep secrets, Holden keeps his secrets and they keep him from growing, while Xiomara ultimately confronts and escapes her secrets through poetry.

Text A: Secrets in Holden's Life (The Catcher in the Rye)

- Holden's secret grief over Allie's death
- Holden's secrets about his own failures
- How these secrets affect Holden

Text B: Secrets in Xiomara's Life (The Poet X)

- Xiomara's secrets from her family
- Xiomara's internal secrets/conflicts
- How confronting secrets transforms Xiomara

Conclusion

- Broader significance of how confronting vs. burying secrets affects personal growth, maybe final insight about literature's power to reveal the consequences of secrets

Part 1 (A&B), Part 2 (A&B), etc.

Introduction

- While both characters keep secrets, Holden keeps his secrets and they keep him from growing, while Xiomara ultimately confronts and escapes her secrets through poetry.

Part 1: How Holden and Xiomara Keep Secrets from Others

- Holden's deception toward authority figures
- Xiomara's hidden actions and thoughts
- Motivations for external secrets for both

Part 2: How They Keep Secrets from Themselves

- Holden's self-deception
- Xiomara's internal conflicts
- Moments of almost-breakthrough for both

Part 3: Different Effects of their Relationship with Secrets

- Holden's stagnation - increasing isolation and cynicism
- Xiomara's breakthrough with poetry as confession and self-discovery
- Contrasting endpoints- Holden's ambiguous future vs. Xiomara's clear direction

Conclusion

- Broader significance of how confronting vs. burying secrets affects personal growth, maybe final insight about literature's power to reveal the consequences of secrets

Mary demonstrates this strategy in her writing. She takes the same thesis and tries two different structures of a compare and contrast essay on The Poet X *and* The Catcher in the Rye.

Lesson 6

Using AI to Generate Potential Structures

STRATEGY

While writers know that drafting is something they want to start on their own, to build their writing muscles and develop their voice, it can be interesting to turn to AI to get some suggestions for different structures. To do this, writers might prepare their AI partner first by talking about their aims, then by sharing notes, explaining their ideas, or describing the student's evidence.

Visit hs-guidetoteaching.org to access the chart, Tips for Training Your AI Partner for Structural Suggestions.

USE THIS STRATEGY... to coach students in how to use AI wisely across the writing process (asking for multiple suggestions, asking for help beyond drafting, teaching your AI about your purpose and audience).

TEACH THE STRATEGY

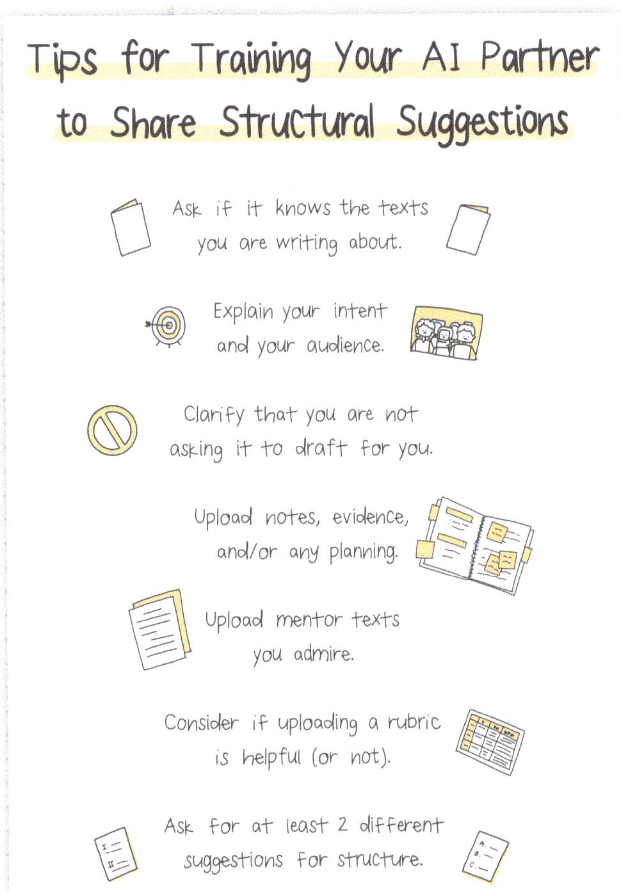

- Suggest to your students that AI can be a helpful partner in suggesting structural possibilities.
- Share a chart with tips for training your AI around structural choices.
- Model uploading your notes and sharing your thesis with your AI partner. Be sure to ask for suggestions for structure, not for AI to write the essay for you (see Classroom Artifacts for a sample).
    - You could also upload a mentor text and ask for a third suggestion, to offer an outline that mirrors the structure of that mentor.
- Invite students to play with an AI partner, suggesting that they ask for at least two different structures, and that they consider uploading a favorite mentor or rubric depending on the task. Remind them they can upload their notes.

PROMPTS TO COACH STUDENTS AND PARTNERSHIPS

Even though your AI partner may suggest that it can help you draft, resist. You want to draft yourself, to build your own writing muscles and develop your own voice.

Give your AI partner as much information as possible so it can personalize its responses for you—share your notes, your goals, your audience, how much freedom you have over the genre, and so on.

When you review structure choices, sometimes it makes sense to choose one that you think you can write, and other times, it makes sense to try something new.

CLASSROOM ARTIFACTS

I'm writing an essay on the Poet X. It's an essay for a ninth grade class on American literature. My thesis is that Xiomara keeps secrets, from others and herself, that are damaging, until she figures out how to use poetry as a form of release and liberation. I'm uploading my notes for my essay. Using these notes, could you suggest 2 different ways to structure this essay? I'd like one version to be a journey of thought essay, where the thesis comes at the end. I don't need help drafting - I want structural suggestions.

Lauren shares her notes and prompts her AI partner.

Structure 1: Traditional Analytical Approach

This structure presents your thesis early and builds evidence around it.

- **Introduction:** Begin with a compelling hook about the power of secrets and self-expression. Introduce *The Poet X* and present your thesis clearly: Xiomara's journey from secrecy to liberation comes through poetry.
- **Part 1 – Secrets from Others:** Analyze how Xiomara keeps secrets from people in her life—especially her mother, father, and the church. Use specific examples to show how her silence causes her emotional suffering.
- **Part 2 – Secrets from Herself:** Examine the secrets Xiomara keeps from herself—her desires, her doubts about faith, her suppressed anger. Show how this self-denial adds to her sense of isolation.
- **Part 3 – Discovery of Poetry:** Identify a turning point when Xiomara begins writing. Analyze early poems that reveal glimpses of her hidden self.
- **Part 4 – Poetry as Liberation:** Explore how poetry evolves from a private outlet to a public act of expression. Highlight scenes like the poetry club and open mic where Xiomara reclaims her voice.
- **Conclusion:** Reinforce the thesis by emphasizing how Xiomara's journey shows that artistic self-expression can be a path toward healing and honesty.

Lauren's AI partner suggests two different structures (continued on next page).

Structure 2: Journey of Thought Essay (Thesis at the End)

This structure mirrors Xiomara's own process of discovering and articulating her truth.

- **Opening Scene:** Start with a vivid moment from the novel that shows how Xiomara feels trapped—by expectations, by silence. Raise questions about why she holds back and what that costs her.
- **Section 1 – The Weight of Secrets:** Explore the secrets Xiomara keeps—about her body, her feelings for Aman, her religious doubts. Analyze how these build distance between her and others.
- **Section 2 – The Price of Silence:** Show how these secrets don't protect her but instead intensify her loneliness and emotional pain.
- **Section 3 – First Words:** Focus on Xiomara's first attempts at writing poetry. Analyze how her notebook becomes a space where she can admit truths she couldn't say aloud.
- **Section 4 – Finding Voice:** Trace how her poetry shifts from private writing to public performance. Highlight moments like the poetry club and slam, where sharing her work brings connection and release.
- **Conclusion – Thesis Revelation:** Now articulate your thesis: that poetry becomes the way Xiomara transforms her relationship to her secrets and finds freedom. The structure of the essay mirrors her path from confusion to clarity.

Lauren's AI partner suggests two different structures.

Lesson 7

Using Concept Maps to Write Engaging Introductions

STRATEGY

Analytical writers craft engaging and informative introductions. One way they can find more to say in an introduction is to start with a concept map. A concept map is a way of connecting ideas and details, showing relationships around a topic or concept. Concept maps can help young writers imagine a few ways their introductions can go or what to include in an introduction.

Visit hs-guidetoteaching.org to download the chart, In Their Introductions, Writers Might ...

USE THIS STRATEGY... when writers are ready to synthesize their ideas in an introduction that frames their thinking and captures readers' attention.

TEACH THE STRATEGY

- Suggest to your readers that an introduction orients and engages your reader, making them interested in the text you're writing about and your ideas.
- Remind students of some of the parts of a strong introduction. Share a chart of some components of introductions.

Lesson 7 (Continued)

- Situate introductions as less of a formula and more of a place for voice, engagement with the audience, and a place to frame a topic or idea.
- Introduce the idea of a concept map to develop ideas for the hook and background information in an introduction. Demonstrate jotting a quick concept map.

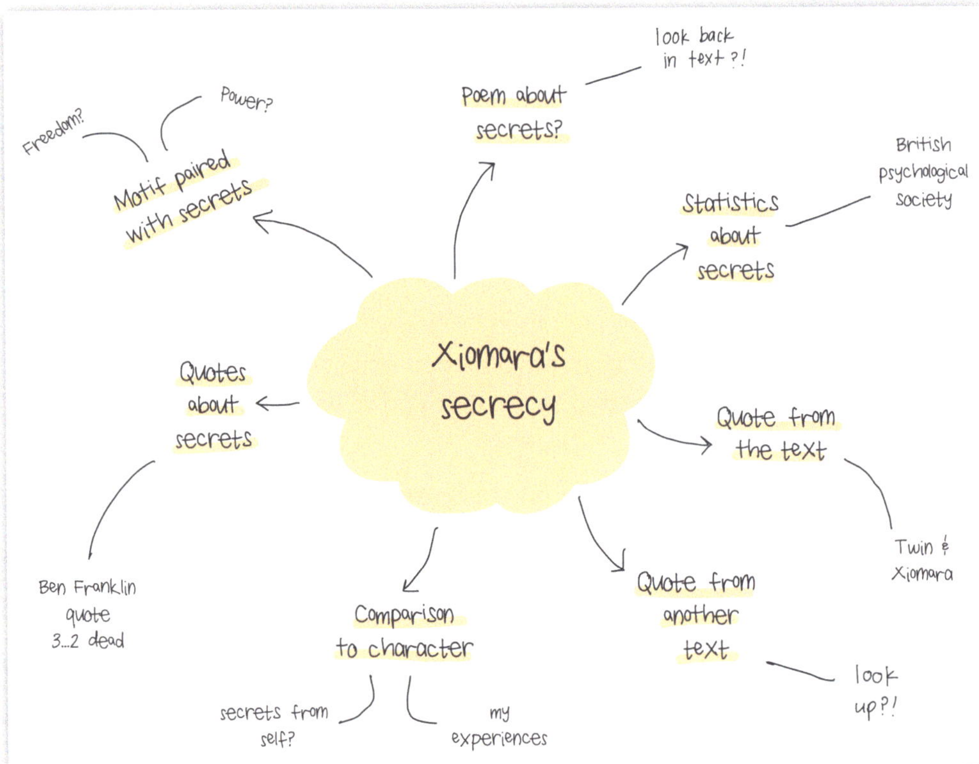

Coley made a concept map to generate ideas for her introduction, specifically for her journey of thought essay about Xiomara's secrecy.

- Invite students to try out a quick concept map, keeping their topic in mind.
- Demonstrate how you select a few different types of introduction to try out, naming which ones would work well for your thesis and your structure. Remind students they can also look at mentor texts for ideas for their introductions.

Intro Version 1

"This is a secret hope we share/that we are both good enough/for each other and maybe the world, too" (Acevedo 73). Usually, we think of secrets as scandalous or shameful, something we are hiding from the world for a reason, oftentimes a negative one. But secrets can also be positive forces—little kernels that we hold onto as just our own, at least for the time being. *The Poet X* demonstrates this perfectly in the way Elizabeth Acevedo depicts Xiomara's journey to find herself and her voice. Although she keeps secrets from everyone around her, those secrets are beautiful versions of her and her life, leading readers to ask: *Why* does she keep secrets from those around her and even from herself?

Intro Version 2

Usually, we think of secrets as scandalous and shameful, something we are hiding from the world for a reason, oftentimes a negative one. Although I certainly have secrets I'm holding onto that aren't pretty, I also have secrets that act as positive forces, secrets that motivate me—my dreams that I am still too shy to share with the world. Similarly, Xiomara, the protagonist in *The Poet X*, also experiences this feeling as she keeps secrets about her poetry, her romantic relationships, and her dreams.

Although Xiomara keeps secrets from everyone around her, those secrets are beautiful versions of herself and her life, leading readers to ask: *Why* does she keep secrets from those around her and even from herself?

Here, Coley experimented with an introduction for her journey of thought essay, using her concept map as a guide. First, she experimented with using a quote from the text as an inroad to her claim and introductory paragraph.

Then, she tried bringing in a story from her own life to tie into her thesis, paralleling her experiences with Xiomara's.

- Send students off to practice this work with their own introductions, reminding them that introductions are places to experiment and find their voice, not necessarily a place to just follow a formula.

PROMPTS TO COACH STUDENTS AND PARTNERSHIPS

Remember that introductions can look more than one way. Decide what's best for your writing style and your topic. You can try out your introduction in a few ways, even making it more than one paragraph.

If you need a little extra support here, you can work with a partner or study mentor texts, looking specifically at introductions. That might give you ideas about how they can go.

You can also use this mind map for your conclusion—return to it once you get there. Or maybe hold onto one of your ideas from your intro and bring it back in your conclusion.

CLASSROOM ARTIFACTS

Reading *Catcher in the Rye* has gotten me more fascinated with how the narrator or the main character understands himself and tells his story (or hers). While reading *Catcher in the Rye* I was also reading Jon Krakauer's *Into Thin Air*. Thinking about Holden so much made me more attentive to how Jon also portrays himself as a hero. Like Holden, he's kind of a flawed hero. But unlike Holden, Jon admits more about his flaws.

The 1920s were the beginnings of female liberation. Girls traded in their corsets and ankle-length ball gowns for cropped, loose, dresses; other girls chopped off their long hair into short, fashionable bobs; some even dared to paint on bright lipstick or eyeshadow. Women had just secured the right to vote, and American families began dreaming about a possible new life full of freedom and luxury.

Cue F. Scott Fitzgerald, a semi-popular author at the time, who decided to throw in his two cents on rebellious women and the new culture of consumerism. When he wasn't worrying about his tumultuous marriage with his wife, Zelda, he was writing. Fitzgerald met his wife when he was stationed in Alabama for the army. Zelda originally rejected him due to his financial status, but later married him after he achieved financial success (sound familiar?).

Today, Fitzgerald is hailed as one of the greatest authors of the twentieth century, and rightfully so. *The Great Gatsby* is a classic critique on American overconsumption and materialism, but it isn't perfect. Daisy Buchanan, the main female protagonist and love interest to millionaire Jay Gatsby, is woefully underdeveloped. Poorly written female characters are not a new phenomenon; complex women in literature is something many male authors continue to struggle with. It clearly stems from implicit biases against women, from the idea that women are not as interesting or compelling as men. For an otherwise insightful book, it begs the question: Did Fitzgerald intentionally underdeveloped Daisy, or did he simply write within the confines of his own biases in line with early 1920s misogyny?

Introductions can be short, like this writer who discusses The Catcher in the Rye, *or several paragraphs, like in the case of this essay on* The Great Gatsby.

Returning to Mentor Texts to Study Conclusions

Lesson 8

STRATEGY

Writers conclude their writing in ways that provide closure and also leave the reader thinking. Studying mentor endings offers writers ideas for their own conclusions.

Visit hs-guidetoteaching.org to access a collection of published mentors and student examples, as well as a collection of mentor endings.

USE THIS STRATEGY... to inspire your writers to outgrow their traditional conclusions of restatement plus one connection. This strategy is especially helpful for fluent writers who are ready to try new techniques.

Inquiry Questions

- What structural choices do writers make to develop ideas across a text?
- What structural choices do published writers make that I might also try?

LAUNCH THE INQUIRY

- Suggest to your writers that just as introductions orient and engage your reader, endings also provide important closure. Remind students that it's often helpful to return to mentors to study how they start and how they end and that today you'll study endings, or conclusions.
- Share the inquiry question, and invite students to join you in studying a mentor ending.

"In 2021, *Ted Lasso* won a Peabody award. The citation recognizes the series for 'offering the perfect counter to the enduring prevalence of toxic masculinity, both on-screen and off, in a moment when the nation truly needs inspiring models of kindness.' If it is indeed the last season of *Ted Lasso*, the show's greatest success is making an alternative, soft masculinity seem possible and worth pursuing, even if it remains a fantasy."

When Mary taught this lesson, she returned to "Ted Lasso and the Fantasy of Soft Masculinity" (Abdelmahmoud 2023) and studied the ending in particular. With her students, Mary named some of these techniques, including:

- sharing awards the story has won
- quoting outside the text
- returning to and expanding on the original thesis
- connecting back to the title of the article

- Make a collection of mentor endings available, or mentor texts overall, and suggest that students study the endings. You might include both published literary analysis and student exemplars, or one or the other.
- Invite students to choose a few texts and study their endings with a partner, and then to choose some techniques they admire that they'd like to try in their own conclusions.
- You might chart some of what students discover. Set up students to draft some sample conclusions for their own piece.

PROMPTS TO COACH STUDENTS AND PARTNERSHIPS

Here are some sentence stems if you need them: "This essay is truly about ..." or "_______ reminds us that ..." and "Beyond the text ..."

You could call back the work you did in your introduction as a place to get ideas for the conclusion.

Feel free to try your conclusion a few ways, just like you would your introduction. Sometimes playing with multiple last lines or sentences and then asking a writing partner for input can be helpful.

At the very end, Nick's voice slips into a kind of historical commentary, as he remarks on the greatest of all human dreams: "for a transitory enchanted moment man must have held his breath in the presence of this continent." He adds that this moment brought man face to face for "the last time in history with something commensurate to his capacity for wonder" (Fitzgerald 180). Nick's more grand voice evokes the possibility that his coming of age, with his stripping of his illusions, his belief in magical possibility, suggests an echo of a greater loss, of man's age of heroes. It's almost as if the entire story has really been a myth, a kind of wish for a past where greatness could exist, where men could make themselves. In Greek mythology, a hero was born a man and becomes a god through his own actions. The belief in heroes marked a belief that man could overcome his mortal limitations. Nick's oscillation from realism to magic to realism may reflect a tension between his longing to believe in heroes, and the punishing aspect of hubris, which punishes mortals who reach above themselves.

Reflecting on Nick's role in a conclusion to an essay on myths in The Great Gatsby.

INTRODUCTION

The novel *Thirteen Reasons Why* tells the tale of a teen, Hannah, who commits suicide, arranging for cassette tapes of her reasons to be delivered to each of the students she wants to know her story. The show has generated a lot of controversy about whether it glorifies suicide. This article isn't about that controversy. It's about the subtexts of alternative music, tragedy, and the outsider that operates through the score of the show.

There are musical references throughout the novel. The narrator, Clay, is interested in music, in a way that sets him apart from other characters. But it's in the Netflix series that music emerges as a force in the narrative, weaving thematic parallels, symbolic allusions, and a subtext of the outsider.

...

CONCLUSION

Layers upon layers. The score is almost always not the original artist, but a cover, continuing the theme of layers—layers of protection, of subterfuge, of near truths—that run through the novel and the show. Always, you are imbued with the sense that there is more, and that if you listened hard enough, you might hear a secret.

This writer ties his conclusion back to his introduction in his analysis of the score in Thirteen Reasons Why.

Chapter Five: Honing and Integrating Evidence

Integrating evidence is a kind of art: There is no one way to do it. Some writers are masters of seamless, natural transitions and framing. Some prefer a highly formal precision. Whether they aim for a conversational tone or a more formal tone, kids will be approximating. They might try a new way to embed their evidence or weave in and out of a quote. They might play with first or second person as published writers do, as in, "We find out in Chapter 4 that Starr ..." or "You never really know what's going on in Holden's head." We encourage you to embrace students' playing with this kind of experimentation, recognizing that it can often lead to writing that has voice and personality.

Knowing that young writers often find integrating evidence tricky—that it takes a lot of thinking work—this chapter offers different ways to support framing evidence. Many of these ways lead students to sort, categorize, weigh, and evaluate evidence. As students consider and reconsider their evidence, they'll also seek new evidence, and they may revise their theses. A lot of important thinking and writing work happens at this stage of the writing process. As we studied mentor writers, we also realized more and more that analysis happens in the framing and integration of evidence, not only in the sentences or commentary following the evidence. Across these lessons, we offer space for students to be writing analytically, even when it comes to framing evidence.

You'll find that a lot of attention in this chapter is given to framing and integrating quotes: How to punctuate them, how to blend them, how to cut them down, when to keep a block quote. We gave these skills so much attention because they are the building blocks of literary analysis, and sometimes young writers need you to teach these skills more than once, from different angles, before they really sink in.

We also want to emphasize, though, the importance of paraphrasing and summarizing, and the fact that these are worthy types of evidence in a literary analysis. Paraphrasing can often be more challenging than adding in a line or two of dialogue from the text. Paraphrasing requires the writer's own words to come through while also representing the voice of the author. This type of evidence expects that students can angle, or retell, the part of the text in a way that supports their thesis and their ideas. During our mentor text study of analytical writing from sources like NPR and the *New York Times*, we found so much of what writers are doing is deliberate, angled retelling of parts of the text. You'll find a few lessons across this chapter that hone these skills.

Whether your young writers are paraphrasing or quoting, it will be helpful to study published mentors, so students become familiar with how evidence is developed and introduced and so they can mirror-write off these texts. While we touch on it in this chapter, you'll also find more lessons on punctuating and citing quotes in Chapter 7, "Attending to Craft and Conventions."

We don't include a lesson on AI in this chapter because we felt that the AI lesson in Chapter 6 (Lesson 8: Inviting New Perspectives with an AI Thought Partner) lets students think with a partner about their evidence and analysis, and whether they may want to return to the text or spend more time thinking about new angles on their evidence. However, students could ask their AI partner for feedback on the framing or paraphrasing of their evidence, gathering suggestions about clarity.

You may find that you can lead some of these lessons as a series of micro-lessons, all in one day. You may decide that some of these lessons are most important only for small groups of students, and there may be a few that you want to teach all your students. Know that in the next chapter, you'll find lessons on developing analysis, or commentary, and in that revision work, students re-think their evidence yet again.

Ultimately, this chapter invites you to support students as they wrestle with the complexity of integrating evidence—encouraging experimentation, deep thinking, and authorial control.

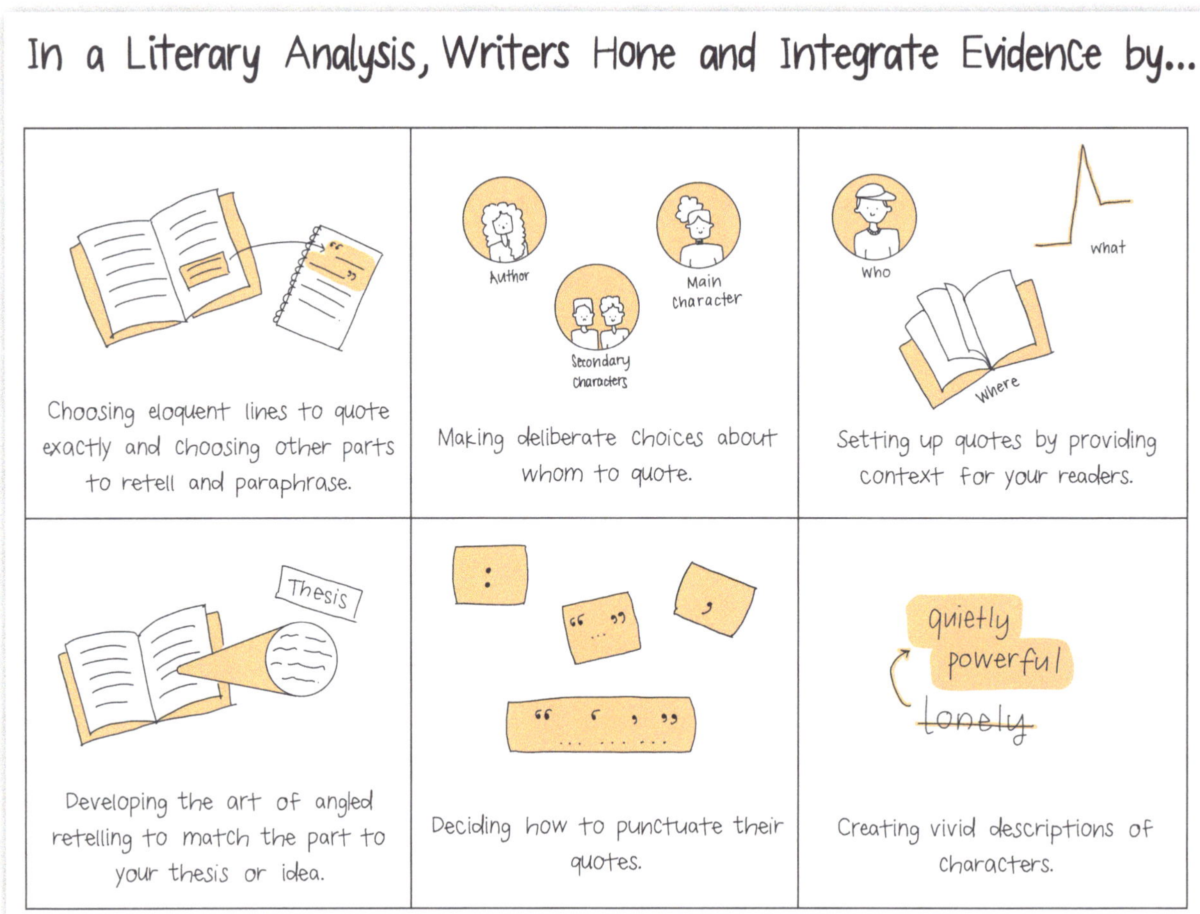

Lesson 1

Setting Up Quotes for Your Audience to Understand

STRATEGY

Writers contextualize the textual evidence they use by explaining when in the text the scene occurs, who is in the scene, where the scene takes place, and what is happening.

Visit hs-guidetoteaching.org to download the following chart.

USE THIS STRATEGY... when your students are drafting and beginning to integrate text evidence in their writing. Also use this strategy when writers are revising and ready to think about making ideas clear to their audience.

TEACH THE STRATEGY

- Remind students that writers keep their audience in mind, and in the case of literary analysis, writers imagine writing to an audience that often includes people who have not read the specific text they are writing about or don't recall it perfectly and, therefore, need plenty of detail about where specific quotes and evidence emerge in the text.
- Demonstrate how to introduce a piece of text evidence so the audience can understand, even if they have not read the text.

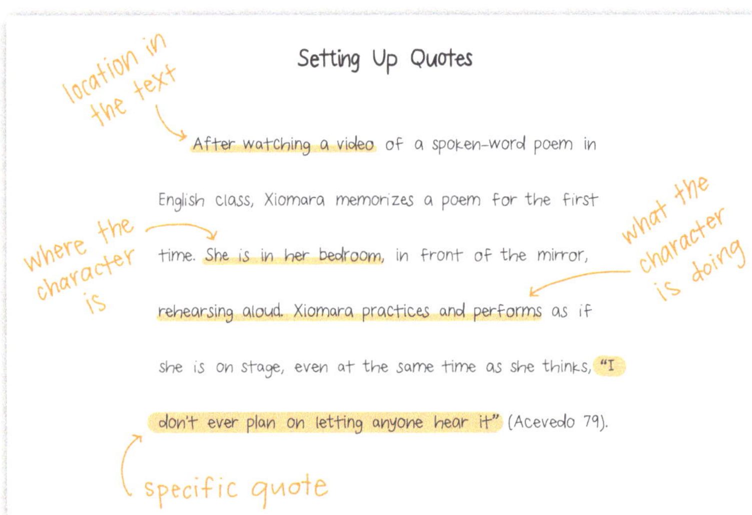

When Lauren taught this lesson, she wanted to use a quote that emphasizes the idea that Xiomara, in *The Poet X*, is highly secretive. To do this, Lauren returned to a moment in which Xiomara memorizes a poem and demonstrated how she explained the context for her quote.

- Share a chart like the one below.

Create Context Around Text Evidence By...

Explaining when in the text the evidence occurs.	Incorporating transitional phrases that suggest time, place, and speaker.	Describing who is in the scene.
• Include events that led to this moment. • Name the part of the text in which the evidence appears. • Indicate the story elements. • Detail where the story elements occur.	• Use words like... ▪ Just after... ▪ Just before... ▪ When... ▪ In this moment... • Introduce evidence or dialogue with phrases like... ▪ For instance, the author writes: "..." ▪ For instance, the character says, "..."	• Reference who is speaking. • Include what the characters are doing. • Provide descriptions of characters. • Name character emotions.

- Encourage students to try this work. They may start by choosing a part of their writing to revise, or by drafting ahead and adding a new quote.

PROMPTS TO COACH STUDENTS AND PARTNERSHIPS

Set the scene for your audience. Even if they haven't read the book, they should be able to understand the context. What details do you need to include so the audience can picture this moment in the text?

Watch me read and give feedback on your partner's writing. Pay attention to how I give feedback on the details they include, and how they connect this moment to other parts in the text.

Now that you've introduced one moment, how can you explain other parts of the text in relation to this? For example, does your next piece of evidence occur shortly after this, much later, or before?

CLASSROOM ARTIFACTS

Perhaps the most iconic My Chemical Romance song is the fifth track, "Welcome to the Black Parade." The song is a five-minute long epic about The Patient greeting the afterlife, which took the form of a marching band similar to the one he saw when he was younger. The Patient seems to be deciding if he should stay or not. He is getting a taste of what the afterlife is to make his decision to keep fighting cancer or to accept death. The song features marching band-like drums and somber piano before switching into heavy guitar. The song then changes tempo completely and becomes more upbeat, with Gerard screaming, "We'll carry on, we'll carry on, and though you're dead and gone, believe me, your memory will carry on." The Patient is told that in death people will always remember him, maybe even as better than he was when he was living. He yearns for a better life, and the marching band is almost luring him in with tales of fame and love that he would receive after he died. The Patient tries to tell the marching band that "[he's] just a man, [he's] not a hero, [he's] just the boy who had to sing this song," to which the afterlife responds with a bellowing "I! DON'T! CARE!"

During the time of the Salem Witch Trials, a young girl named Abigail Williams accuses many women of being witches. To keep herself out of trouble, she decides to blame it on the first person she sees. When Hale asks her, "What are you concealing? Have you sold yourself to the devil?" Abigail responds with, "I never sold myself! I'm a good girl! I'm a proper girl!" When Tituba, a slave, enters, instantly, Abigail points at her and says, "She made me do it! She makes me drink blood!" (Miller 40–41). Once these words come out of Abby's mouth, Salem will never be the same again.

Setting the scene for specific quotes with plenty of textual detail, while analyzing a song by My Chemical Romance and The Crucible.

Cut, Condense, and Combine Evidence

Lesson 2

STRATEGY

Writers decide which parts of a quote are the most significant and which parts aren't as relevant to keep their evidence lean and targeted. They do this by bolding or highlighting the most important part and then deciding how they can trim the less important parts (unless the entire block quote is significant).

USE THIS STRATEGY... when writers have collected lots of powerful evidence, but they've inserted large block quotes that might be too long and dense for the reader, or they could benefit from combining pieces of evidence, especially if they have too much evidence.

TEACH THE STRATEGY

- Suggest to students that there are moments in literary analysis when it makes sense to include a block quote, when you are analyzing a section of the text and you are going to closely read all of it, for instance. *And* it often makes sense to focus on smaller quotes, so that the flow of your own words isn't so interrupted.
- Display a long block quote that you've selected for your writing.
- Model bolding/highlighting the most important words/phrases from the quote, showcasing how you consider your thesis statements and how you intend to use the quote.
    - Consider also crossing out parts that are less significant.
- Name back the steps to students, so they can try out this process with their own evidence.
    - Study your thesis and analysis before making decisions.
    - Select parts to keep or parts to let go of by asking yourself how each connects to your thesis.
    - Decide which chunks to directly quote by picking out the most important language.
    - Consider paraphrasing parts in between quotes.
- Demonstrate moving from the highlighted and crossed-out quote to a leaner quote, showing how you paraphrased some parts, removed others, and integrated the quote properly, all in service of your ideas.

Lesson 2
(Continued)

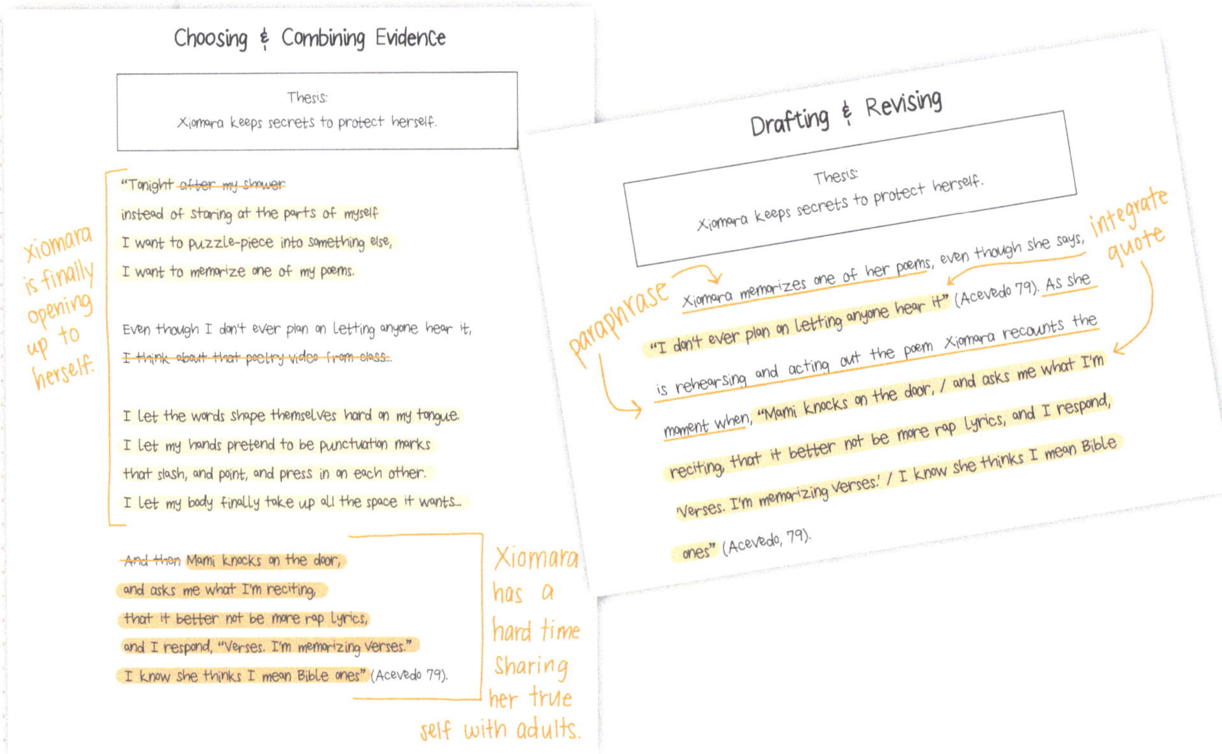

Coley displayed her thesis and a longer quote to demonstrate highlighting the important parts and model cutting parts that are less relevant to her thesis about secrecy.

Coley explained that what's important in this quote is dependent on how she uses it. If she uses it as evidence about how Xiomara has a difficult time sharing her true self with adults, then she'll focus on the parts about Mami, but if she wants to use it to explore how Xiomara is finally opening up to her own-self, the first part of the quote will be more important. To show this, she highlighted it in two different colors and crossed out irrelevant parts.

Coley then modeled paraphrasing the first half of the quote, setting up the rest of the quote, and directly quoting the second half because her goal is to describe how Xiomara is hiding her true self from her mother to protect herself.

- Invite students to experiment with these strategies as they are looking to make their quotes leaner, giving them the option to do this digitally or on paper. Either way, aim for them to do this in a place separate from their drafting. We find students will be more experimental this way.

PROMPTS TO COACH STUDENTS AND PARTNERSHIPS

I see you crossed out a few chunks. Which parts will leave out entirely? Which parts might you want to paraphrase? Remember, when you omit something you can use an ellipses to convey that.

You could try analyzing this full quote first, then consider which parts were relevant and which were less crucial.

There might be times when you want to keep a full block quote. It's okay to have block quotes, especially when the language of the quote is important for the analysis. Trust your instincts.

CLASSROOM ARTIFACTS

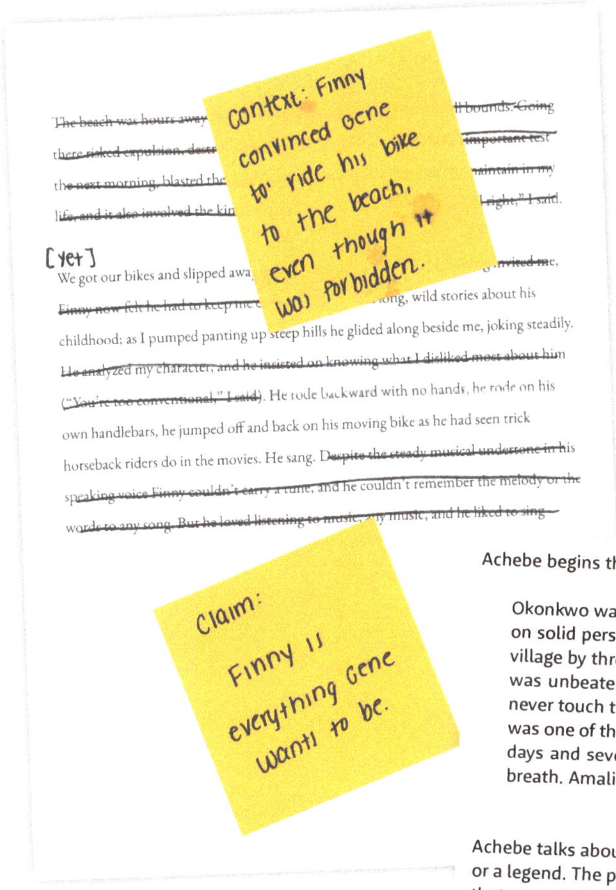

A writer revises his block quote to something leaner.

Achebe begins the novel with a passage that evokes pre-colonial Africa:

> Okonkwo was well-known throughout the nine villages and even beyond. His fame rested on solid personal achievements. As a young man of eighteen he had brought honor to his village by throwing Amalinze the Cat. Amalinze was the great wrestler who for seven years was unbeaten, from Umuofia to Mbaino. He was called the cat because his back would never touch the earth. It was this man Okonkwo threw in a fight which the old men agreed was one of the fiercest since the founder of their town engaged a spirit of the wild for seven days and seven nights. The drums beat and the flutes sang and the spectators held their breath. Amalinze was a wily craftsman, but Okonkwo was as slippery as a fish in water.
>
> (Achebe 3)

Achebe talks about Okonkwo in this passage as if he were talking about a character in a fairy-tale, or a legend. The point of view is one that rests with the spectators; the villagers who were there at that event. By telling the reader that "that was twenty years ago, twenty years or more, and during this time Okonkwo's fame had grown," Achebe's language sets Okonkwo up to be a sort of larger-than-life figure, saying, "he was well-known throughout the nine villages," and "he had brought honor to his village." The reader hasn't even met Okonkwo, really, but knows that he is famous. Achebe uses point of view to set Okonkwo as an honored man, as well as part of a fabled history. This makes his suicide later all the more painful, and symbolic of the death of the pre-colonial culture that was evoked at the beginning of the novel.

This writer decided to keep their block quote and analyze parts of it in the following paragraph in their analysis of Things Fall Apart.

Lesson 3

Quoting Quotes

STRATEGY

Writers use conventions to make clear who they are quoting—the narrator, another character, or someone else who is quoted in the text.

Visit hs-guidetoteaching.org to download the chart, Three Ways to Integrate Quotations.

USE THIS STRATEGY... when your literary essayists are drafting sections of their essays and integrating quotations, or revising their writing for precision and clarity. It can also help writers find interesting quotes by widening the range of voices they might quote.

TEACH THE STRATEGY

- Suggest to students that sometimes it can be confusing for a reader to know who is really being quoted, inside of a literary essay.
- Show your students a paragraph of your writing in which you want to add a quotation that is a combination of characters speaking and narration.
- Introduce three ways you might quote: by separating the narration and the dialogue, by nesting the dialogue, or by separating the quote with analysis in between. You could create your own writing or use this chart.

Three Ways to Integrate Quotations

Option	Example
Include the moment the character is talking and the moment of narration separately.	Xiomara tells Aman she doesn't feel good, that she has to leave, but "Aman tugs at [her] hand," and says, "Read me a poem, X? I want to remember your voice when I think about tonight" (Acevedo 169).
Use nested quotations.	Xiomara recounts her evening with Aman in her journal: "Aman tugs at my hand: 'Read me a poem, X? I want to remember your voice when I think about tonight'" (Acevedo 169).
Spread the quotes out with analysis in between.	Xiomara tells Aman she doesn't feel good, that she has to leave, but "Aman tugs at [her] hand," and says, "Read me a poem, X?" His request isn't just about poetry—it's about connection, as he says, "I want to remember your voice when I think about tonight" (Acevedo 169).

When Mary taught this lesson, she pulled a quote from *The Poet X* focused on Xiomara and Aman's relationship. She introduced a chart with different ways she might format the quotation in her essay. While all three options could work, after discussion, Mary and the students determined Option 1 works best for the fluidity of her writing.

- Invite students to analyze the different examples, considering when and why writers might use each in a literary essay, and choose one for your essay.
- Send off students to try this work, looking over their text for new ideas for quotes and their essays for places to insert and frame these quotes.

PROMPTS TO COACH STUDENTS AND PARTNERSHIPS

As you're writing, pause anytime you're integrating evidence that quotes a character, and think about the main point you want to emphasize with that quote. Then, use the structure that will most reveal your point. For example, it might be you want to:

- *show the character's feelings*
- *reveal a contrast between what the character says and how they act*
- *reveal the character's innermost thinking*

Imagine you were introducing this quote to someone who doesn't clearly remember this part of the story. How might you introduce it?

When you're stuck, it can help to talk through your ideas with a partner. You can say to each other, "Can you help me with this part? I'm trying to ... How can I ...?"

CLASSROOM ARTIFACTS

The important line substitute here is the Chromatics' cover of Neil Young's, "It's Better to Burn Out Than to Fade Away." That line plays behind Alex as he floats upside down in the pool. Alex comes up for air, but others who knew that line haven't. "It's better to burn out than to fade away" was quoted by Kurt Cobain in his suicide note. There's something else important. Critics of the show fear that it will inspire teen suicide-glamorize it, romanticize it. Neil Young himself was haunted by Cobain's use of his lyric in his suicide note. He wrote and dedicated his 1994 album, *Sleeps with Angels* to Cobain, and inspired a generation of new punk bands, perhaps in the way that Hannah's tapes inspire her listeners to confront their own pain and tell their own stories.

Achebe shifts the point of view so that you have access to Okonkwo's inner thinking. Yet at the same time, there will be, across the novel, small moments when you hear the author's voice—or a voice and point of view, at least, that are not Okonkwo's. For instance, as Okonkwo listens to the crier's voice as the start of Chapter 2, and "discerned a clear overtone of tragedy in the crier's voice," Achebe also inserts: "darkness held a vague terror for these people" (9). The first phrase brings the reader closer to Okonkwo. His inner thinking portrays him as perceptive. The second phrase, though, is a distancing one. "These people" suggests a kind of outside view, and one that is not necessarily antagonistic but definitely distant. Achebe didn't say "his people" or "the people of the village."

These writers clarify the speaker of their quotes carefully, while analyzing the score of Thirteen Reasons Why *and point of view in* Things Fall Apart.

The Art of Angled Paraphrasing and Summarizing

Lesson 4

STRATEGY

Literary essayists, and all those who write about stories, don't only write about specific lines or quotes. They also describe and analyze what happens in the story. Literary essayists, therefore, develop the art of angled paraphrasing, where they retell parts of the story, highlighting the parts that support their ideas.

USE THIS STRATEGY... to help your powerful writers mirror the authentic writing about books they'll see in published literary criticism and book reviews. This strategy is also helpful for novice writers who need support in angling their paraphrasing so they are more purposeful.

Visit hs-guidetoteaching.org to download mentor excerpts of angled retellings, from published literary criticism and book reviews.

Inquiry Questions

How do writers paraphrase parts of a story in ways that:

- engage the reader?
- suggest themes?
- support their ideas about the text?

LAUNCH THE INQUIRY

- Suggest to students that literary essayists not only include quotes as evidence, they also retell parts of the story to support their ideas, much as film critics retell parts of a film.
- Invite students to study some excerpts from published reviews, (artful retellings alongside the ideas these authors develop), and to try to name some of the moves these writers make in supporting their ideas.
- Summarize (and elevate) what students notice about effective retellings, perhaps creating a chart or annotated excerpt to support students.
- Invite students to consider where angled retelling might be helpful in their own writing, and what ideas they want to highlight through these retellings, and set them to trying this out.

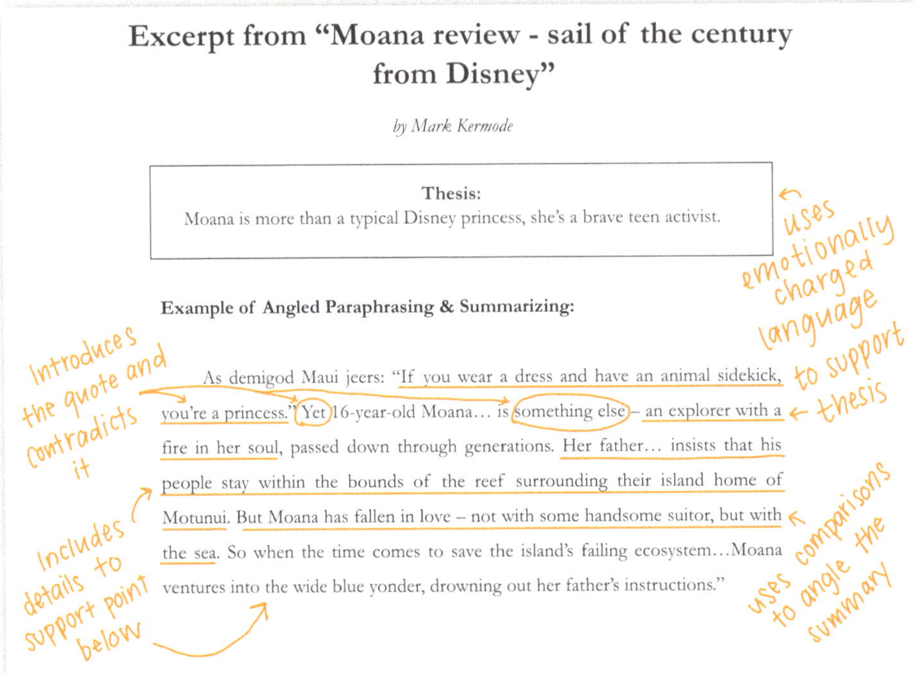

Excerpt from "Moana review - sail of the century from Disney"

by Mark Kermode

Thesis:
Moana is more than a typical Disney princess, she's a brave teen activist.

Example of Angled Paraphrasing & Summarizing:

As demigod Maui jeers: "If you wear a dress and have an animal sidekick, you're a princess." Yet 16-year-old Moana… is something else – an explorer with a fire in her soul, passed down through generations. Her father… insists that his people stay within the bounds of the reef surrounding their island home of Motunui. But Moana has fallen in love – not with some handsome suitor, but with the sea. So when the time comes to save the island's failing ecosystem…Moana ventures into the wide blue yonder, drowning out her father's instructions."

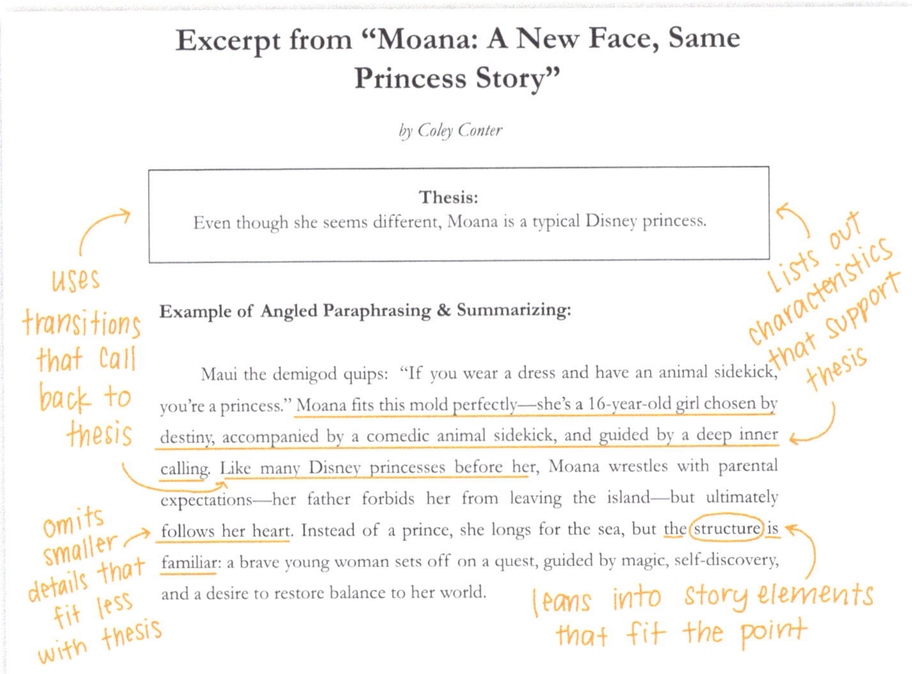

Excerpt from "Moana: A New Face, Same Princess Story"

by Coley Conter

Thesis:
Even though she seems different, Moana is a typical Disney princess.

Example of Angled Paraphrasing & Summarizing:

Maui the demigod quips: "If you wear a dress and have an animal sidekick, you're a princess." Moana fits this mold perfectly—she's a 16-year-old girl chosen by destiny, accompanied by a comedic animal sidekick, and guided by a deep inner calling. Like many Disney princesses before her, Moana wrestles with parental expectations—her father forbids her from leaving the island—but ultimately follows her heart. Instead of a prince, she longs for the sea, but the structure is familiar: a brave young woman sets off on a quest, guided by magic, self-discovery, and a desire to restore balance to her world.

When Coley taught this lesson, she worked with a class to collaboratively annotate a review of Moana from *The Guardian* (Kermode 2016) and a version she created herself.

LANGUAGE TO COACH STUDENTS AND PARTNERSHIPS

Sometimes angled retelling is really helpful in the introduction, to lead into and build up to your idea.

You can retell part of the text as your evidence, choosing which moments or incidents seem most important, and summarizing them—and being deliberate in how you describe these moments.

The adjectives you use to describe a moment often lead the reader to understand your sympathies. Was a moment dreadful, brutal, or lovely?

CLASSROOM ARTIFACTS

Patrick surprises David during an open mic night at Rose Apothecary. In front of a small audience, he dedicates a performance to David and sings an acoustic version of Tina Turner's, "Simply the Best." As Patrick sings, David is emotional and a little uncomfortable with the public attention. The performance becomes a powerful act of love. It's a turning point in their relationship, showing just how much Patrick cares.

Phoebe sees movies with Holden, and they talk about them. Holden really admires her, and he lets slip that they have seen some movies, like Hitchcock's *The Steps*, over a dozen times, and that Phoebe has memorized whole parts. The way Holden admires Phoebe for being so smart tells us that he really admires intelligence. Perhaps he wishes he was like Phoebe—especially the way everyone admires her. Holden seems to want to be treated with the kind of respect, love, and caring that Phoebe is.

These writers angle their retellings so that their plot summaries support their ideas about Schitt's Creek *and* The Catcher in the Rye.

Lesson 5

Finding and Introducing Delicious Lines

STRATEGY

Writers make choices about what information to summarize and which words, phrases, or lines to quote by thinking about which words or phrases are most important, use a specific craft or technique, or are too complex to summarize.

USE THIS STRATEGY... when writers identify climatic scenes but still need to think about which parts to quote and which parts to paraphrase. This strategy also supports students who are writing about longer texts, where parts of the plot—what happens—are important to their ideas.

Visit hs-guidetoteaching.org to download the chart.

TEACH THE STRATEGY

Essayists identify striking lines by...

- looking for lines from the text that are so beautiful, poignant, or well-worded, they couldn't say it better themselves.
- choosing lines in which the author uses a craft technique, like alliteration, metaphor, or repetition, that would be lost when summarizing the moment.
- choosing dialogue that shows something important about a character's relationships, motivations, or growth.
- picking out words, phrases, or dialogue that demonstrate strong emotion

- Revisit a key part of the text you want to use to support your thesis. Model rereading, differentiating between parts that move the plot forward and lines that stand out as particularly poignant.
- Highlight standout words, phrases, and lines that could be good fodder for quotes.
- Give students a few tips on where they might find these powerful lines, namely, at the end of chapters or scenes.
- Draft a few lines of your own, showing how you paraphrase the plot to set up the quote, and then quote a key moment in the text.
- Set up students to quickly practice this work, replicating the steps from the demonstration with an example the teacher creates or in their own work.

PROMPTS TO COACH STUDENTS AND PARTNERSHIPS

Sometimes you'll come across a line that just feels particularly poetic, and you know you want to write about it.

Often evocative lines involve some kind of symbolism. You can look back at your text for where you jotted any annotations about symbolism.

It can be interesting to look at narration—when the author describes parts. Sometimes there are gems hidden in the narration.

CLASSROOM ARTIFACTS

Collecting Evidence

Page 192-193

Important plot points:

- Mami yells
- Xiomara discovers why Mami is yelling
- Twin comes over to comfort Xiomara
- Xiomara feels badly

Important Quotes

- Xiomara slides "down to put my head between my legs" (192)
- Twin "crouches next to me, but I can't warn him of the storm that's coming" (193)
- She tries "to make all the big of me small, small, small" (193).

Drafting

paraphrase plot

In the middle of the text, Xiomara floats home after kissing Aman on the train. However, she's greeted by yelling as she opens the door to her home, and Xiomara knows she's in deep trouble. After a moment with Aman in which she feels expansive, it's almost as if she shrinks when she arrives home. As her mother shouts and Twin comes to comfort her, Xiomara crouches down and slides her head between her legs. She narrates, "I try to make all the big/ of me small, small, small" (Acevedo 193).

* striking quote

When Lauren modeled this, she first separated the moment into parts to paraphrase and parts to quote directly, then she did some drafting in front of the class.

Lesson 6

Leading into and out of Quotes with Voice

STRATEGY

Writers often study mentors who are skilled at leading into and out of quotes in interesting ways. By studying mentors, they can figure out a few techniques to try themselves.

Visit hs-guidetoteaching.org to download a chart of techniques for leading into and out of quotes and a curated list of mentors.

USE THIS STRATEGY... when your writers need more support framing quotes or with maintaining a sense of voice in their writing.

Inquiry Questions

- How do writers lead into and out of quotes in a way that maintains their voice, develops their ideas, and highlights key passages?

LAUNCH THE INQUIRY

- Suggest to students that there are many ways to lead in and out of quotes, and it can be interesting to study mentors to get ideas.
- Post the inquiry question and invite students to work with a partner to study some excerpts from mentor essays that frame quotes gracefully. Ask students to name some of the techniques they are noticing the mentor writers are using to lead in and out of quotes.
- Collect some of what students say, developing their thinking as needed, and share a chart, like the one here.
- Send off students to revise their own writing, trying out some of these techniques in their own writing, mirror-writing using the examples you provide.

Leading In & Out of Quotes with Voice

Technique	Example
Fit the quote naturally into your own sentence.	Her body now "takes up more room" than her voice (Acevedo 5).
Introduce an idea and tuck the quote in as an example.	Xiomara is used to standing out: she's tall with "too much body for a young girl" (Acevedo 5).
Start with your idea and analytical thinking, ending with the quote to prove your point.	Xiomara's pain reveals how her body is a source of joy and embarrassment. Xiomara is "unhide-able" (Acevedo 5).
Let the reader know what the quote will describe first, and then give the quote.	Xiomara's mother constantly reminds her of how difficult she finds her daughter when she says, "Pero tu no eres facil" (Acevedo 10).
Start with a quote by blending it into a sentence and saying more about what it demonstrates.	"Pero tu no eres facil" is something Xiomara has heard her whole life that turns into a mirror of how she sees herself (Acevedo 10).
Blend the quote into your sentence. Then, explain this moment in the story and why it is significant.	Xiomara is, as she proclaims, "unhide-able" (Acevedo 5). In this moment in the story, Xiomara's inability to hide causes her more pain than joy.

PROMPTS TO COACH STUDENTS AND PARTNERSHIPS

You could try introducing your quote out loud, as if you were explaining it to a partner. Then write that in to see how it flows.

Remember you can link two parts of a quote together in the same sentence using a "…"

One thing writers do is try on different types of punctuation when leading into quotes to see what works best.

Lesson 6 (Continued)

CLASSROOM ARTIFACTS

"November's Book Club Pick: Speaking Truth, Beautifully, to Shattered Young People" by Julia Fogliano, New York Times, 2018

Xiomara is lost. . . . Although she still inhabits the same body, the same pious Dominican family and the same Harlem neighborhood, nothing is the same. Her body now "takes up more room" than her voice and has become a target for relentless catcalls from boys and insults from girls. Her once adored mother has become a constant source of rules and disapproval, and the church that was once a place of joy now feels like a house that is "no longer one I want to rent."

"*The Poet X*" by Elizabeth Acevedo, Kirkus Review, 2018

Fifteen-year old Xiomara ("See-oh-MAH-ruh," as she constantly instructs teachers on the first day of school) is used to standing out: she's tall with "a little too much body for a young girl." Street harassed by both boys and grown men and just plain harassed by girls, she copes with her fists.

"Caught Between Worlds? For Elizabeth Acevedo, It's a Familiar Feeling" by Concepción de León, New York Times, 2020

Xiomara, her protagonist in "The Poet X," expresses this sentiment when she describes the moment she hears spoken word for the first time. "We're different, this poet and I. In looks, in body,/ in background," she says. "But I don't feel so different/ when I listen to her. I feel heard."

Teacher Demonstration Writing

There is a moment in Part 1 that is particularly moving, when Xiomara laments, "When your body takes up more room than your voice you are always the target of well-aimed rumors" (Acevedo 5). Xiomara's cry of pain reveals how Xiomara's body is a source of joy and embarrassment. Xiomara is, as she proclaims, "unhide-able" (5). In this moment in the story, Xiomara's inability to hide causes her more pain than joy...

Xiomara's mother constantly reminds her of how difficult her daughter is when she says, "Pero, tú no eres fácil," something Ximomara has heard her whole life that turns into a mirror of how she sees herself. These five words sum up Xiomara's way of walking through the world - uneasily, at war within herself and with the world.

"The Poetry X: A Review by Eben Roddis," Young Poets Network

The first of these experiences is the daily challenge faced by young women every day. Whilst 'Harlem is opening its eyes to September', Xiomara has to battle with the eyes and flirtatious taunt of every guy on her block. This remains a crucial theme throughout the book and the frustration it causes is both powerful and moving.

...By page 60 we see the first rebellion. After refusing to take the bread and wine of Communion, we see Xiomara and Mami face off via Xiomara's resentful poetry. We also begin to learn more about Papi, who seems like a ghost in many scenes, only there in spirit. His tongue is described as 'slick with compliments', and we find out the twins were 'miracles' as they were born despite Papi's infertility, and that they simultaneously saved him and condemned him to a mundane life.

Mentor text excerpts to study how authors lead in and out of quotes.

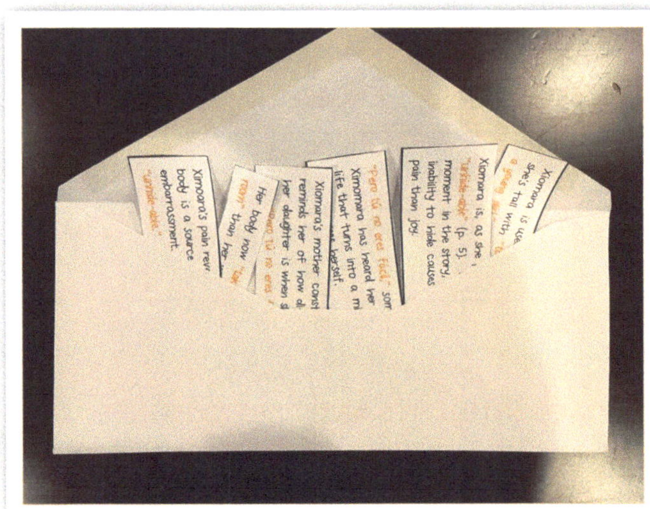

Writers match techniques and excerpts.

Creating Vivid Character Descriptions

Lesson 7

STRATEGY

Writers often include vivid character descriptions to introduce characters they'll discuss in their writing and to support their ideas about characters.

USE THIS STRATEGY... so that your writers have varied forms of evidence they can include, and so that they have more to say across their pieces. This strategy also supports writers in matching their descriptions with their ideas.

Visit hs-guidetoteaching.org to download mentor character descriptions from published literary criticism and book reviews.

TEACH THE STRATEGY

- Suggest to your writers that literary essayists often include vivid character descriptions to introduce characters they'll discuss in their literary analyses and to support their ideas about characters.
- Share a small collection of mentor character descriptions from published reviews, and invite students to choose one to study with a partner, thinking about how this writer describes that character and what their purpose might be.
- Demonstrate two ways to describe a familiar character.

Idea: Xiomara's secrets in *The Poet X* cause her to be unhappy and confused.

Xiomara is a lonely tenth grade girl living in Harlem, attending a private school. Her body has changed faster than her soul. She comes to school with a woman's body, curvaceous and sexy, but inside, Xiomara is unsure and faltering. Her frightened uncertainty about herself bleeds into her damaged relationships with others, as she pulls in and at the same time pushes at her boyfriend, Aman, and even her brother, whom she calls Twin.

Idea: Xiomara's secrets in *The Poet X* keep her safe.

Xiomara is a quietly powerful tenth grade girl living in Harlem, attending a private school. She has a lot to keep secret, including her uncertainty about religion, her hidden pleasure that she is attractive to boys, and her pride in her writing. Xiomara carefully chooses not to speak about any of these openly, and that wise caution keeps her safe and gives her time to grow.

When Coley taught this lesson, she used vivid language that highlights different aspects of Xiomara from *The Poet X*, to support different ideas. It can help to highlight some of that language, or you can suggest students highlight it.

- Invite writers to try this work in their drafts, looking for places where they might describe a character deliberately.

COACHING LANGUAGE TO SUPPORT STUDENTS AND PARTNERSHIPS

The first time you introduce a character, you can decide how you'll describe them, especially if you'll describe them in positive or negative ways.

Sometimes what you want to emphasize about a character is their complexity, and then you might describe different sides of a character.

When you study mentor writers, they often give background on a character, emphasizing the parts they'll develop later in their writing.

CLASSROOM ARTIFACTS

From his first days at Hogwarts, the young, green-eyed boy bore the burden of his destiny as a leader, coping with the expectations and duties of his role, and in this volume, he is clearly more Henry V than Prince Hal, more King Arthur than young Wart: High-spirited war games of Quidditch have given way to real war, and Harry often wishes he were not the de facto leader of the Resistance movement, shouldering . . . responsibilities, but an ordinary teenage boy—free to romance Ginny Weasley and hang out with . . . friends.

Excerpt: "An Epic Showdown as Harry Potter is Initiated into Adulthood." Review of *Harry Potter and the Deathly Hallows*, New York Times, July 19, 2007.

Elwood has always fundamentally thought of himself as the kind of person who doesn't get into this sort of trouble. He's the kind of person who follows the rules and plays whatever game he's asked to play, even when it's rigged against him. At his after-school job at the neighborhood cigar store, he informs on his classmates when he catches them stealing candy, although his boss keeps explaining to him that a little candy theft is built into the overhead and it's fine to let it go. His classmates beat him up afterward. Elwood believes that the game is fair. It never occurs to him that he might be getting scammed just by playing in the first place.

Excerpt: "Colson Whitehead's Spare, Riveting, Horrifying Nickel Boys," Vox, July 18, 2019.

These published writers create vivid images of the characters they analyze.

Chapter Six: Bolstering Analysis, Developing Commentary

There are lots of names for deep, analytical thinking: reasoning, commentary, analysis, elaboration, explanation. Whatever you choose to call it (and we suggest using many terms), thinking is at the heart of this genre, and we're always excited to see where students take their ideas.

We know analyzing literary texts can be challenging for students. If it was easy, we probably wouldn't put so much emphasis on young writers developing and refining this skill. Knowing that it's a challenge, we can think strategically about how we can set up students to do this work, how we can coach them. One of the most effective pedagogies is for students to see you developing your own analysis and refining it. When we do this messy work in front of students and show our own process, they come to better understand that it's inherently challenging, that it's okay to waffle back and forth on an idea, that they can ask a bunch of questions and turn the answers into an analysis.

Beyond your own demonstration, it's also helpful to coach students to do this thinking work out loud with a partner, recording it on a big sticky note, in a notes app—anywhere but in the middle of the paragraph they are writing. Oftentimes, when students try to weave their analysis into their writing beautifully, as they are also actively thinking through what they are going to say, it leads to frustration and sometimes a less developed analysis. Young writers, and probably most writers, analyze more deeply when they can first experiment outside of their drafts and then dip back in to craft their ideas into coherent and well-developed sentences. Also, most of your students will say more than they write, so rehearsing their thinking out loud helps them develop that thinking.

Most of all, we want students to have explicit strategies they can use as they analyze their evidence and support their thesis statement. For some students, all we have to say is, "Why is this quote important?" or "How does this bit connect to your thesis?" and they are off and writing. For other students, sentence stems are a really helpful tool. But most young writers also benefit from mentor texts or models of how analysis can look, or specific angles to lean into or moves to try. This chapter aims to do just that, sharing lessons that teach students a variety of strategies to get to deeper thinking. Our goal is for students to have a repertoire of strategies they can turn to anytime they have to analyze a text.

We appreciate Hochman and Wexler's thesis in *The Writing Revolution* (2017) that sometimes students' ideas stay simplistic because their language is simplistic—they lack the academic language to construct more complex sentences and, thus, more complex ideas. We play here with asking students to deliberately experiment with adding in interesting conjunctions and other phrases such as "even though …" or "in spite of …," which lead the writer to new thinking.

Sometimes analysis in literary essays can feel a bit forced or formulaic, and that's usually because we're thinking only of the "writing for school" version of literary analysis. Similar to structure, when we studied the commentary and analysis of published writers, we realized how open analysis can be. Some writers set it up before the evidence; other writers weave it in the same sentence as the evidence, blending the two components seamlessly. Others analyze text alongside their own experiences or by asking questions. We invite you to lean into this, to show young writers all that analysis can be. When we open the doors for them, the depth of their ideas only seems to grow.

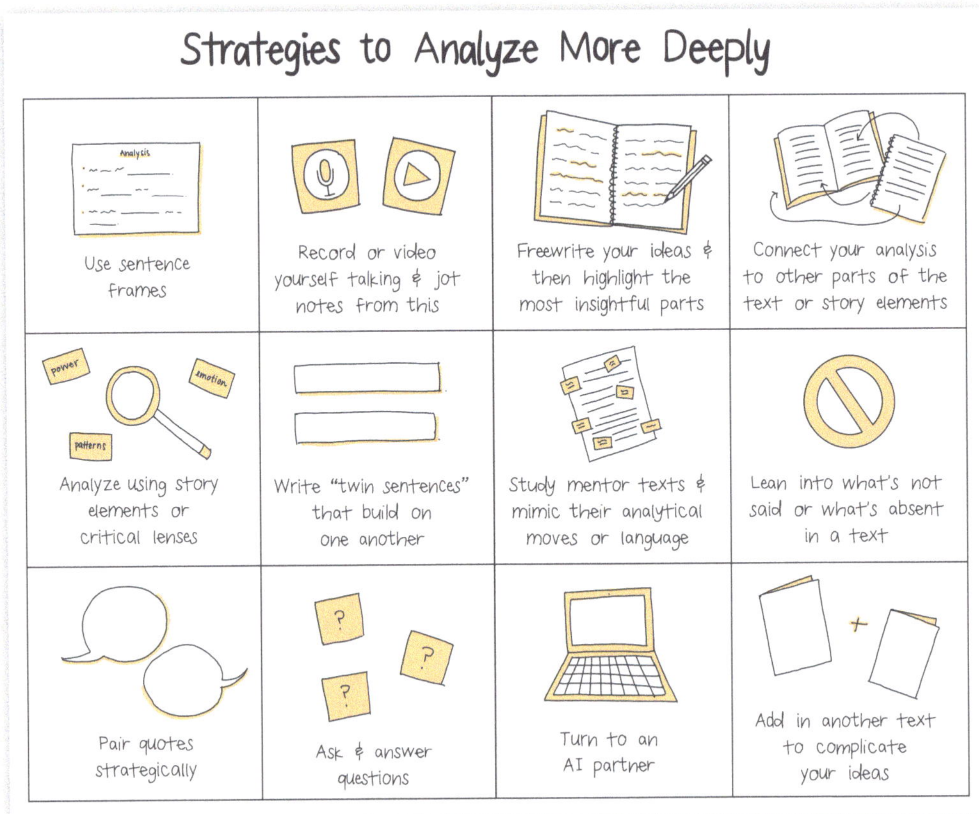

Lesson 1

Rehearsing Literary Explanations

STRATEGY

Writers know that it's not enough to insert evidence into their drafts—they need to unpack and discuss that evidence. One way to develop this kind of analysis is to talk through with a partner why the writer included that evidence, explaining how it relates to an overall thesis or to a subtopic.

Visit hs-guidetoteaching.org to download cue cards for developing literary explanations.

USE THIS STRATEGY... to help writers have more to say about their evidence and to help them link their evidence to ideas—to move up and down a ladder of abstraction. This strategy especially supports the many young people who say more than they write.

TEACH THE STRATEGY

- Suggest to students that once analytical writers have gathered and inserted their evidence, they often need to develop commentary that explains the significance of that evidence.
- Suggest, as well, that sometimes a writer might need to explain how a detail links to their overall thesis, and other times they're explaining its relevance to that *part* of the thesis—a subtopic. Explain that prompts can help writers develop this contextual analysis.
- Model for students how you find a piece of evidence, such as a quote, in your draft, and talk through a literary explanation for its significance. Ask one student to be your partner, and suggest that they prompt you with a couple of cue cards for developing literary explanations.

Cue Cards for Elaboration

This quote/ scene/ passage reveals...	One reason this quote/scene/passage is so significant is that...	Here, the character/author...
What makes this line powerful is...	The deeper meaning behind this quote/scene/passage is...	This detail/these words help readers understand...
At first glance it seems... but actually...	The author's choice of words here reveals...	This quote/ scene /passage reveals...
This line reflects the character's internal conflict...	What's illuminated in this quote/scene/ passage is...	This moment echoes/ reinforces/ interrupts an earlier scene...

Elaborating with Cue Cards

Xiomara describes her conflicting emotions: "I'm disgusted at myself/for the slight excitement/that shivers up my back/at the same time that I wish/my body could fold into the tiniest corner/for me to hide in" (47). Here, Xiomara engages in almost a form of self-deception, unable to process her own reactions. In this space—the pages of her journal—she works to conceal feelings not just from others, but even from herself.

When Lauren did this work with her class, for instance, she returned to a quote from *The Poet X*. When her partner asked her to say, "Here, the character...," Lauren spoke about how here, Xiomara engages in almost a form of self-deception.

- Suggest that students do similar work, finding quotes and other bits of evidence in each part of their writing, and working to develop literary explanations for their significance, using these cue cards as a support.
- Remind students after a few minutes to make sure to add their new thinking to their own work.

PROMPTS TO COACH STUDENTS AND PARTNERSHIPS

Sometimes it's really helpful to develop literary explanations verbally. To capture these, you might ask a partner to transcribe, or you might use an AI note-taker or any speech-to-text program.

It's always interesting to consider whether this bit of evidence connects not only to your overall thesis but also to another part of your idea or another part of the text.

If you're a little stuck, you can start by saying something like, "I included this quote because ..." and then you can develop a fancier transition later. You can also help a partner by suggesting they start with this phrase.

CLASSROOM ARTIFACTS

"Don't tell anybody anything. If you do, you start missing everybody."

This line reflects Holden's internal conflict in how it suggests that Holden, on this last page of the novel, in his last words to the reader, shuts down. Despite the moments when it seemed as if Holden were opening himself to emotion, in these final words, Holden shows his distrust of himself and the world. What makes this line so powerful is how it reflects the depth of Holden's wounds, and what makes it so poignant is it hints at Holden's yearning for others, how he does, inside, miss everybody.

The moment when Celie finally says, "I'm poor, I'm black, I may be ugly and can't cook.... But I'm here" (Walker 207) is an important moment for Celie. This quote reveals Celie's transformation from silence toward finding her voice. At first glance, it seems Celie is simply acknowledging her own limitations, but actually, she is reclaiming her identity even though she experienced years of abuse.

Combining sentence starters leads to deeper analysis of The Catcher in the Rye *and* The Color Purple.

Analyzing with Lenses

Lesson 2

STRATEGY

Writers often use lenses to deepen their analyses or explore new thinking. They can start by selecting evidence to analyze, and then considering which lenses are best for their theses. Then they try out a few lenses, layering them or selecting the one that works best.

USE THIS STRATEGY... to deepen students' analytical skills and to help students try analyzing a quote several different ways before deciding which interaction works best for the thesis.

Visit hs-guidetoteaching.org to download the chart of literary analysis lenses.

TEACH THE STRATEGY

- Suggest to students that analytical writers are always striving to see more in the text and deepen their analysis. Introduce the idea of analyzing with lenses as one way to go deeper, showing students a chart with several lenses.

Lesson 2 (Continued)

- Demonstrate selecting a part of your writing to work on and a specific piece of evidence, deciding which lenses will best support your work. Then, model choosing a few lenses, thinking or jotting to show how these lenses help you develop thinking related to your overall thesis or a subtopic off your thesis.

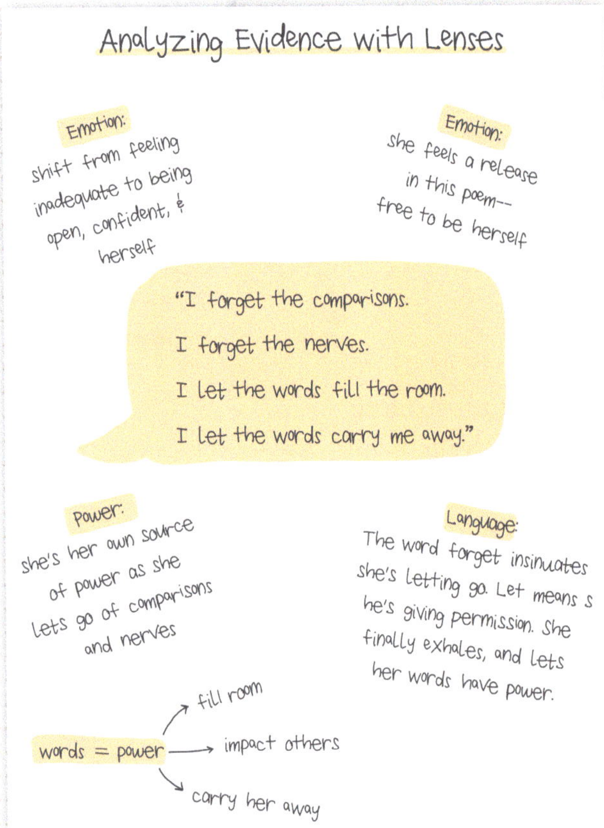

Xiomara's transformation during the poetry slam marks a turning point where she moves from being constrained by self-doubt to embracing the strength of her voice. The repetition of the word "forget" insinuates that Xiomara is ready to let go of the part of her identity that was housing nerves and insecurity. In contrast, the repetition of the word "let" means she's finally giving permission to let her voice take up space and for her words to be a source or power. Her words have power over her, as they "carry her away" and allow her to let go, but they are also powerful in that they impact others by "filling the room."

When Coley modeled this work, she returned to the poem "The Mic Is Open," from *The Poet X*. She demonstrated revisiting this excerpt through the lenses of language, emotion, and power, jotting some thinking in her notebook, showing students how you can leave your essay to develop more thinking, and then come back to it with new ideas.

Then, Coley modeled how she returned to her essay to add new analysis, typing directly into the part of her essay where her new thinking fit.

Last, Coley double-checked that this analysis connected to her focus for this part of her essay and thesis statement, making any necessary adjustments.

- Guide students to engage in this same process with their own writing, encouraging them to talk through new ideas based on these lenses with a partner, and then do some jotting and writing.

PROMPTS TO COACH STUDENTS AND PARTNERSHIPS

There are so many lenses to analyze from. You could think of different critical lenses or story elements that feel important to the part you're analyzing.

Sometimes it helps to look at your thesis and ask yourself: Which lens is this thesis calling on me to analyze with? Alternatively, you could let go of your thesis a bit, analyze with lenses, and then revise your thesis as needed.

You might want to try out a new angle, where you think of what most people would say about this quote, and then try it with a fresh perspective.

CLASSROOM ARTIFACTS

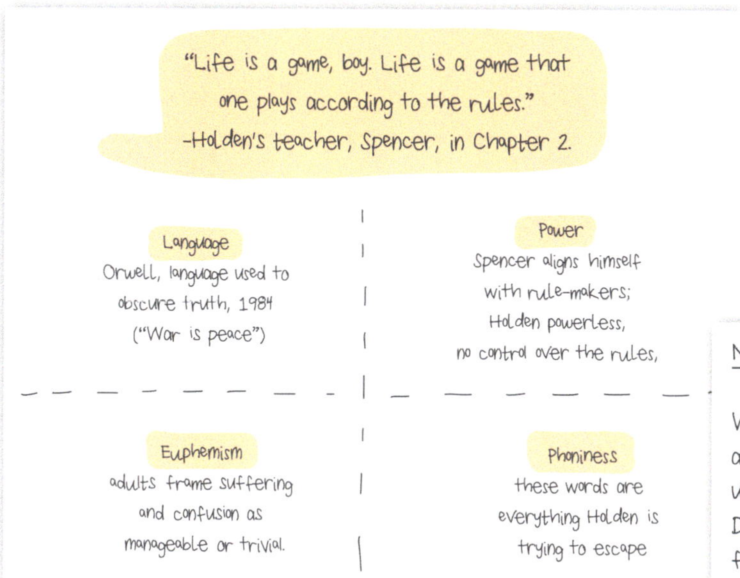

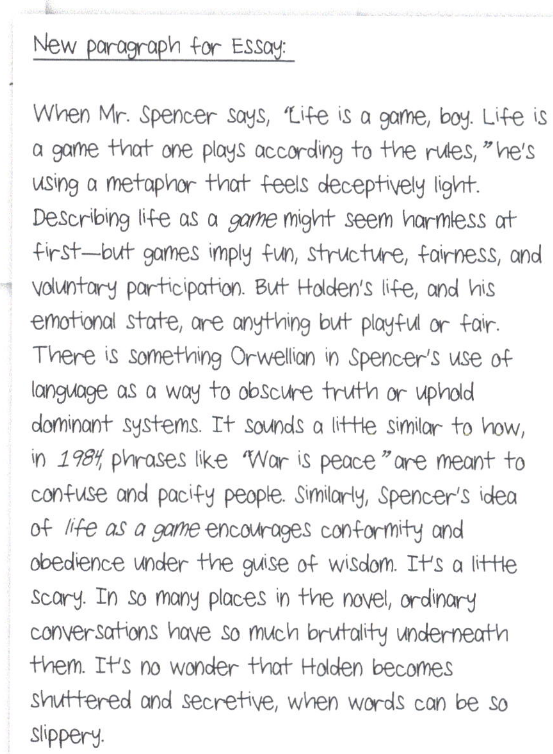

New paragraph for Essay:

When Mr. Spencer says, "Life is a game, boy. Life is a game that one plays according to the rules," he's using a metaphor that feels deceptively light. Describing life as a *game* might seem harmless at first—but games imply fun, structure, fairness, and voluntary participation. But Holden's life, and his emotional state, are anything but playful or fair. There is something Orwellian in Spencer's use of language as a way to obscure truth or uphold dominant systems. It sounds a little similar to how, in *1984*, phrases like "War is peace" are meant to confuse and pacify people. Similarly, Spencer's idea of *life as a game* encourages conformity and obedience under the guise of wisdom. It's a little scary. In so many places in the novel, ordinary conversations have so much brutality underneath them. It's no wonder that Holden becomes shuttered and secretive, when words can be so slippery.

Jotting outside of the essay helps Mary develop an entire new paragraph to add to her essay on The Catcher in the Rye *and* The Poet X.

Lesson 3

Studying Mentor Texts to Deepen Our Understanding of Analysis

STRATEGY

Writers return to mentor texts often across the writing process. One time when it can be very helpful to look back at a mentor is when a writer wants to deepen their analysis. Often, published writing will suggest new analytical moves that writers can try out in their own literary analyses.

Visit hs-guidetoteaching.org for a curated collection of mentor texts and to download the chart.

USE THIS STRATEGY... when writers are using the same kinds of analyses across their writing or when they are ready to try out some new ways to analyze texts. This work also inculcates the habit of returning to mentor texts across the writing process.

Inquiry Questions

- How do published writers analyze text?
- What moves do they make that I could try?

LAUNCH THE INQUIRY

- Suggest to students that mentor texts can often give writers new ideas for analysis.
- Pose the inquiry questions for students and set them up to read a few mentor texts, focusing on the analysis and commentary in the pieces. Invite students to circle, underline, and annotate on print texts and to jot notes on digital texts.
- Collect a list of strategies for analyzing texts as a class.
- Encourage students to try these strategies by mirror-writing the sentence frames from the writer or by thinking how this particular technique might play out in their own writing. Encourage writers to jot in their notebooks first or a separate document, before returning to their essays, if that's helpful.

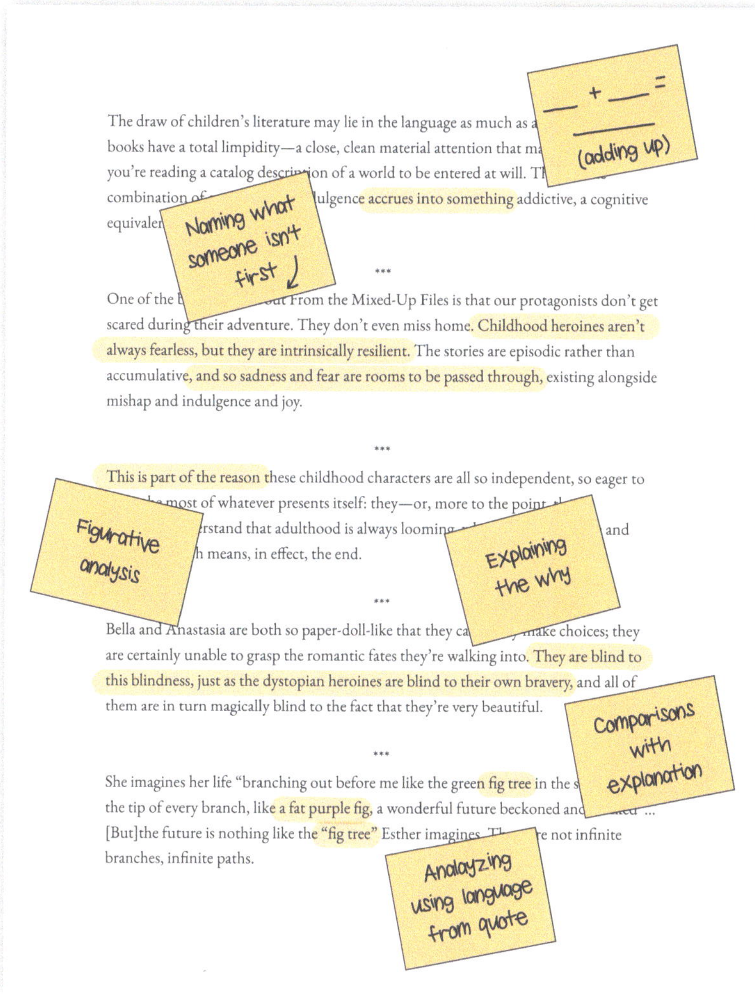

When Coley did this work with her class, she used the mentor text "Pure Heroines" in Jia Tolentino's essay collection, *Trick Mirror* (2019). She invited students to help her name strategies Tolentino used, and collected these on sticky notes.

PROMPTS TO COACH STUDENTS AND PARTNERSHIPS

Sometimes it's helpful to leave your draft and jot some new sentences in your notebook or in a new document. Then you can weave these new sentences back into your draft.

You could also combine some of these moves to build a layered and complicated analysis.

Verbally rehearsing your analysis or recording your analysis is a helpful starting point. Try that before diving into the writing.

CLASSROOM ARTIFACTS

Writers Analyze Texts by...

Adding up parts

- The combination of ____ and _____ adds up to ______
- Example: The stylistic combination of economy and indulgence accrues into something addictive...

Naming what we know

- We know ______ from ______.
- Example: We know everything we need to know about twelve-year-old Claudia from this accumulation of nouns.

Indicating, not this, but that

- ______ isn't _____, but she is ______.
- As much as _____ is about _____, it's also about _____.
- Example: Childhood heroines aren't always fearless, but they are intrinsically resilient.

Explaining the Why

- The reason for ________ is because ______
- _____ stems from ______.
- Example: This is part of the reason these childhood characters are all so independent...they—or...their creators understand that adulthood is always looming.

Using comparisons

- ______ is the _____ used to represent _______.
- Example: The Lisbons' bodies are the rubric through which all else in the town is interpreted.

Exploring similarity and difference

- ______ is ______, just like ________.
- ______ juxtaposes the idea that _______.
- Example: They are blind to [their romantic fates], just as the dystopian heroines are blind to their own bravery.

Returning to specific language from the text

The use of the word _____ illustrates the idea that

When ______ says _____ it means ______

Example: She imagines her life "branching out before me like the green fig tree in the story. From the tip of every branch, like a fat purple fig, a wonderful future beckoned and winked"... [But]the future is nothing like the "fig tree" Esther imagines. There are not infinite branches, infinite paths.

*Examples are from *Pure Heroines (2019)* by Jia Tolentino

Coley collects sentence frames from "Pure Heroines," and uses them to mirror write sentences she can use in her own essay.

Lesson 4

Using What's Missing to Jumpstart Analysis

STRATEGY

Writers analyze the text by looking at what's missing or what's *not* said as well as what's included. They do this by examining what could have happened or been said in a part of a text and its potential outcome on the character or overall trajectory of the narrative.

USE THIS STRATEGY... to show students a subtle way to analyze text and when students are ready to make their analyses more sophisticated.

Visit hs-guidetoteaching.org to download the chart.

TEACH THE STRATEGY

- Remind students of the strategies they know for strengthening analysis (or have them name their favorite strategies), then name a new and subtle strategy for students: analyzing what's not said or what's missing in the text.
- Demonstrate this type of analysis by sharing your thesis and an excerpt from the text you are studying. First, quickly think through and analyze what is said. Then move into what's not said, trying out new thinking using the bank of sentence frames.

Essay Question:

Why does Xiomara keep secrets from those around her and even from herself?

In "Whispering with Caridad Later That Day," Xiomara begins to reveal a secret, saying, "There's this boy at school..." Her best friend Caridad replies with things like, "This is why your mom should have sent you with me to St. Joan's" and "It's wrong to lust, Xia. You know it's a sin" (71). Caridad could've said tell me more, or asked a question, but instead she led with judgment, shutting down Xiomara from telling her anymore. In this moment Xiomara was looking for someone to understand her. Caridad responded with her religion instead of with her friendship at the forefront. Xiomara keeps secrets, even the positive ones about her life, because she lacks support from those that love her.

Analyzing with the Lens of What's Missing

- The author could've said ________, but said ________, instead.
- The silence around ________ suggests that the author might be emphasizing ________...
- Even though no one talks about ________, it feels like ________.
- The character doesn't say ________, so maybe they are ________.
- Nothing is said about ________, which might mean ________.
- It's quiet when ________ happens, so I wonder if ________.
- Here, what might have happened ________, but instead ________.
- No one ever talks about or refers to ________.
- We never get to know about ________.
- One thing that is never fully explained is ________.
- By omitting ________, the author invites readers to question or consider ________.
- The author's deliberate choice not to address ________ implies ________ about the underlying message or theme.

Lesson 4
(Continued)

When Coley did this work with her class, she went back to the question she was focusing her essay around and an excerpt that helped her answer this question. From here, Coley thought about ways the character could have responded, but didn't, and the impact that had on the story.

- Coach writers to try this work with a sample excerpt in partnerships, sharing sentence stems to prompt their thinking.
- End by sending students off to try this analytical method with their own writing. Suggest that sometimes this strategy leads to such big thinking that it might need thesis revision.

PROMPTS TO COACH STUDENTS AND PARTNERSHIPS

Look for excerpts where you were surprised how things turned out. It could be an important part of the text where a character's perspective is missing, or when you think the opposite happened of what the character might have imagined.

Sometimes you can think not only about a single excerpt but about whole perspectives that are missing, or people who disappear, or events that are never fully explained.

This can work well with a craft essay, too, where you're thinking of what language the author could've used or the technique that would have shifted the mood or trajectory of the text.

CLASSROOM ARTIFACTS

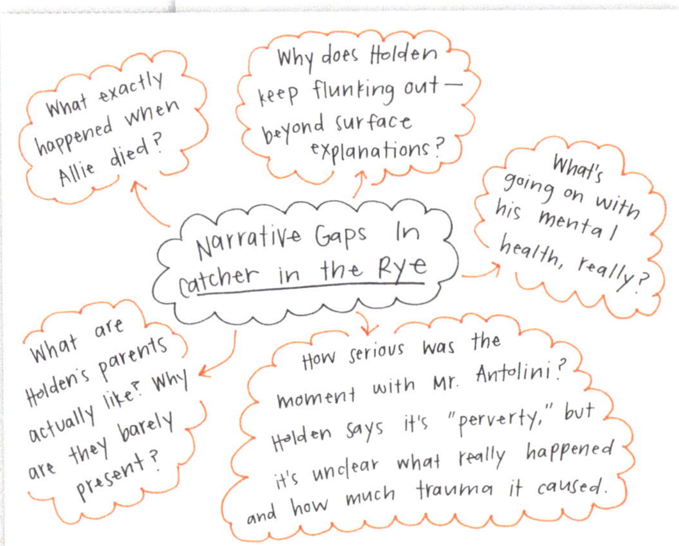

Mary analyzes what's missing in The Catcher in the Rye.

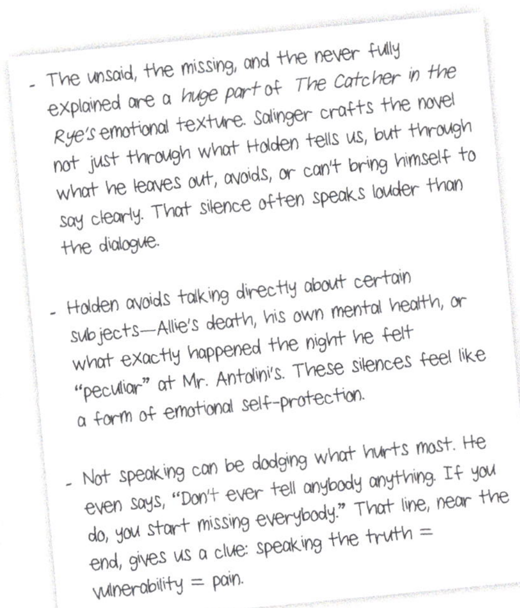

- The unsaid, the missing, and the never fully explained are a huge part of The Catcher in the Rye's emotional texture. Salinger crafts the novel not just through what Holden tells us, but through what he leaves out, avoids, or can't bring himself to say clearly. That silence often speaks louder than the dialogue.
- Holden avoids talking directly about certain subjects—Allie's death, his own mental health, or what exactly happened the night he felt "peculiar" at Mr. Antolini's. These silences feel like a form of emotional self-protection.
- Not speaking can be dodging what hurts most. He even says, "Don't ever tell anybody anything. If you do, you start missing everybody." That line, near the end, gives us a clue: speaking the truth = vulnerability = pain.

Expanding Our Sentences (and Our Thinking)

Lesson 5

STRATEGY

Experimenting with expanding sentences can often lead to expanded thinking. Writers, therefore, sometimes write a sentence (often a topic sentence or framing sentence) and see what happens if they expand it with phrases such as *but …*, *in spite of …*, *as if to say*, and other phrases that lead to new thinking.

USE THIS STRATEGY… to support students in developing more complex sentences and language to develop more complex ideas.

Visit hs-guidetoteaching.org to access a chart of phrases for expanding sentences.

Inquiry Questions

What new thinking might I develop by expanding some sentences?

LAUNCH THE INQUIRY

- Suggest to your writers that sometimes expanding sentences is a way to develop more complex thinking and that there are phrases that help writers develop this skill.
- Share a collection of phrases to expand sentences, asking students to study them, considering which ones might work best in their own writing.

Writers try these phrases to expand their sentences (and their thinking)		
Phrases to try at the end of a sentence		
...because...	...but...	...so...
...perhaps because...	...at the same time...	...although beneath the surface...
...as if...	...even though...	...as a result of...
...which leads to...	...and so...	...which seems to suggest...
Phrases to try at the start a sentence		
Surprisingly/disconcertingly...	Despite...	Although...
At first...	It turns out....	Even though...
In fact,	What's more...	In other words,
Tragically...	Hopefully...	Remarkably...
Others may say.../ people say...	Ironically...	Because of...
Ultimately...	In a way...	Not only that, but...

- Demonstrate trying one or two of these phrases, showing how you add the phrase, and pause to think: "What could I say?" Then try new versions of your sentence, asking students to notice how the idea shifts with different words and phrases.

> - Xiomara doesn't even fully express herself to her brother, Twin, perhaps because she senses his preoccupation with his own secrets.
>
> - Xiomara doesn't even fully express herself to her brother, Twin, as if she doesn't fully trust him with her greatest vulnerabilities.
>
> - Ironically, Xiomara doesn't even fully express herself to her brother, Twin, despite her assertions that he is almost a part of her.

When Mary taught this lesson, she modeled expanding one sentence, about Xiomara in *The Poet X*, in a few different directions, to deepen her thinking, staring with, "Xiomara doesn't even fully express herself to her brother..."

- Invite students to try this method, suggesting they revise some existing sentences and try drafting some new ones.

PROMPTS TO COACH STUDENTS AND PARTNERSHIPS

You could try different kinds of sentences. Sometimes the ones we frame our quotes with can be interesting.

Sometimes it's interesting to try two, or even three, of these phrases inside one sentence.

You can do this work with a partner, where you say one of your sentences and your partner gives you a phrase to add on with, which you have to respond to.

Starr never really feels comfortable at Williamson Prep.

In a way, Starr never really feels comfortable at Williamson Prep, perhaps because she can never bring her full identity to this space.

Despite how Starr never really feels comfortable at Williamson Prep, this discomfort doesn't keep her from deciding to take risks.

In episode one, Clay, the narrator, gets into a car with his friend Tony. Tony offers to play Clay a cassette tape. It has a penciled name on it. *Joy Division*. As Clay and Tony pull into the street, the sounds of "Love Will Tear Us Apart" fills the car. At first, it seems like the choice of the late seventies band Joy Division signals that Clay and Tony are different. They're nostalgic; they're into subculture.

But the music is playing an entirely other role. It has a subtext to it. Joy Division was a band in the late seventies. They were headed by Ian Curtis, a fantastically talented songwriter and singer. He was also a tortured figure who killed himself when he was twenty-three. Curtis suffered from depression, from epilepsy at concerts, from a sense that his life was fragmenting around him. He poured that into his music.

People loved to say that Joy Division is "moody," and they would say that as if Curtis's lyrics shouldn't be taken seriously. Yet later it turned out that he was pouring out his soul. He really meant it when he wrote that love would tear him apart. This song was one of the last songs Ian Curtis sang when he was alive. Joy Division only really released two albums. This song is at the end of the second album. In fact, it's not even on the original album—it was added as a live version to the collectors' edition after Curtis killed himself. Hannah, it turns out, was moody, and no one took her words seriously. No one was even able to listen to her words, until after she died.

Expanding sentences can lead to surprising new insights about The Hate U Give *and the score of* Thirteen Reasons Why.

Lesson 6

Pairing Quotes to Synthesize and Analyze

Visit hs-guidetoteaching.org to access the chart from this lesson.

STRATEGY

Writers sometimes pair quotes strategically, thinking about how quotes work together to enhance an argument. Writers ask themselves: How do these quotes connect? And: How will my analysis be deeper if I look at these two pieces of evidence together?

USE THIS STRATEGY... when students are using more than one quote in a paragraph or section of their writing and they are ready to think more deeply about how they can connect multiple pieces of evidence to make their analysis more complex.

TEACH THE STRATEGY

- Suggest to students that writers often pair quotes or multiple pieces of evidence to prove their point, extend their thinking, add complexity to their ideas, or develop counterarguments.
- Generate a chart alongside students, naming the different reasons to pair quotes.

When Pairing Quotes...

- look for quotes that complement/build on each other
- choose quotes that show difference, contradiction, counterargument
- find quotes that demonstrate a cause and effect relationship
- consider quotes from different characters that reinforce an idea
- avoid selecting quotes that are too similar to each other

Original Quote

I forget the comparisons.
I forget the nerves.
I let the words fill the room.
I let the words carry me away.

Pairing to Extend Ideas

"No music today, X./Instead I want to hear you /Read me something" (111)

Aman invited her to share her voice and waited for her to share it with him. As he yearns to know her, he helps her get to the place where she can share with the world.

Complicating Ideas/Counterargument

"All of Friday and the weekend/the world I've lived in/wears masking tape/over its mouth (223).

Xiomara felt nervous about sharing her voice with the world, but having it taken away from her, without her consent, gives her the power to share it with others.

Exploring Cause and Effect

"'That gave me chills', I say, /'I felt it in here,' I say. /'You should finish it,' I say" (284).

After sharing her voice with the world, she understands the power of feeling seen and passes on the confidence to Isabella. Her words are carrying her not only in performing, but in supporting other writers and young women.

When Lauren experimented with this lesson, she shared a quote she planned to use in her own writing. She discussed how this quote shows Xiomara finding herself and her voice. Then, Lauren modeled thinking about a few quotes she might pair it with, specifically thinking about quotes that contradict, extend, or complicate her ideas about the quote she used.

PROMPTS TO COACH STUDENTS AND PARTNERSHIPS

Consider which quote should go first and how you'll move fluidly from one to the other. How will you frame the partnership between the pieces of evidence?

Sometimes, when you read a second quote, it makes you reconsider the significance of the first. Perhaps there was foreshadowing, which you see only now, or perhaps there is a shift in perspective, or another change.

You could try pulling a big idea or phrase from one quote and applying it to the other. Sometimes that helps to forge connections between them.

Lesson 6 (Continued)

CLASSROOM ARTIFACTS:

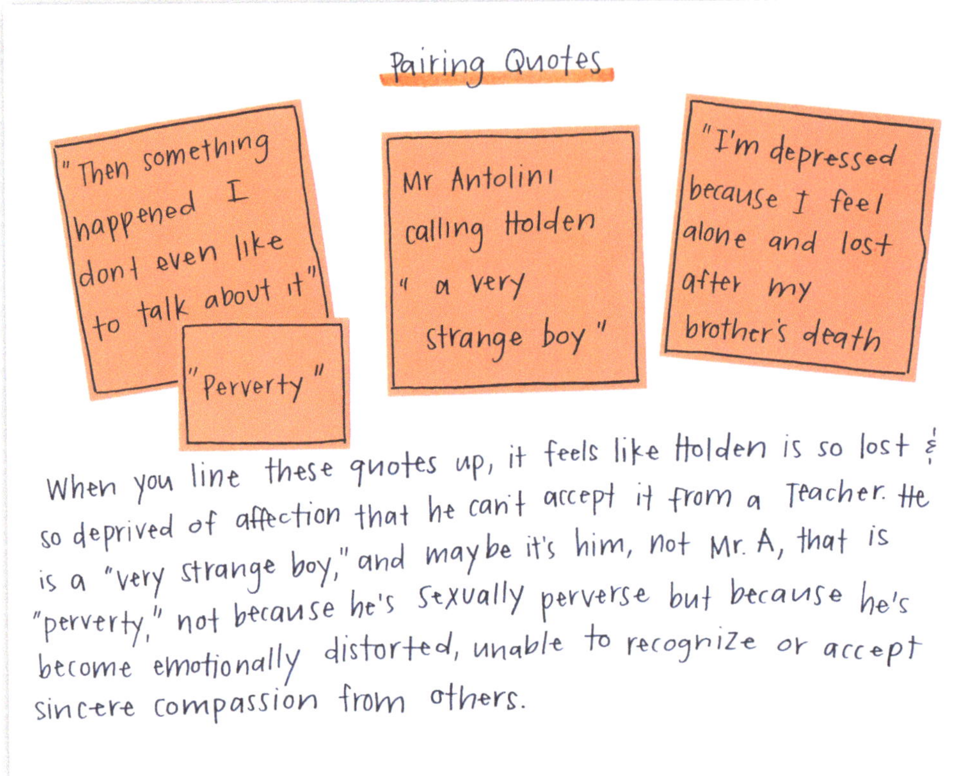

Mary experiments with pairing quotes using The Catcher in the Rye.

In *The Great Gatsby*, Jay Gatsby's American Dream is to win Daisy's love, but he's driven by his obsession with wealth. Gatsby plans on impressing Daisy with his mansion. Since Nick lives next door, he has a meeting set up at Nick's home. "Why didn't he ask you to arrange a meeting?' 'He wants her to see his house,' she explained. 'And your house is right next door.'" This displays Gatsby's belief that money can buy happiness, which ultimately results in his death. In *The Great Gatsby*, the rich are greedy and continuously wanting more, whereas, in *The Grapes of Wrath*, the poor are people desperate to live a better life. The Joads' dream of living a better life in California away from the desolate fields of Oklahoma. Granpa Joad says he's "Gonna get me a whole big bunch of grapes off a bush, or whatever, an' I'm gonna squash 'em on my face an' let 'em run offen my chin." Unfortunately, he died of a stroke, so his dream will never come true. Both *The Grapes of Wrath* and *The Great Gatsby* show that the rich and poor are not so different. The rich have everything and take it for granted, whereas the poor have nothing and wish for more. Regardless, both can lead to misguided ambitions, ultimately causing their downfall.

Writers experiment pairing quotes in a comparison of The Great Gatsby *and* The Grapes of Wrath.

Tucking in Precise Language to Elevate Analysis

Lesson 7

STRATEGY

Writers can lift the level of their writing by paying attention to language. Often, they do this by first writing their analyses, then going back and attending to their own language as well as the language or craft in the quote.

USE THIS STRATEGY... when writers are ready to revise their writing and their analysis is already strong, so they will benefit from making small tweaks to lift the level of their thinking.

Visit hs-guidetoteaching.org to access the chart from this lesson.

TEACH THE STRATEGY

Introduce the idea that there are large-scale ways to analyze a text and then there are micro-moves that writers can make that offer a big impact on their analyses, such as paying attention to language.

- Pull from the following chart to name a few ways writers might make tiny moves to develop their analyses.
- Demonstrate adding a few moves from the chart into your own writing, modeling this work in front of students, adding specific language in a different color, or showing them two pieces of writing, one before your revisions and one after, asking them to notice the strategies you tried.
- Support students as they try this work in their own writing, noting that some of your students, but not all, might be ready for this step.

Tiny Moves to Elevate Your Analysis

- Tuck in discussion craft and language
- Use figurative language or a comparison
- Include appositive phrases to add in extra details
- Select precise and intentional verbs
- Identify the text structure
- Indicate the story element
- Mirror the language/style of the text

Caridad, obedient and faithful, is Xiomara's best friend, though the two couldn't be more opposite. Where Caridad "recites bible verses and promotes peace, [Xiomara] curse[s] up a storm and [is] always ready to knuckle up" (30). Although the two of them are juxtaposed in this poem, Xiomara feels their friendship is powerful and enduring, like a rosary strung tight—different beads, same thread. But this is complicated when the two of them are whispering during Confirmation class, and Xiomara begins to reveal a secret, revealing, "There's this boy at school…" Caridad replies with things like, "This is why your mom should have sent you with me to St. Joan's" and "It's wrong to lust, Xio. You know it's a sin" (71). Although Caridad is bringing her true self to the friendship, this is surely stopping Xiomara from sharing more about her feelings and relationship with Aman, forcing her to harbor secrets and hide her true self. If Caridad was more open to the conversation, what might Xiomara have shared?

When Coley demonstrated this, she added appositives, figurative language, precise verbs, and specific language, using different colors to highlight her writing moves as she made insertions.

PROMPTS TO COACH STUDENTS AND PARTNERSHIPS

You could pick one of these moves to focus on at a time. Maybe just try to sharpen your verbs, or find places to add in some figurative language.

Sometimes this work will lead you to bigger ideas to add to your analysis. It's okay for it to take you down a rabbit hole. Experiment and see where it leads you!

For work like this, studying mentor texts can be helpful! Pick one we've studied as a class and see what you notice.

Nick goes on to describe the party with rhythm: "the halls and salons and verandas are gaudy with primary colors, and hair shorn in strange new ways, and shawls beyond the dreams of Castile" (p. 40). Nick sees this as a dreamlike place, where "the bar is in full swing, and floating rounds of cocktails permeate the garden outside, until the air is alive with chatter and laughter, and casual innuendo and introductions forgotten on the spot" (p. 40). The combination of assonance in the chatter and the laughter, and the alliteration of the full and floating, contrast sharply with the unsentimental tone with which Nick had described his family. Nick creates a fairy-tale vision, in which the Rolls Royce becomes an "omnibus," and the station wagons a "yellow bug" that meets and transports the guests. It seems as if Gatsby has, after all, created a magic that can seduce.

This student revises, adding words that describe the language of The Great Gatsby.

There's a thing I hardly ever talk about because I don't know how to talk about it. It's this: I have a sort-of-step-sister, and it's hard to have her as a sister, and I feel badly about that, because it's not her fault, it's mine, for not loving her more. But we'll get to that later.

Right now, let's talk about the novel I just read. It's called *Extremely Loud and Incredibly Close*, and it's by this guy Jonathan Safran Foer, who had already published this other novel, *Everything Is Illuminated*, which had gotten great feedback from the press. So, when he came out with this second novel, expectations were high. Then it came out; it failed to impress.

Maybe people didn't love the novel because they didn't love Oskar. Oskar is the fictional hero of the novel. Oskar's a little like my sort-of-sister. Not so easy to love. You find yourself not loving them because they're imperfect in a way that you don't empathize with. Or, I empathize with Oskar, but not with my sister. Maybe because it's harder in real life, or maybe it's because you can see how hard Oskar finds it to connect with anyone. It's hard to talk about this stuff because it can make you feel like a horrible person. When people are damaged, you're supposed to love them more. But you don't, always; sometimes it has the opposite effect. You find yourself wishing they were different. Let's not talk about my sister, though. It's easier to admit that Oskar can be hard to be around. He's extraordinarily intelligent in some aspects and almost missing a sense in others. My sister's like that too. Anyways.

This writer mirrors the language and tone of Jonathan Safran Foer, as he discusses hard parts of the text and his life.

Lesson 8

Inviting New Perspectives with an AI Thought Partner

STRATEGY

Contemporary thinkers and writers know that one role an AI partner can play is to offer new perspectives. They prompt their AI partner by suggesting that they'd like their partner to troubleshoot their ideas and lead them to consider new angles.

USE THIS STRATEGY... to help your students become more adept at training an AI partner in ways that will increase their criticality, and to help students who would benefit from listening to a partner's thinking about some of their evidence.

Visit hs-guidetoteaching.org to access the chart from this lesson.

TEACH THE STRATEGY

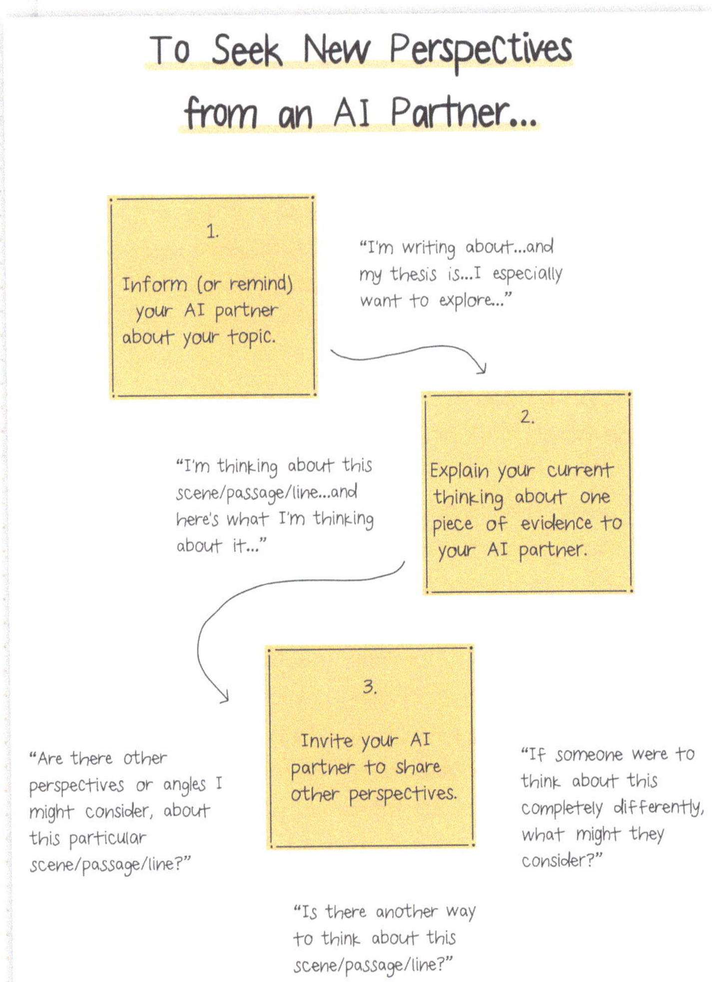

- Suggest to your students that sometimes it's helpful for writers to hear a completely different perspective about their ideas or their evidence and that an AI partner can play this role.
- Share a chart with some ways to prompt an AI partner, to invite new perspectives.
- Model for your students how you might ask an AI partner to suggest alternate perspectives for one part of your essay.
- Encourage students to follow these suggestions, asking AI to first clarify how well they know the text.

PROMPTS TO COACH STUDENTS AND PARTNERSHIPS

Make sure that your AI partner knows your text well—ask it to be sure.

Be sure to upload the part of your writing you most want to focus on, so your AI partner can focus.

If your AI partner gives you too many suggestions, ask it to offer only one or two alternatives.

CLASSROOM ARTIFACTS

I'm writing a literary essay about The Poet X, and my thesis is that across the novel, Xiomara is highly secretive, but the way in which she keeps and reveals secrets changes with the different spaces she inhabits. I especially want to explore how Xiomara, the protagonist, learns to navigate spaces in which she feels pressure to make herself small. Growing up in a strict religious household, Xiomara learns that certain thoughts, feelings and desires must be kept hidden. Therefore, secrecy becomes a form of self-preservation. Do you know the novel well enough to be a thought partner for me as I develop parts of my analysis?

I'd like to share a paragraph I'm writing, that explores Xiomara's secrets that involve Aman, and I'd like you to offer other ways to think about these parts of the text. Are there other perspectives or angles I might consider, about this particular scene/passage/line? Here's my thinking: Xiomara both hides and reveals secrets at the smoke park. The smoke park is a public space, but it feels semi-hidden, outside the control of her family, school and church– a place where she goes to secretly spend time with Aman without her family knowing. It is here that she begins to share parts of herself with him. In their first visit at the smoke park, they sit in companionable silence, listening to a Kendrick Lamar album. While they don't say much, Xiomara admires his smell, and lets her hand linger holding his. The next time they visit the park, Aman asks Xiomara to read him a poem, and she does. She reads him a "poem about Papi." It's the first time Xiomara reads her work to someone, and her heart is pumping in her chest. Xiomara writes, "when I'm done I can't look at Aman./ I feel as naked as if I'd undressed before him" (112). In this moment, we see how vulnerable Xiomara feels, both exhilarated and terrified at the way she's shared a part of herself.

1. Contrast Between Physical and Emotional Intimacy

You hint at this already, but you might deepen it: Xiomara lets Aman hold her hand and later reads him a poem—both moments of intimacy, but the second is far riskier for her emotionally. The fact that the poem is about *Papi*, not a love poem, is also worth noting—it's a kind of misdirection, but also a revelation. Why *that* poem? What does choosing to share that particular secret with Aman reveal about where she is emotionally?

Angle to explore:

> The act of sharing a poem—not a romantic confession, but a complex family secret—suggests Xiomara is testing emotional safety. The smoke park becomes not just a hiding place for romantic transgressions, but a testing ground for emotional truth.

2. What Makes the Smoke Park Feel Safe?

You call it "semi-hidden" and outside the control of family, school, and church. You might go further and ask: what is it about this *lack of structure* that allows Xiomara to experiment with revealing herself? How does the physical environment contribute to the sense of freedom?

Possible thread:

> The smoke park lacks the surveillance and expectations that define Xiomara's other spaces. There are no rules to follow, no scripts to read from—just music, silence, and shared presence. This absence of structure gives her permission to create a new kind of self.

3. Sensory Language as a Clue to Secret Desire

The way Xiomara observes Aman's scent, the physical touch, and later describes the vulnerability of reading her poem—all suggest how sensory experience is tied to hidden longing. Even when she isn't speaking, Xiomara's body and senses are telling a secret.

Angle to explore:

> In the absence of words, Xiomara's body becomes the bearer of secrets—her lingering hand, her racing heart, her inability to meet Aman's gaze. These physical cues hint at the powerful undercurrent of self-expression she is just beginning to explore.

4. Foreshadowing Her Later Poetic Liberation

This may be one of the first times she reads her poetry aloud, which foreshadows the later moment when she performs her work publicly. The smoke park scene can be seen as a rehearsal, a kind of emotional stretching.

Angle to explore:

> This quiet moment with Aman is an early rehearsal for the poet she will become—a person who dares to speak her truth, even when it feels like undressing.

Lauren explains both her thesis and what she was interested in exploring in her essay overall. She shares the part of her essay she's looking for other perspectives on. Notice how this AI partner summarizes the writer's words first.

Lesson 9

Analyzing the Language of Particularly Expressive Quotes

STRATEGY

Sometimes the author writes with such eloquent, specific language that the literary essayist needs to quote those specific words. Often these parts include evocative language or literary techniques. Literary essayists, then, analyze the language as well as the content of these quotes.

USE THIS STRATEGY... to help writers notice language and literary techniques more, find poignant lines to quote, and begin to analyze form as well as content.

TEACH THE STRATEGY

- Suggest to students that when literary essayists choose particularly evocative quotes, they often analyze the language, as well as the content of these quotes.
- Explain that essayists often identify these lines, in the narrative and in their essay, by ...
  - looking for lines from the text that are so beautiful, poignant, or well worded, they couldn't say it better themselves.
  - choosing lines in which the author uses a craft technique, like alliteration, metaphor, or repetition, that would be lost when summarizing the moment.
- Demonstrate how you can discuss the language of a quote as part of your analysis, returning to a familiar text.
- Name the moves you made while drafting, including returning to evocative lines, ones that feel particularly moving, and lingering in your analysis to talk about the language of the quote, in your essay.
- Set up students to quickly practice selecting quotes and studying language in their own work.

Aman doesn't write poetry, as Xiomara does, but sometimes he seems to speak in the language of poems, as when he says:

> I can remember Trinidad:
> the palm trees behind my grandmother's house,
> the taste of backyard mangoes,
> The song in the voice every time someone spoke.

Aman's words evoke the taste of fruit, the music of voices, the palm trees he clearly, openly still longs for and remembers, even as he shuts away any longing for his mother. The way Aman references 'the song in the voice," of everyone he remembers speaking creates a sense of nostalgic, remembered musicality and intimacy, echoed by the 'backyard' mangoes and the palm trees 'behind my grandmother's house.' All of Aman's language is simple but lyrical, like the island he remembers.

When Lauren did this work in class, she revisited the poem in *The Poet X*, "And Then He Does," where Aman speaks of his memories of Trinidad, and showed students how she lingered in thinking about Aman's language, the specific words that he uses and their simplicity and lyricism.

PROMPTS TO COACH STUDENTS AND PARTNERSHIPS

Sometimes you'll come across a line that just feels particularly poetic, and you know you want to write about it.

Often evocative lines involve some kind of symbolism. You can look back at your text for where you jotted any annotations about symbolism.

It can be interesting to look at narration, when the author describes parts of the story, as well as moments of dialogue. Sometimes gems are hidden in the narration.

CLASSROOM ARTIFACTS

Because Nick's initial tone and content are overall so starkly realistic, it's even more dramatic when his tone shifts to one of wonderment. This happens when Nick first attends a party at Gatsby's house. It's not just that Nick describes a magical party. It's that his descriptions are lyrical, seductive, and... seduced. "There was music from my neighbor's house through the summer nights. In his blue gardens men and girls came and went like moths among the whisperings and the champagne and the stars" (39). Nick's metaphoric language, the "blue gardens," and the men and girls fluttering "like moths," enhance the sense of him being drawn in like a moth to a flame, believing, in this moment, in the possibility of Gatsby's transformational magic.

The Great Gatsby

This writer lingers in his analysis of language in The Great Gatsby.

Chapter Seven: Attending to Craft and Conventions

We love artful craft and conventions, because we love writing and we are readers. We also realize that not all of our students feel the same, and so we need to a) lure them into caring enough about their writing to attend to craft and conventions, and b) teach them about language, syntax, and citation so they can apply their knowledge of these to elevate their writing.

The truth is, it would be impossible to teach individual strategies for everything there is to learn about interesting sentence structure and accurate and artful punctuation. And it is even more impossible to simply teach students to write with that oh-so-coveted and oh-so-ambiguous quality: voice. All of these things come, usually, from doing a lot of reading. If we had lots and lots of time, we would set kids to listening to podcasts and reading book reviews and devouring literary criticism, so by the time they were writing their own pieces, they were full of language in the way that only comes from an immense amount of reading. If you ever do have the time, try this—have kids read not one or two mentor texts but dozens, so they become experts in the language of those who talk a lot about books.

We can do a lot to interest kids in craft and convention by teaching some strategies directly and immersing them in mentor texts so they can absorb innumerable other techniques. You'll see that's what we've done in these lessons. We send students back to mentor texts to study voice, we send them back to practice mimetic writing of individual sentences, we send them back to study transitions, and we send them back to study citation. All of this "returning to mentor text" work is deliberate. When we teach young people to seek and study mentor texts across the writing process, we teach them to outgrow us, to know that they have agency to learn from published authors, for any genre, at any time.

You will find some checklists embedded in these lessons (especially Lessons 4 and 5), as checklists help students self-assess, set goals, and strive to meet these goals. For conventions, it's always helpful to focus on those that are specific to that genre, so here, we zoom in on the conventions that are of particular importance to literary analysis (the biggest of which have to do with titles, capitalization, and citation). We know that students can simply turn to AI to fix up their conventions, but we also want to improve their knowledge, so they are better prepared for on-demand assessments, and so that their overall expertise with language grows.

Expect that your writers will use AI before publishing pieces. Where students used to use a spell and grammar check, they'll probably use a more comprehensive EdTech or open AI platform, depending on what your school and classroom promote. Teens need a lot of practice with this work as well as direct instruction on referencing AI. We model our practices on those that adult writers use, so that students become adept at wise and ethical AI use.

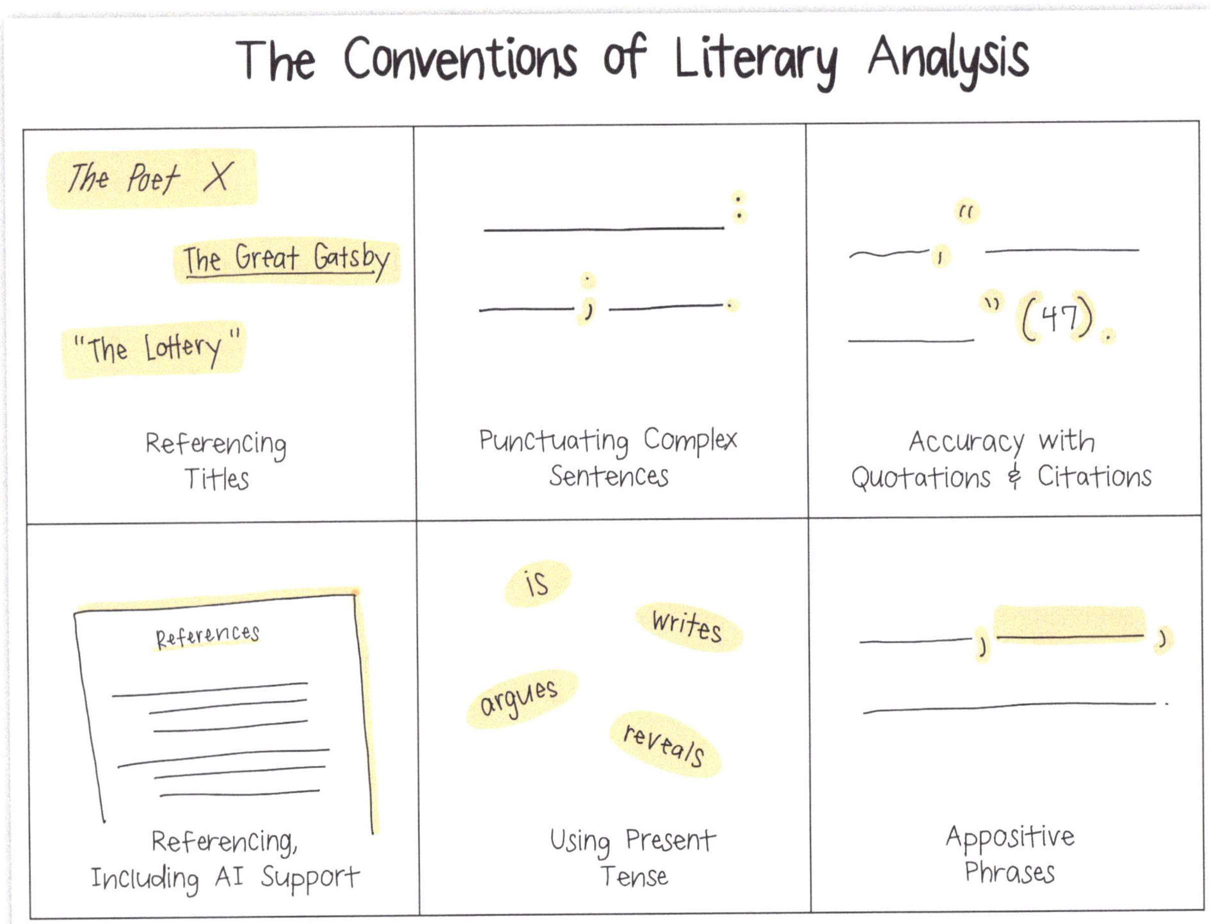
The Conventions of Literary Analysis
The Poet X
The Great Gatsby
"The Lottery"
Referencing Titles
Punctuating Complex Sentences
(47)
Accuracy with Quotations & Citations
References
Referencing, Including AI Support
is
writes
argues
reveals
Using Present Tense
Appositive Phrases

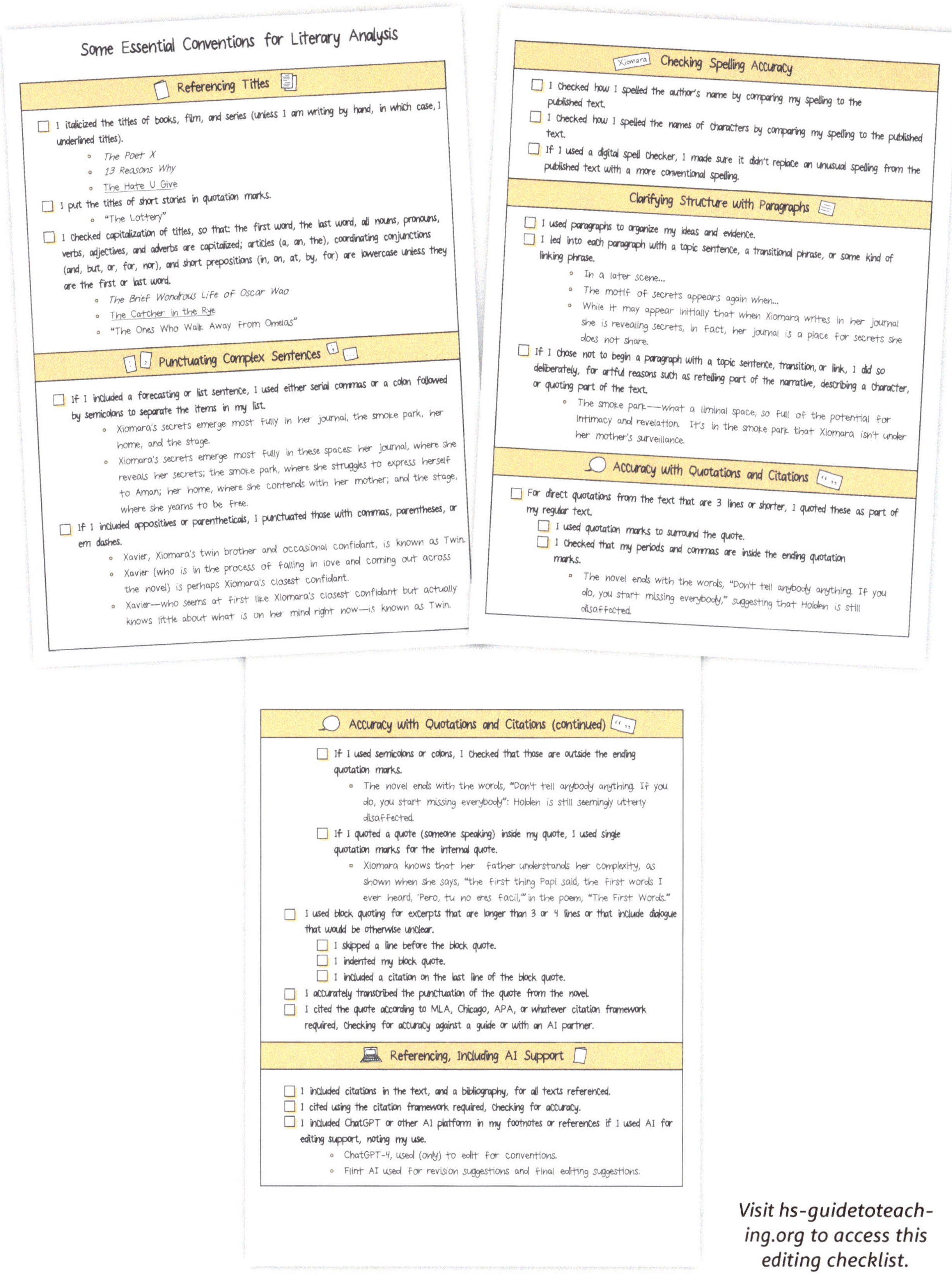

Some Essential Conventions for Literary Analysis

Referencing Titles

- ☐ I italicized the titles of books, film, and series (unless I am writing by hand, in which case, I underlined titles).
  - *The Poet X*
  - *13 Reasons Why*
  - *The Hate U Give*
- ☐ I put the titles of short stories in quotation marks.
  - "The Lottery"
- ☐ I checked capitalization of titles, so that: the first word, the last word, all nouns, pronouns, verbs, adjectives, and adverbs are capitalized; articles (a, an, the), coordinating conjunctions (and, but, or, for, nor), and short prepositions (in, on, at, by, for) are lowercase unless they are the first or last word.
  - *The Brief Wondrous Life of Oscar Wao*
  - *The Catcher in the Rye*
  - "The Ones Who Walk Away From Omelas"

Punctuating Complex Sentences

- ☐ If I included a forecasting or list sentence, I used either serial commas or a colon followed by semicolons to separate the items in my list.
  - Xiomara's secrets emerge most fully in her journal, the smoke park, her home, and the stage.
  - Xiomara's secrets emerge most fully in these spaces: her journal, where she reveals her secrets; the smoke park, where she struggles to express herself to Aman; her home, where she contends with her mother; and the stage, where she yearns to be free.
- ☐ If I included appositives or parentheticals, I punctuated those with commas, parentheses, or em dashes.
  - Xavier, Xiomara's twin brother and occasional confidant, is known as Twin.
  - Xavier (who is in the process of falling in love and coming out across the novel) is perhaps Xiomara's closest confidant.
  - Xavier—who seems at first like Xiomara's closest confidant but actually knows little about what is on her mind right now—is known as Twin.

Checking Spelling Accuracy

- ☐ I checked how I spelled the author's name by comparing my spelling to the published text.
- ☐ I checked how I spelled the names of characters by comparing my spelling to the published text.
- ☐ If I used a digital spell checker, I made sure it didn't replace an unusual spelling from the published text with a more conventional spelling.

Clarifying Structure with Paragraphs

- ☐ I used paragraphs to organize my ideas and evidence.
- ☐ I led into each paragraph with a topic sentence, a transitional phrase, or some kind of linking phrase.
  - In a later scene...
  - The motif of secrets appears again when...
  - While it may appear initially that when Xiomara writes in her journal she is revealing secrets, in fact, her journal is a place for secrets she does not share.
- ☐ If I chose not to begin a paragraph with a topic sentence, transition, or link, I did so deliberately, for artful reasons such as retelling part of the narrative, describing a character, or quoting part of the text.
  - The smoke park—what a liminal space, so full of the potential for intimacy and revelation. It's in the smoke park that Xiomara isn't under her mother's surveillance.

Accuracy with Quotations and Citations

- ☐ For direct quotations from the text that are 3 lines or shorter, I quoted these as part of my regular text.
  - ☐ I used quotation marks to surround the quote.
  - ☐ I checked that my periods and commas are inside the ending quotation marks.
    - The novel ends with the words, "Don't tell anybody anything. If you do, you start missing everybody," suggesting that Holden is still disaffected.

Accuracy with Quotations and Citations (continued)

- ☐ If I used semicolons or colons, I checked that those are outside the ending quotation marks.
  - The novel ends with the words, "Don't tell anybody anything. If you do, you start missing everybody": Holden is still seemingly utterly disaffected.
- ☐ If I quoted a quote (someone speaking) inside my quote, I used single quotation marks for the internal quote.
  - Xiomara knows that her father understands her complexity, as shown when she says, "the first thing Papi said, the first words I ever heard, 'Pero, tu no eres facil,'" in the poem, "The First Words."
- ☐ I used block quoting for excerpts that are longer than 3 or 4 lines or that include dialogue that would be otherwise unclear.
  - ☐ I skipped a line before the block quote.
  - ☐ I indented my block quote.
  - ☐ I included a citation on the last line of the block quote.
- ☐ I accurately transcribed the punctuation of the quote from the novel.
- ☐ I cited the quote according to MLA, Chicago, APA, or whatever citation framework required, checking for accuracy against a guide or with an AI partner.

Referencing, Including AI Support

- ☐ I included citations in the text, and a bibliography, for all texts referenced.
- ☐ I cited using the citation framework required, checking for accuracy.
- ☐ I included ChatGPT or other AI platform in my footnotes or references if I used AI for editing support, noting my use.
  - ChatGPT-4, used (only) to edit for conventions.
  - Flint AI used for revision suggestions and final editing suggestions.

Visit hs-guidetoteaching.org to access this editing checklist.

Lesson 1

Mentor Text Immersion: Bringing Voice to Literary Analysis

STRATEGY

Writers know that they may choose to write with unleashed voices, or with tightly controlled voices, depending on their audience and purpose. One way to develop more voice as a writer is to immerse oneself in mentor texts, asking: How do these writers bring voice into their writing?

Visit hs-guidetoteaching.org to download the chart and a list of mentor texts.

USE THIS STRATEGY... when your writers have been creating formulaic responses, so that their writing becomes prosaic, and when you want to inspire students to really look at how writers in the world speak and write about texts.

Inquiry Questions

- How do writers bring voice into their analytical writing?
- Who is the writer's intended audience? How does that impact their voice?

LAUNCH THE INQUIRY

- Suggest to students that literary analysis calls forth a strong sense of voice in some writers, and in others—especially when writing essays for school—it can lead to a constrained, controlled voice. *And* suggest that it's always powerful to write with voice, in any genre.
- Invite your writers to study two versions of an introduction and to name what gives the second version more voice.

Both *The Catcher in the Rye*, by J.D. Salinger, and *The Poet X*, by Elizabeth Acevedo, are narratives of escape and liberation. *The Catcher in the Rye* tells the story of Holden, who leaves his boarding school, to the freedom of New York City. *The Poet X* tells the story of Xiomara, who longs for escape from the restrictions of her religious upbringing, her femininity, and her inability to express her dreams. Both young people are damaged by their own secrets, and both experience transformations.

Both *The Catcher in the Rye*, by the secretive-reclusive-sequestered J.D. Salinger, and *The Poet X*, by outspoken-spoken-word-activist Elizabeth Acevedo, are narratives of escape and liberation. *The Catcher in the Rye* tells the story of Holden, who escapes the confines of his boarding school, and the generations of adult entrapment the school symbolizes, to the untamed freedom of New York City. *The Poet X* tells the story of Xiomara, who also yearns for escape, but hers is a longing for escape from the oppressive restrictions of her religious upbringing, the terror of her shifting femininity, and her tortured inability to express her dreams. Both young people are damaged by their own secrets, and both experience transformations, though the nature and result of these transformations are very different (perhaps mirroring the private/public nature of their authors).

When Mary did this work with her class, students spoke about the power of descriptive adjectives, strong verbs, and, mostly, a sense that the author loves the books, cares about the characters, and makes judgments or connections.

- Share a collection of mentor texts, and invite students to study a couple of texts with a partner, investigating how these authors bring voice to their writing. You might create a class chart of these writing moves.
- Finish by giving students some time to try some of this work in their own writing.

What contributes to a lively sense of voice?

- Vivid descriptions
- A sense that the author cares about the story, the characters
- Glimpses of the author as a reader
- Strong emotional response to parts
- Celebrations of language and word choice
- Personal judgments and insights
- Sympathy for the characters
- Surprising comparisons
- Direct address to the audience
- Literary techniques (poetic language, allusions, short and long sentences and paragraphs)

PROMPTS TO COACH STUDENTS AND PARTNERSHIPS

Voice is mysterious. Just ask yourself: What do I really like about this writing?

Sometimes essay writers use literary techniques, like figurative language. If you notice any, they probably add to the voice.

Try out your writing a few ways, with a few different craft moves, and see which way works best. Consider the context of the text you're using.

CLASSROOM ARTIFACTS

Nathaniel Hawthorne's *The Scarlet Letter* tells the tale of forbidden and destructive loves. The central love focus is ostensibly Hester Prynne, whose histories with the minister, Dimmesdale, and relations with her own husband, Chillingworth, are shrouded in secrets. The greater intimacy in the story, though, is between Dimmesdale and Chillingworth. This relationship, despite its suppressed, secret, and hidden qualities, is what ultimately subsumes Dimmesdale in a way his relationship with Hester never did.

There is something oddly disturbing about the way Jekyll talks about giving in to Hyde (a murderer), as if he is indulging a weakness. And consider the time this was written in—a period of sexual repression, when desire itself could be a crime. Stevenson wrote this story in the same period when Oscar Wilde was first living flamboyantly in London, and then was prosecuted and imprisoned, essentially for being openly gay—for not being secretive about that side of himself. So, when Jekyll, for instance, talks about how he indulges his secret appetites, and how drawn he is to this darker, forbidden side, there is something tragic about it. It just feels as if the notion of having a darker side, a secret side, that is also compelling and urgent and desperate, might have felt very real to some men in London at the time—men like Oscar Wilde, or anyone who felt as if they couldn't fit in that society's mores.

These writers use figurative language, they speak to the audience, and overall, they write with a strong authorial voice about The Scarlet Letter *and* The Strange Case of Dr. Jekyll and Mr. Hyde.

Tailoring Literary Analysis for Specific Audiences

Lesson 2

STRATEGY

Writers consider the audience for their literary analyses, and then they tailor their language to reach that audience. For instance, they consider word choice, what examples to include, and, overall, how best to reach their chosen audience.

USE THIS STRATEGY... to help students imagine and reach real audiences, and to support students writing with a more personal, individual voice and perspective.

Visit hs-guidetoteaching.org to download the Audiences for Literary Analysis Chart.

TEACH THE STRATEGY

- Suggest to students that writers always write best when they write for a specific audience, and ask students to consider possible audiences for literary analysis—Who might read what writers have to say about the stories they are reading?
  - Initially students may name their teacher, but push them to think about other audiences in the world, and why people write about stories.
- Next, invite students to imagine with you some of the ways writers might tailor their work to especially reach a specific audience. Share a chart of these audiences.

Audiences for Literary Analysis

Book Lovers
- Describe types of settings, characters, or plots
- Recall other stories by this author
- Compare the text to others in the genre.

Book Banners/Book Haters
- Anticipate their fears and arguments
- Offer counter-arguments
- Be passionate about the need the book fills

Teen Readers
- Use colloquial language
- Add references they'll know
- Use inclusive language (we, our, etc.)
- Use anecdotes from your own life

Literary Critics
- Acknowledge the significance of the text, its tradition
- Make comparisons to other texts
- Discuss the language as well as the content

Academics
- Use sophisticated language
- Try out critical lenses
- Make comparisons to other texts
- Reference other critics and authors

Yourself
- Ask reflective questions
- Connect to moments in your own life
- Share why the book made an impression

Someone Specific

If you're writing to the author, a friend, a caretaker....

- Talk to the reader directly
- Share stories, anecdotes, and examples they'll connect to

People Unfamiliar with Text

If your audience hasn't read the text yet....

- Avoid spoilers, embrace trailers
- Discuss big themes and issues
- Describe enticing characters
- Invite them to read the book

A Certain Demographic

If you're writing to poets, parents, young women, etc.

- Cater examples and commentary to that group
- Use domain-specific vocabulary (words that group will know)

Lesson 2 (Continued)

- Share a sample chunk from a literary analysis with small groups of students. Demonstrate how you might alter a text for a specific audience.
  - This works best with a shared text that all students know!

<u>Original Paragraph</u>

In *The Poet X*, Caridad is Xiomara's best friend, though the two couldn't be more opposite. Where Caridad "recites bible verses and promotes peace," Xiomara describes herself as likely to "curse up a storm and always ready to knuckle up" (30). Although the two of them act in opposite ways, Xiomara feels their friendship is powerful and enduring. But this friendship becomes complicated when the two whisper during Confirmation class. Xiomara begins to reveal a secret, saying, "There's this boy at school…" Caridad replies, saying, "This is why your mom should have sent you with me to St. Joan's" and "It's wrong to lust, Xio. You know it's a sin" (71).

<u>Paragraph Tailored to Persuade Book Banners/ Book Haters of a Book's Value</u>

The Poet X teaches important lessons about caring for friendships, and standing up for oneself, challenges that all young people face. For example, in *The Poet X*, Caridad is Xiomara's best friend, though the two couldn't be more opposite - showing readers that teens can make friendships across differences. Where Caridad "recites bible verses and promotes peace," Xiomara describes herself as likely to "curse up a storm and always ready to knuckle up" (30). It's not that Xiomara, or the novel, are anti-religious. It's that Xiomara finds the rules she faces in church confusing. Although the two of them act in opposite ways, Xiomara feels their friendship is powerful and enduring. But this friendship becomes complicated when the two whisper during Confirmation class. Xiomara begins to reveal a secret, saying, "There's this boy at school…" Caridad replies, saying, "This is why your mom should have sent you with me to St. Joan's" and "It's wrong to lust, Xio. You know it's a sin" (71). It happens a lot in friendships that friends are mean to each other. The novel helps readers think about their own friendships, and their own behaviors, so that readers learn to be both stronger, and kinder. While Xiomara isn't certain about religion, she is certain she wants to be kind.

Here, Coley adds phrases deliberately aimed to speak back to those who might challenge or want to ban this novel. She models anticipating what these book fearers might dislike and speaking directly to these points.

- Invite students to give this a try, either assigning them an audience to alter the same part that you worked on (if students know the text well) or by having students revise a snippet from their own writing. Encourage students to color-code the moves they try out.

LANGUAGE TO COACH STUDENTS AND PARTNERSHIPS

Consider your thesis, your writing style, and your text. These things can help decide which audience will work best for your literary analysis.

You could have your partner read your writing and suggest possible audiences. This will give you a sense of how you might revise.

Depending on the audience you select, you can also think about a modality beyond writing. Consider creating a podcast, or a video essay.

CLASSROOM ARTIFACTS

Paragraph Tailored for Young Women

In *The Poet X*, Caridad is Xiomara's best friend, though the two young women couldn't be more opposite in how they express their gender. Where Caridad "recites bible verses and promotes peace," Xiomara describes herself as likely to "curse up a storm and always ready to knuckle up" (30). Although the two of them act in opposite ways, as can happen in many female friendships, Xiomara feels their friendship is powerful and enduring. But this female friendship becomes complicated when the two whisper during Confirmation class. Xiomara begins to reveal a secret, saying, "There's this boy at school..." Caridad replies, saying, "This is why your mom should have sent you with me to St. Joan's" and "It's wrong to lust, Xio. You know it's a sin" (71).

Paragraph Tailored for People Unfamiliar with the Text – New readers

The Poet X is ultimately a story of one young woman, Xiomara, but the novel also explores friendships, especially Xiomara's friendship with Caridad, her best friend. The two couldn't be more opposite. They have their biggest dustups around religion, particularly during Confirmation class, a site of turmoil for Xiomara. Where Caridad "recites bible verses and promotes peace," Xiomara describes herself as likely to "curse up a storm and always ready to knuckle up" (30). Although the two of them act in opposite ways, Xiomara feels their friendship is powerful and enduring. As you read on, though, you'll see that this friendship becomes complicated. Pause when you get to the scene where the two whisper during Confirmation class. Listen to the girls' dialogue, and you'll hear the emerging conflict. Xiomara begins to reveal a secret, saying, "There's this boy at school..." Caridad replies, saying, "This is why your mom should have sent you with me to St. Joan's" and "It's wrong to lust, Xio. You know it's a sin" (71). No one likes to be called a sinner by their best friend.

Tailoring the same paragraph on The Poet X *for other different audiences.*

Lesson 3

Student-Created Checklists for Formatting and Citing Quotes

STRATEGY

Anyone who writes literary analyses knows that formatting and citing quotations can be challenging. Even published writers will remind themselves of correct form, usually by studying samples. One way to capture what writers learn from studying samples is to create a checklist that writers can then use for their own formatting and citing.

Visit hs-guidetoteaching.org to download the sample quotes and the checklist.

USE THIS STRATEGY... when students are inserting quotes and references, when they are finding formatting and citing quotes challenging, or when you need an engaging way to remind students of these conventions.

Inquiry Questions

- What can I learn about how quotes are formatted and cited by studying mentor texts?
- How can I apply these conventions to my own writing?

LAUNCH THE INQUIRY

- Console students that all writers find citations to be challenging and tedious, and suggest that even very experienced writers will often check a mentor text for citation conventions.
- Put students in small groups or partnerships to share a mentor text. Share the goal of creating their own checklist for formatting and citing quotes.
- Come together as a class to share the different checklists students created, or have partnerships share with another partnership, reviewing the expectations for formatting and citing quotes.
- Set up students to go back to their own writing to use their checklists, as well as available mentors, to double-check and revise their citations.

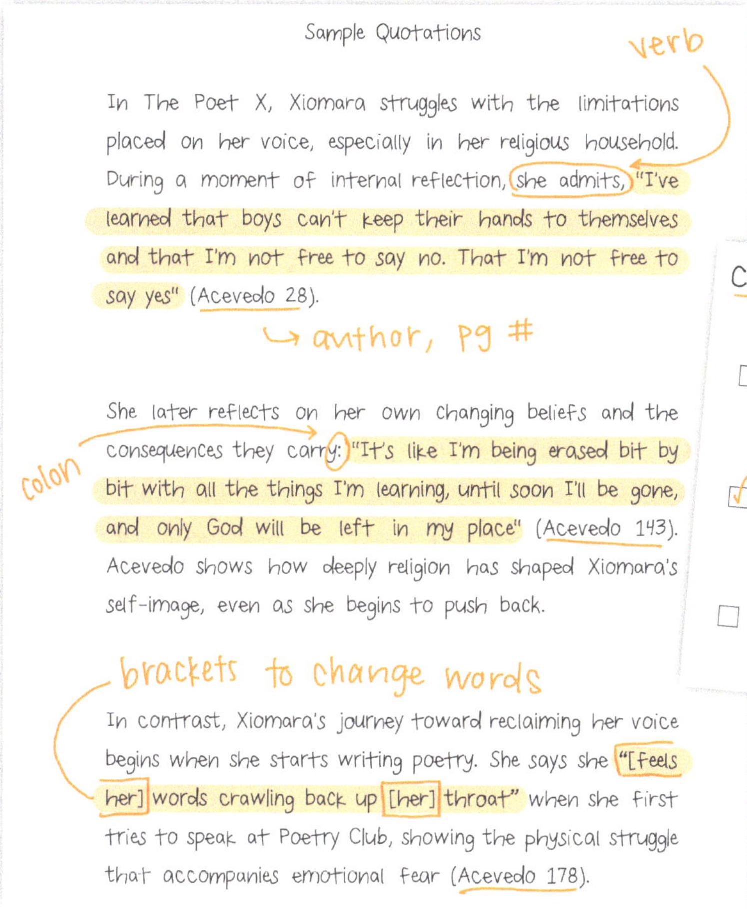

Sample Quotations

verb

In The Poet X, Xiomara struggles with the limitations placed on her voice, especially in her religious household. During a moment of internal reflection, she admits, "I've learned that boys can't keep their hands to themselves and that I'm not free to say no. That I'm not free to say yes" (Acevedo 28).

↳ author, pg #

She later reflects on her own changing beliefs and the consequences they carry: "It's like I'm being erased bit by bit with all the things I'm learning, until soon I'll be gone, and only God will be left in my place" (Acevedo 143). Acevedo shows how deeply religion has shaped Xiomara's self-image, even as she begins to push back.

colon

brackets to change words

In contrast, Xiomara's journey toward reclaiming her voice begins when she starts writing poetry. She says she "[feels her] words crawling back up [her] throat" when she first tries to speak at Poetry Club, showing the physical struggle that accompanies emotional fear (Acevedo 178).

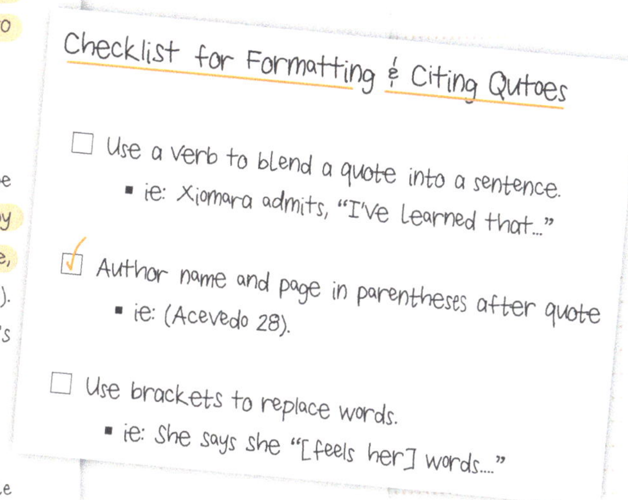

Checklist for Formatting & Citing Qutoes

- ☐ Use a verb to blend a quote into a sentence.
  - ie: Xiomara admits, "I've learned that..."
- ☑ Author name and page in parentheses after quote
  - ie: (Acevedo 28).
- ☐ Use brackets to replace words.
  - ie: She says she "[feels her] words..."

When Lauren did this with her class, she used sample snippets from essays that show quotes integrated and formatted several different ways. She studied and annotated the quotations and demonstrated jotting the beginning of a quick checklist, to model for students the work they would do in groups.

LANGUAGE TO COACH STUDENTS AND PARTNERSHIPS

Remember, there are multiple ways to format a quote correctly. You can try it a few ways, depending on the quote and the context.

It can be helpful to ask an AI partner about quote formatting and citations. You'll have to give them some info about what type of citations you're looking for and what type of writing you're doing.

Blending quotes seamlessly into a sentence is sophisticated and challenging. Be sure to read the sentence all the way through to make sure it makes sense and include a citation at the very end of the sentence.

Lesson 3 (Continued)

CLASSROOM ARTIFACTS

Commas	Colons	Citations & End Punctuation
• Commas after a verb to introduce a quote • Example: Offred explains, "We learned to whisper almost without sound" (Atwood 4).	• Colons can be used when a full sentence comes before a quote or when there is going to be listed evidence. • Example: Later, Offred reflects on how dangerous it feels to say anything at all: "The truth is that she is my spy, as I am hers" (Atwood 18).	• Citation = Author's last name and the page number • End Punctuation AFTER the citation • Example: (Atwood 68).
Brackets	**Ellipses**	**Quoting Quotes**
• Use the [brackets] to show you changed something • Example: She describes her secret desire "to steal something" because it would "make [her] feel that [she] ha[s] power" (Atwood 23).	• Use the ... to show you are excluding part of a quote • Example: She remembers, "Nothing changes instantaneously: in a gradually heating bathtub you'd be boiled to death before you knew it. . . . There were stories in the newspapers" (56).	• Use ' inside of " to show you are quoting dialogue • Example: Aunt Lydia says, "'There is more than one kind of freedom'" (24).

One group's student-generated checklist to use when formatting and citing quotes using MLA.

Use Brackets to Modify Quotations

At lunch, Xiomara finds "comfort in apples and [her] journal" (Acevedo 104).
Change pronouns

She chooses a table where she can "[share] space, but not words" (Acevedo 104).
Shift verb tense

Although Xiomara is having trouble at home, "[i]n school things feel so different" (Acevedo 104).
Adjust capitalization

Xiomara explains "how at any moment [her body] is going to pop open/and surprise the whole damn world" (Acevedo 105).
Clarify a word/phrase

A group makes a quick guide on brackets.

Choosing Verbs That Suggest ... Reveal ... Prove

Lesson 4

STRATEGY

Writers who tackle literary analysis know that verbs that replace "show" are particularly significant in this genre. They also know that there is a continuum of these verbs, from ones that suggest evidence is ... suggestive, to ones that suggest evidence is indisputable in supporting a point, and they choose their verbs accordingly.

USE THIS STRATEGY... to help students move beyond "show" in their literary analysis, and also to help writers evaluate the overall strength and type of evidence they present.

Visit hs-guidetoteaching.org to access the charts in this lesson.

TEACH THE STRATEGY

- Suggest to students that many writers keep a list of verbs that replace "show" and other basic verbs when they are writing a literary analysis.
- Introduce a chart of helpful verbs, and suggest that they are ordered along a continuum that supports what type and overall strength a piece of evidence is.
- Demonstrate how you might choose among and/or revise your verbs for a snippet of your literary analysis, depending on the purpose and strength of a piece of evidence.

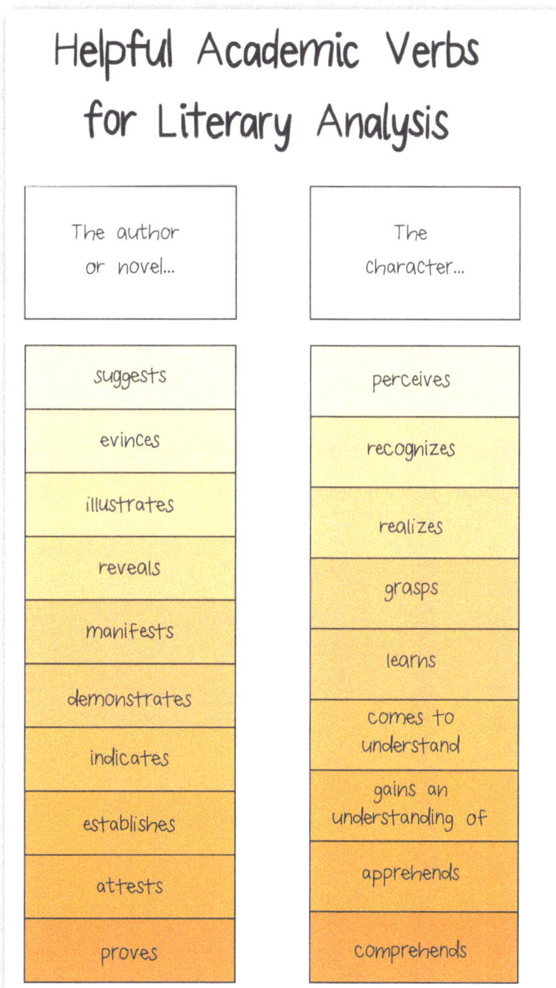

Lesson 4 (Continued)

Xiomara writes in her journal: "While some girls are pretty/and some are pretty smart, /I got a body that makes grown men turn their heads, /and girls call me conceited" (5). The economy of Xiomara's words and their brutal honesty reveal Xiomara's dilemma, suggesting the way she is caught between self-loathing and the possibility of self-love.

When Lauren demonstrated this work, she considered with her students which verb would best fit her analysis, choosing, in her case, verbs that fit the exploratory nature of her investigation.

- Send students off to do similar work of looking over their verb choices to consider which verb best fits that particular bit of literary analysis.

LANGUAGE TO COACH STUDENTS AND PARTNERSHIPS

If you are exploring an idea or hypothesis, then you'll want to use verbs such as suggests, illustrates, reveals, *which support more exploratory ideas.*

When you are proving a claim that you think is indisputable, then verbs such as indicate, establish, attest *will assert your confidence in your idea.*

You can turn to a similar kind of continuum for words as well, such as words to replace important, *or words to replace* beautiful.

Words for *Important*

powerful
compelling
decisive
revelatory
convincing
significant
revealing
representative
telling
suggestive

Words for *Excerpt*

scene
passage
excerpt
moment
interaction
sequence
section
fragment
snippet
selection

Words for *Beautiful/Moving*

profound
striking
vivid
dramatic
moving
eloquent
evocative

Words for *Disturbing/Troubling*

disruptive
troublesome
problematic
challenging
demanding
confusing
awkward

Word lists related to literary analysis help any writer vary their word choice purposefully.

Lesson 5

Conventions That Are Important to Literary Analysis

STRATEGY

Writers know that as they get their writing ready for publication, it's helpful to consider conventions. One way to zoom in on and improve one's grasp of conventions is to consider the conventions that are especially important to the genre. Another is to use a checklist to remind writers of these conventions.

Visit hs-guidetoteaching.org to access an editing checklist, specifically for a literary analysis.

USE THIS STRATEGY... to support writers in self-assessing conventions (before turning to an AI editor) to reinforce the process of internalizing conventions. This strategy also supports writers who will sometimes be writing in on-demand situations, without access to digital editing tools.

TEACH THE STRATEGY

- Suggest to your students that as they prepare for publication, writers usually do a quick editing check, looking back over their writing to consider essential conventions. Suggest, as well, that especially for young writers, who will be assessed sometimes without the ability to use technology, it's worth it to deepen their control of conventions.
- Remind your writers that it's very hard to edit your own writing, and often a checklist is helpful, to remind you of the things you want to check. Introduce a checklist of some essential conventions for literary essays.
- Demonstrate how you might use this checklist to check one convention.

Both The Catcher in The Rye, by J.D. Salinger, and The poet X, by Elizabeth Acevedo, are narratives of escape and liberation.	Both *The Catcher in the Rye*, by J.D. Salinger, and *The Poet X*, by Elizabeth Acevedo, are narratives of escape and liberation.

When Mary demonstrated this work, she modeled considering the first sentence of her literary essay, in which she references the titles of two texts. Then she and her students used the checklist to edit her titles so that they were in italics and followed conventions for capitalization inside of titles.

- Invite students to do similar work with their own pieces, choosing one convention at a time, and using the checklist to help them edit.

LANGUAGE TO COACH STUDENTS AND PARTNERSHIPS

Be sure to check with your teacher about what style they want for a citation. Some prefer APA, whereas others prefer Chicago, or MLA, or another. It's always important to check.

If you're unsure about punctuating or citing a quote, go look at an example from a citation guide or a mentor text.

Remember, your partner can also help you edit. You can trade your writing to help each other attend to conventions and teach each other conventions.

CLASSROOM ARTIFACTS

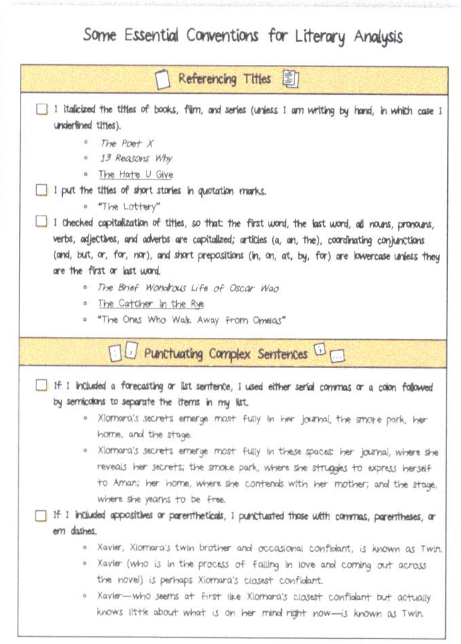

Some Essential Conventions for Literary Analysis

Referencing Titles

- ☐ I italicized the titles of books, film, and series (unless I am writing by hand, in which case I underlined titles).
    - *The Poet X*
    - *13 Reasons Why*
    - The Hate U Give
- ☐ I put the titles of short stories in quotation marks.
    - "The Lottery"
- ☐ I checked capitalization of titles, so that: the first word, the last word, all nouns, pronouns, verbs, adjectives, and adverbs are capitalized; articles (a, an, the), coordinating conjunctions (and, but, or, for, nor), and short prepositions (in, on, at, by, for) are lowercase unless they are the first or last word.
    - *The Brief Wondrous Life of Oscar Wao*
    - The Catcher in the Rye
    - "The Ones Who Walk Away from Omelas"

Punctuating Complex Sentences

- ☐ If I included a forecasting or list sentence, I used either serial commas or a colon followed by semicolons to separate the items in my list.
    - Xiomara's secrets emerge most fully in her journal, the smoke park, her home, and the stage.
    - Xiomara's secrets emerge most fully in these spaces: her journal, where she reveals her secrets; the smoke park, where she struggles to express herself to Aman; her home, where she contends with her mother; and the stage, where she yearns to be free.
- ☐ If I included appositives or parentheticals, I punctuated those with commas, parentheses, or em dashes.
    - Xavier, Xiomara's twin brother and occasional confidant, is known as Twin.
    - Xavier (who is in the process of falling in love and coming out across the novel) is perhaps Xiomara's closest confidant.
    - Xavier—who seems at first like Xiomara's closest confidant but actually knows little about what is on her mind right now—is known as Twin.

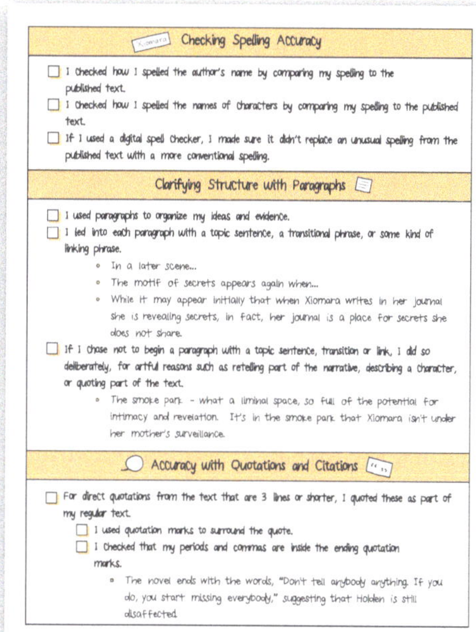

Checking Spelling Accuracy

- ☐ I checked how I spelled the author's name by comparing my spelling to the published text.
- ☐ I checked how I spelled the names of characters by comparing my spelling to the published text.
- ☐ If I used a digital spell checker, I made sure it didn't replace an unusual spelling from the published text with a more conventional spelling.

Clarifying Structure with Paragraphs

- ☐ I used paragraphs to organize my ideas and evidence.
- ☐ I led into each paragraph with a topic sentence, a transitional phrase, or some kind of linking phrase.
    - In a later scene...
    - The motif of secrets appears again when...
    - While it may appear initially that when Xiomara writes in her journal she is revealing secrets, in fact, her journal is a place for secrets she does not share.
- ☐ If I chose not to begin a paragraph with a topic sentence, transition or link, I did so deliberately, for artful reasons such as retelling part of the narrative, describing a character, or quoting part of the text.
    - The smoke park - what a liminal space, so full of the potential for intimacy and revelation. It's in the smoke park that Xiomara isn't under her mother's surveillance.

Accuracy with Quotations and Citations

- ☐ For direct quotations from the text that are 3 lines or shorter, I quoted these as part of my regular text.
    - ☐ I used quotation marks to surround the quote.
    - ☐ I checked that my periods and commas are inside the ending quotation marks.
        - The novel ends with the words, "Don't tell anybody anything. If you do, you start missing everybody," suggesting that Holden is still disaffected.

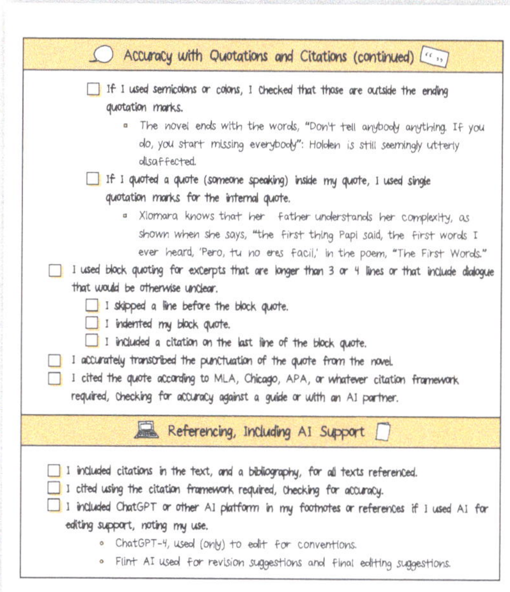

Accuracy with Quotations and Citations (continued)

- ☐ If I used semicolons or colons, I checked that those are outside the ending quotation marks.
    - The novel ends with the words, "Don't tell anybody anything. If you do, you start missing everybody": Holden is still seemingly utterly disaffected.
- ☐ If I quoted a quote (someone speaking) inside my quote, I used single quotation marks for the internal quote.
    - Xiomara knows that her father understands her complexity, as shown when she says, "the first thing Papi said, the first words I ever heard, 'Pero, tu no eres facil,' in the poem, "The First Words."
- ☐ I used block quoting for excerpts that are longer than 3 or 4 lines or that include dialogue that would be otherwise unclear.
    - ☐ I skipped a line before the block quote.
    - ☐ I indented my block quote.
    - ☐ I included a citation on the last line of the block quote.
- ☐ I accurately transcribed the punctuation of the quote from the novel.
- ☐ I cited the quote according to MLA, Chicago, APA, or whatever citation framework required, checking for accuracy against a guide or with an AI partner.

Referencing, Including AI Support

- ☐ I included citations in the text, and a bibliography, for all texts referenced.
- ☐ I cited using the citation framework required, checking for accuracy.
- ☐ I included ChatGPT or other AI platform in my footnotes or references if I used AI for editing support, noting my use.
    - ChatGPT-4, used (only) to edit for conventions.
    - Flint AI used for revision suggestions and final editing suggestions.

Writers use the checklist, "Some Essential Conventions for Literary Analysis" to edit their work.

Lesson 6

Leveling Up Transitional Words and Phrases

STRATEGY

Writers can elevate their transitions, or links between parts, by studying mentor texts, exploring how other writers transition smoothly from one sentence to another or from one section to another. Then, they use this knowledge to elevate their own transitions.

Visit hs-guidetoteaching.org to access this mentor text.

USE THIS STRATEGY... when students have simple transitions such as "furthermore" and "however" and are ready to explore more elegant transitional phrases.

TEACH THE STRATEGY

- Suggest to students that just as writers think about how to move in and out of quotes, they also think about how to link paragraphs, move from one part to another, and even from one sentence to another.
- Give students a few minutes to sift through their writing, highlighting their transitions between sections, paragraphs, and sentences. Collect some of the common words/phrases they seem to be using.
- Introduce the idea that writers study the way other writers make these transitions, trying out the ones that might work well in their own writing.
- Study a mentor text together and collect some of the transitions the author is using. Here we used "Is 'Wicked' Really a Resistance Musical?" from the *New York Times*.

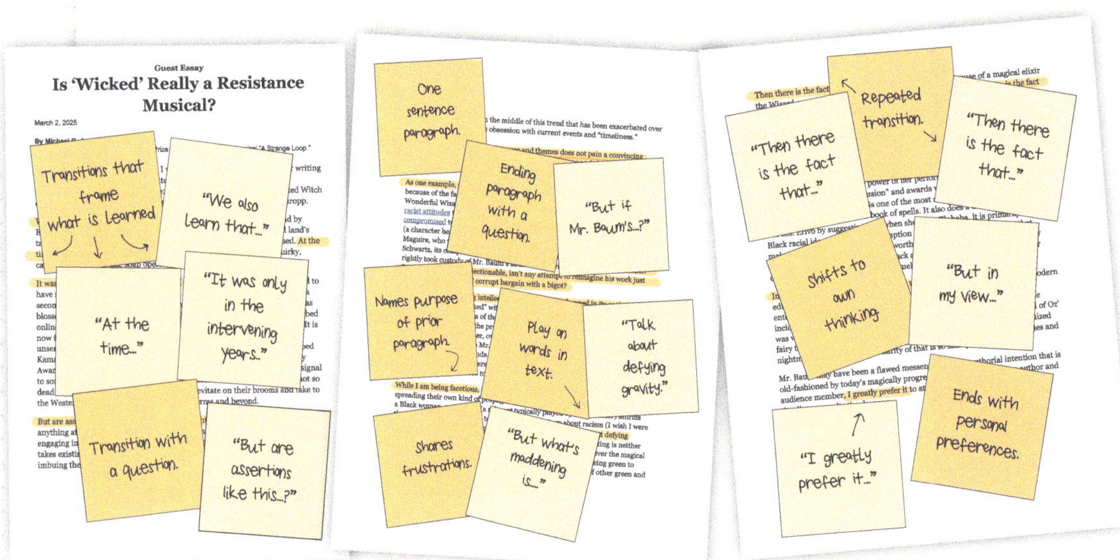

When Coley did this lesson with young writers, together, they annotated the mentor text above, "Is Wicked Really a Resistance Musical," by Michael Jackson (2025). Annotating texts together helps students learn the art of close reading.

- Model pointing to a few places in your own writing where you might consider elevating your transitions.
- Send off students to experiment with these leveled-up transitions in their own writing.

LANGUAGE TO COACH STUDENTS AND PARTNERSHIPS

Try thinking about the content of one paragraph and the content of the next paragraph. Consider how they are connected and the thread between them. Use that to transition between these parts. You can also try this with sentences. Think: How do these ideas connect?

It can help to maintain a conversational tone, as if you were giving a podcast—that often leads to natural transitions.

Of course, it's okay to have some one-word transitions or use the ones that are familiar to you—those are great, too! It just helps to vary your language and sentence structure.

CLASSROOM ARTIFACTS

In the short story, "The Dentist," Curt Lemon, a soldier in the Vietnam War, goes trick-or-treating wearing nothing but a ghost mask. This is a conscious identity claim. He actively chooses to trick-or-treat naked, making himself appear secure and bold. What shows more of his true identity is the time he is deeply embarrassed by his fear of the dentist (O'Brien 84). The reader realizes Curt Lemon has fears. This emotional reaction is an unconscious identity claim because Curt Lemon is not able to regulate his emotions, and, therefore, he is also unable to regulate how others perceive him. These unconscious moments are important because conscious identity claims do not necessarily show who people really are, but who they want to be.

In the short story, "The Dentist," Curt Lemon, a soldier in the Vietnam War, goes trick-or-treating wearing nothing but a ghost mask. This is a conscious identity claim. He actively chooses to trick-or-treat naked, making himself appear secure and bold.

But what actually shows his true identity? The time he is deeply embarrassed by his fear of the dentist (O'Brien 84). It is this moment that the reader realizes Curt Lemon has fears. This emotional reaction is an unconscious identity claim because Curt Lemon is not able to regulate his emotions, and, therefore, he is also unable to regulate how others perceive him. Ultimately, these unconscious moments are important because conscious identity claims do not necessarily show who people really are, but who they want to be.

Varying transitions in an analysis of "The Dentist" from The Things They Carried.

Lesson 7

Mimetic Writing of Complex Sentences

STRATEGY

Writers often craft complex sentences inside of narrative, and they can do similar work inside of literary analysis. One way to imagine more complex sentences is to study mentor sentences and to mirror their structure.

Visit hs-guidetoteaching.org to access a collection of mentor sentences.

USE THIS STRATEGY... to support writers who are ready to play with and learn more complicated syntax, and to support all writers in turning to mentor texts regularly to raise the level of their own writing.

TEACH THE STRATEGY

- Explain to your students what mimetic writing is—mentoring yourself at the sentence level to a published writer, mirroring their exact syntax or sentence structure, and substituting your content, to develop more vibrant sentences.
- Introduce a collection of mentor sentences.
- Model how you choose a sentence and mirror-write, weaving in your own content from your literary analysis. Sometimes it helps to tap the parts of the mentor sentence and circle the punctuation.

Nickel presents itself again and again as a school: to the state, to taxpayers, to people like Elwood and his family when Elwood is facing the chance of jail time and Nickel seems like a better alternative.

"Colson Whitehead's Spare, Riveting, Horrifying *Nickel Boys*" (2019).
—by Constance Grady for *Vox*

Xiomara's secrets present again and again as damaging: to Twin, to Aman, to Xiomara herself when she hides her thinking in her journal and never expresses it aloud.

We know everything we need to know about twelve-year-old Claudia from this accumulation of nouns: no to the insects and the sun and the cupcake icing; yes to the Metropolitan Museum of Art.

"Pure Heroines," excerpted from *Trick Mirror: Reflections on Self-Delusion (2019)*, by Jia Tolentino

We know everything there is to know about Holden from how he dreams of Phoebe: entirely with love and loyalty; always with loss and longing.

When Mary modeled this work, she mirrored the structure and punctuation choices in the mentor sentences and inserted her own content. As she drafted, she paused to name the parts of the mentor sentences and to call attention to the interior punctuation, naming what she liked about these.

- Encourage students to select a mentor sentence to try this with, and a part of their literary analysis to situate the content of the sentence.

LANGUAGE TO COACH STUDENTS AND PARTNERSHIPS

Sometimes you can take a sentence or two you've already written and redraft them, mirroring the mentor exactly.

When you mirror-write, it's also okay to make most of your sentences the same as your mentor and change one part; that can also lead to interesting sentences.

Often, you'll find yourself mirroring the tone and content, which can lead to new surprises in your own writing.

CLASSROOM ARTIFACTS

While the series might make for a compelling dumpster fire of relational drama and unresolved trauma (which is hard to turn away from), it's worth interrogating what social relations and ideologies "Love Is Blind" reproduces—and how we might be internalizing these.

"Love Is Blind," reviewed by Noor Norman for ABC

While *To Kill a Mockingbird* makes for a compelling story of courtroom drama and neighborhood activism (it's impossible not to love Atticus and Scout), it's worth interrogating the roles of Black Victim and White Savior that Toni Morrison discusses—and how the novel might reinforce these.

The show, which debuted in the U.S. in 2020, has become a global phenomenon with adaptations based in Brazil, Japan and Sweden, and at least four more versions planned for Argentina, Germany, the U.K. and the UAE (I regret to inform you the last one is titled "Love Is Blind, Habibi")

"Love Is Blind," reviewed by Noor Norman for ABC

The novel, which was published in 2017, has won literary acclaim with multiple awards, including as an honor book for the National Book Award, the Michael L. Printz Award, the Coretta Scott King award, and more than fifty weeks on the *New York Times* bestseller list (as well as being turned into a movie).

These writers practice mimetic writing, creating artful sentences that make their analysis of To Kill a Mockingbird *and* The Hate U Give, *more artful.*

Lesson 8

How to Train, Learn from, and Reference an AI Editor

STRATEGY

When writers turn to AI for editing support, it's important to:

- train an AI partner to personalize its feedback,
- think about what one learns from your AI partner, so the writer becomes a more skilled writer/editor,
- reference AI support.

Visit hs-guidetoteaching.org to download a chart on training AI as a personal editor.

USE THIS STRATEGY... to help your writers learn wise ways with AI, especially avoiding letting AI overwrite their pieces, and to help your writers become more confident with referencing AI.

TEACH THE STRATEGY

- Suggest to students that digital editing tools can be very helpful, that writers almost always turn to these before sharing any high-stakes writing, and that AI is so powerful that it changes the ways we interact with digital editors. AI will do a sweeping revision inside of an edit, in ways that can overwrite and distort the original writer's voice, style, and even content.
- Suggest that it's important to train your AI partner, especially by providing samples of your writing, and to reference AI support. It's also important to read its suggestions carefully and reject those that don't fit your goals and style.
- Share a chart of ways to train an AI partner, and demonstrate how you might work with an AI partner to edit your demonstration writing.

- Invite students to work with an AI partner (such as an EdTech partner like MagicSchool, SchoolAI, or Flint), encouraging them to take the time to teach and train their AI partner to sustain their voice and intentions as they edit their writing.

PROMPTS TO COACH STUDENTS AND PARTNERSHIPS

It helps to work on one part of your writing at a time, so you can learn from what your AI partner suggests.

When you train your AI partner with your writing, share pieces in any genre. It can get to know you as a writer by studying your poetry, your stories—any writing you like that highlights your voice.

You can reference AI support by a simple footnote at the end: "ChatGPT version 4.0 supported editing for conventions. I trained it not to interfere with my voice or style or content".

CLASSROOM ARTIFACTS

Suggestions and Reasoning:

1. **Clarify and Simplify Author Descriptions:**
    - *Original:* "the secretive-reclusive-sequestered J. D. Salinger"
    - *Edit:* "the famously reclusive J. D. Salinger"
    - **Why:** The original string of adjectives is colorful but a bit overloaded. "Famously reclusive" is concise, clear, and retains the intent.
2. **Consistency in Parallel Structure:**
    - *Original:* "tells the story of Holden"/"tells of Xiomara"
    - *Edit:* "follows Holden Caulfield"/"centers on Xiomara"
    - **Why:** Keeps the sentence structure balanced and elegant; avoids repetition of "tells."
3. **Refine Diction for Precision and Flow:**
    - *Original:* "to the untamed freedom of New York City"
    - *Edit:* "for the chaotic freedom of New York City"
    - **Why:** "Untamed" is vivid, but "chaotic" fits better with Holden's disorientation and matches the tone of the sentence more closely.

4. **Polish Abstract Phrasing:**
   - *Original:* "the terror of her shifting feminity"
   - *Edit:* "the turmoil of her emerging femininity"
   - **Why:** "Feminity" should be "femininity" (typo), and "turmoil" softens and deepens the tone—more aligned with the nuanced struggles Xiomara faces.

5. **Grammar and Clarity:**
   - *Original:* "and both experience transformations though the nature and result of these transformations are very different"
   - *Edit:* "and both experience transformation. However, the nature and outcome of their transformations differ"
   - **Why:** Breaking this into two sentences improves clarity and allows for a smoother transition. Also, "transformation" reads better in singular here to emphasize the arc, and "outcome" pairs more smoothly with "nature."

6. **Refine Parenthetical Ending:**
   - *Original:* "(perhaps mirroring the private/public nature of their authors.)"
   - *Edit:* "—perhaps reflecting the private and public sensibilities of their respective authors."
   - **Why:** Integrating the aside into the sentence with an em dash makes it feel more intentional and elevated. "Sensibilities" is a more literary and precise term.

Mary asks her AI partner to explain its reasoning for its suggestions, so she can make considered decisions about her revisions.

Conclusion: Publishing, Reflection, and Assessment

The books that the world calls immoral
are the books that show the world its own shame.
—Oscar Wilde

Writing about books and stories is more than simply writing for school. A writer who has ideas about their reading is someone who is different—has become different—because they are a reader. As Oscar Wilde suggests, when societies become afraid of ideas, one of their first acts is to destroy or ban literature. When people stand up for ideas, one way they show that determination is by standing up on behalf of literature.

As you consider where and how your students will publish their work, you might think about the long history of writing about books and stories and where their writing fits. Are your students writing the kinds of pieces that act as recommendations to other readers? Are they writing literary criticism? Are they defending literature they think is important (and challenged)? Are they writing for others who have read the same book, and their writing is a way to join a literary conversation? Whatever their purpose, your students' writing merits an audience, and that means thinking about publishing as you also consider grading and assessment.

Publishing

Literary analysis is a harder genre to imagine publishing than, say, memoir or fiction or poetry—genres that many readers read for pleasure. But the truth is, plenty of readers love to read book reviews and literary criticism. Other readers learn about books by reading about them. They learn about ideas, they delight in language, and they love to agree and disagree with critics.

With the goal of speaking to other readers, you might gather your students' writing into *literary journals*, which you could display in the local coffee shop or public library. You'll be surprised how many readers there are out there who will pick up a journal to read an essay about a book they know or one they're interested in.

Or you could have your student publish their writing digitally and make it accessible through a QR code that gets placed directly inside the book (this works especially well if the books are displayed in the school or classroom library, or you could make them available in a lending library). When a reader is considering one of these books, they can access the content to give them new ideas as they read. Or the next book club might read the last book club's work to compare their thinking.

Finally, you might consider inviting students to speak on their ideas about a text as part of a panel discussion or "coffee house chat." Or they might speak to the school board or the librarian or the parents association about books they think are important. The ability to engage in literary conversation is learned academic and social capital. Foster your students' analytical and verbal skills.

The main thing is that something needs to happen with students' writing, even with this esoteric genre. Writers need an audience, and books need advocates.

Reflection

Literary analyses are reflections—on texts, on stories, on the act of reading. Your writers have reflected on the stories they've encountered through the act of drafting and revising. Now is a good moment for them to also reflect on their growth as writers. You might put students into very small groups, have them share their pieces, and invite them to give each other compliments. You can also have writers reflect on their own writing.

Some students will benefit from simple sentence starters or cue cards to help them reflect on themselves as writers. Partners can "play a card," and the other partner can talk off of it, as one way to help writers launch these conversations, or they can freewrite from these cards.

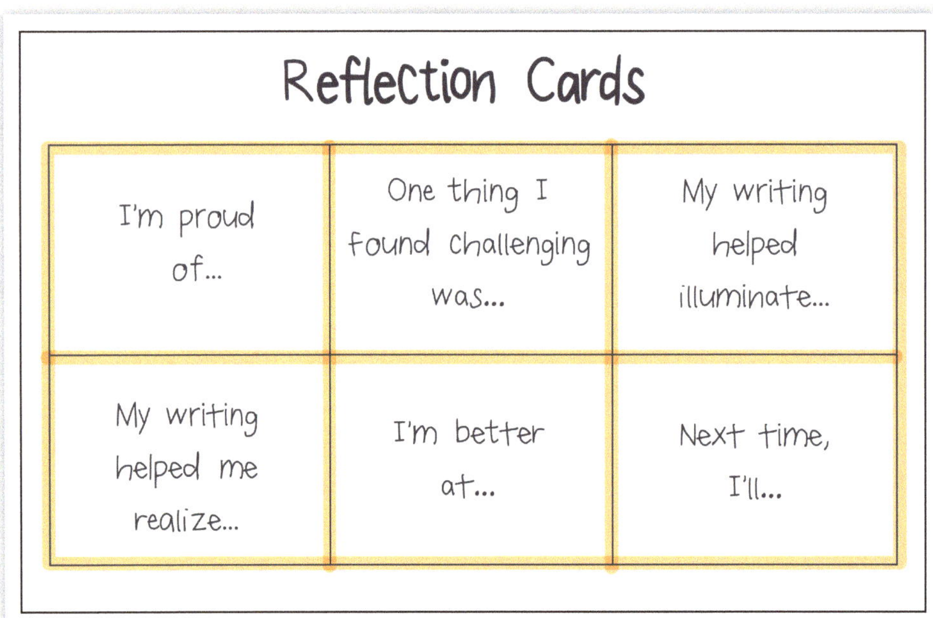

Celebrate your own work, as well. Teaching kids to write analytically is challenging, and teaching them to write with insight and voice is even more challenging. Let your students' parents know how proud you are of their work. Send home a literary journal, or even better, let them know it's in the library, so they'll visit. Let your principal know how much the kids have grown. Writing is hard, so don't stay quiet about your accomplishments.

Assessment

We think about assessment and grading as slightly different things, with grading being one part of and one way to assess. Assessment is something you are doing every day, every time you talk with a kid about their writing, or listen to their partnership conversation, or skim their EdTech chats, or study their drafts. Assessment is something you do like breathing. You're learning about your kids, making judgments, adjusting your instruction, the way birds adjust to wind shifts—it's all the time, and you don't pause to document it all.

Grading is different. All secondary teachers know that grading is the bête noire that haunts us. It is the thing that leaves us feeling uneasy, unsure about the precise fairness of our grades, absolutely sure that we take too long to give grades, and quietly worried about the effect (and lack of effect) of the grades we give students. We've spent a lot of time studying assessment and grading. We share some of that thinking here.

Grading

For a deep discussion of grading, including ways to reform grading practices so that they support student achievement (and do the least harm possible), we suggest starting with Joe Feldman's *Grading for Equity* (2024), as a powerful and thought-provoking text. Great texts to pair with it are *Making Thinking Visible* (2011) by Ritchhart et al. and *Collective Student Efficacy* (2021) by Hattie et al., and two watershed (and very short) texts to consider are Doug Reeves's (2004) "The Case Against the Zero," and Howard Johnston's (2011) "Best Practices in Grading." We also love Guskey et al.'s (2024) *Grading with Integrity*, and Guskey's (2006) article, "Making High School Grades Meaningful." Visit hs-guidetoteaching.org to access a list of texts you might consider for a study group on grading.

What all of these scholars agree on is that grading has the potential to do harm to students: to limit their motivation to write, to damage their confidence as writers, or to create writers whose only motivation is a letter or a number. Feldman looks closely at how grading affects motivation, and he encourages teachers to think about practices that will inform students and families of their progress toward important benchmarks, rather than their compliance within sometimes very old systems. Reeves reminds us that a very low score, especially when schools use numerical systems of 0–100, can make it impossible for students to recuperate and don't offer students any way to grow and change. It's all worth reading, and we encourage you to do your best as an individual to grade ethically and in a way that doesn't harm young people, and to form committees to read and research contemporary practices in grading.

We also know that you work within a system that you may have little control over or voice within. And so, we offer a few tools that may be helpful as you work with assessment, self-assessment, and grading. These include checklists, which are most helpful for kids, and rubrics, which are necessary for teachers.

A note about rubrics. We did a lot of studying of rubrics, particularly with Ray Pecheone, executive director of SCALE (Stanford Center for Assessment, Learning, and Equity) at Stanford. We developed a few characteristics of effective student-facing rubrics in our collaboration that we share here.

Characteristics of Student-Facing Rubrics	
Accessible language	Rubrics are most often useful for the people who wrote them, usually because their language is so arcane. To make rubrics useful to students, use language that bridges social and academic language.
Formative, "how-to" steps to advance levels	A lot of rubrics (IB, AP, SAT) are *summative*, which means they are useful only for scoring. Students need *formative* rubrics, ones that include practical steps they can follow to raise the level of their work.
Asset-based criteria	Avoid all deficit language, such as "did not . . ." or "only . . ." A student's first step should be to get on the rubric, and that's a positive step. Then they can look at the next criterion, and say, "if I do that, I can move up . . ." and that, too, should be a positive step.
Include only the benchmarks that are an option	Don't include the "well below benchmark" as an option. Start your rubric with an accessible starting point, so that students can enter the rubric, and focus on the levels they can work within and strive for.
Allow for interstices	Instead of wordsmithing the spaces between levels, leave those as blanks, as there are a lot of ways writing may grow and change, and that leaves you and students room for flexibility (the score of 3.5, for example).

Feedback

It's important to distinguish between grading and feedback. John Hattie's (2023) review of over 2,100 meta-analyses show how significant feedback can be to accelerating achievement—feedback that is given in the moment, is calibrated, and is followed by the immediate opportunity for repeated practice (Frey et al., 2018). Good feedback helps students cultivate awareness of their decision-making within the learning processes, and the steps they can take to revise their work and move it forward (Frey et al., 2018). Feedback is what you give your students every time you talk to them about their writing while they are writing. It is what a peer partner and an AI partner can give across the writing process. Overall, we try to maximize the time and effort we put into feedback, and to make our grading as concise and civilized as possible.

It's also important to conceive of student work *as* feedback. "First and foremost, teachers have to see student work and performance as feedback to themselves" (Frey et al., 2018). As you study student work across the writing process, think about it as feedback for how students are responding to instruction, to curriculum.

Self-Assessment

We do believe in self-assessment and in collective assessment. It's tremendously helpful for students to self-assess their writing and their writing process, so they can note how they are growing and set goals for themselves for their next writing project. Frey et al. (2018) remind us it's important for students to develop an internal compass that drives independent learning, rather than being dependent on a teacher to determine next steps. Tools are helpful in this process—checklists and rubrics. We've provided samples of each of these. In general, checklists are most helpful for kids, as they reflect on what they've done and set goals for next steps.

We learned a few things from Ray Pecheone (2015) that transformed the effectiveness of our checklists. They include:

- Write the checklist in an "I" voice—it makes it more personal.
- Include checkboxes. Checking off a list is satisfying.
- Include practical "how-to" steps for how to reach criteria.
- Pair checklists with annotated exemplars.
- Teach students to practice self-assessment and annotation with a partner.

A Writer's Checklist for Literary Analysis

Meaning

- ☐ I explored an idea about a character, issue, motif, theme, and/or literary device that feels deeply significant in the text.
- ☐ I suggested the significance of this idea through the depth of my analysis, and the clarity of my language.
- ☐ I developed and supported my idea with:
  - ☐ related text evidence.
  - ☐ insightful analysis.

Structure

- ☐ I structured my piece deliberately, perhaps to:
  - ☐ develop the parts of my idea.
  - ☐ layer an argument.
  - ☐ lead the reader on a journey of thought.
- ☐ I led my reader considerately from one part to the next, using transitional phrases, topic sentences, or other cues so that the reader can follow:
  - ☐ shifts in ideas and thinking.
  - ☐ introduction of new evidence.
- ☐ I may have experimented with structure and/or modalities as a way to deepen my expression and/or reach an audience.

Evidence and Analysis

- ☐ I carefully framed and integrated my evidence, for instance, by:
  - ☐ providing relevant background information and context.
  - ☐ blending quotes fluidly into sentences.
  - ☐ clarifying who is speaking when quoting dialogue.
  - ☐ citing accurately.
- ☐ I developed analysis or commentary, for instance, by:
  - ☐ explaining the significance of these details/evidence to my overall idea.
  - ☐ exploring the relevance of these details/evidence to this part of my essay.
  - ☐ analyzing how these details/evidence echo, reinforce, or contrast with other moments in the text.
  - ☐ exploring the relevance of text details to their life and/or community when appropriate to the genre.

Rubrics theoretically help teachers and kids envision how to raise the level of their writing, but to work this way, rubrics need to be asset-based, with practical "how-to" steps, so that first, they get on the rubric (a good thing), and then they can see how to work their way up levels. Overall, we focus on formative rubrics—ones that will help students improve. We may, eventually, find ourselves needing to use a summative

Craft

- [ ] I oriented my reader at the start of my piece, sharing essential information about:
  - [ ] the author, title, and genre of the text I am writing about.
  - [ ] my thesis, theory, or question.
- [ ] I developed the context of this text, perhaps by:
  - [ ] angled retelling.
  - [ ] describing its publishing and reception.
  - [ ] discussing its place in a literary tradition.
  - [ ] describing its personal significance.
- [ ] I used nonfiction literary techniques to make the essay engaging, perhaps through:
  - [ ] vivid language.
  - [ ] clear and artful paragraphs.
  - [ ] artful sentence structures.
  - [ ] addressing the audience.
  - [ ] references to my own emotions and thoughts as a reader.
- [ ] I provided some resolution or closure at the end, such as:
  - [ ] new thinking about the characters that emerges from my analysis.
  - [ ] personal connections to the text.
  - [ ] an extension to my thesis or theory.

Conventions

- [ ] I used all my strategies to edit my writing myself, so that my control of conventions grew. I did this by...
  - [ ] rereading.
  - [ ] using a checklist.
  - [ ] working with a partner.
- [ ] I used a digital editing tool or AI partner to wisely edit for conventions, and I attended to these suggestions carefully.
- [ ] I was careful with citations and references, including all texts I included, and any AI support.

Find the full checklist on our website: hs-guidetoteaching.org.

rubric such as an IB or AP rubric, but we know that along the way, students need more supportive tools. AI can partner with you in creating asset-based, formative rubrics that include practical steps for writers to raise the level of their work. Know that the rubric we designed for this unit is flexible and could be the rubric you use to score students, or it might be a jumping off point—something you study with your team to design an assessment tool that meets the needs of your students and your teaching.

A Rubric for Literary Analysis

Emerging 2.0	2.5	Proficient 3.0	3.5	Advanced 4.0
Meaning				
☐ The writer explored an idea about a character, issue, motif, theme, or literary device. ☐ The writer supported their idea with details from the text.		☐ The writer explored an idea about a character, issue, motif, theme, and/or literary device that feels deeply significant in the text. ☐ The writer suggested the significance of this idea through the depth of their analysis and the clarity of their language. ☐ The writer developed and supported their idea with: ☐ related text evidence ☐ insightful analysis		☐ The writer explored a layered or nuanced idea or theory about a character, issue, motif, theme, or literary device that feels especially meaningful in the text. ☐ The writer suggested the deeper meaning or impact of this idea, showing clarity, control, and depth in their language and analysis. ☐ The writer developed their idea with well-chosen, relevant text evidence and added insightful analysis that deepens the reader's understanding of the text.
Structure				
☐ The writer used a clear structure to organize their thinking. They grouped ideas in a straightforward way that reflects early planning and purposeful intent.		☐ The writer structured their piece deliberately, perhaps to: ☐ develop the parts of their idea ☐ layer an argument ☐ lead the reader on a journey of thought		☐ The writer structured their piece with intention and complexity, leading their reader through: ☐ layered thinking ☐ juxtapositions or ambiguity ☐ shifting perspectives ☐ the evolution of an idea
Structure (continued)				
☐ The writer marked new points or evidence with: ☐ clear topic sentences ☐ transitional phrases		☐ The writer led their reader considerately from one part to the next, using transitional phrases, topic sentences, or other cues so that the reader can follow: ☐ shifts in ideas and thinking ☐ introduction of new evidence ☐ The writer may have experimented with structure and/or modalities to deepen their expression and/or reach an audience.		☐ The writer used a variety of transition strategies to signal changes in thinking or emphasis, including: ☐ subtle language shifts ☐ framing phrases ☐ reflective commentary ☐ The writer may have experimented with structure and/or modalities across the piece or within a part to deepen their expression and/or reach an audience.
Evidence and Analysis				
☐ The writer included relevant evidence, including: ☐ quotes ☐ angled retelling of parts of the text		☐ The writer carefully framed and integrated their evidence, for instance, by: ☐ providing relevant background information and context ☐ blending quotes fluidly into sentences ☐ clarifying who is speaking when quoting dialogue ☐ citing accurately		☐ The writer framed and blended evidence with precision and voice, for instance, by: ☐ offering just enough context ☐ seamlessly weaving quotes into analysis and fluidly integrating quotes into the writer's sentences ☐ clearly clarifying speaker and situation when needed ☐ citing all evidence accurately and consistently ☐ making sure that the speaker, tone, or context of dialogue was always easy to follow and relevant to the argument
Evidence and Analysis (continued)				
☐ The writer included analysis, for instance by: ☐ explaining how their evidence connects to their main idea ☐ exploring why details matter—how they support the argument or reveal something important about a character, theme, or conflict.		☐ The writer developed analysis or commentary, for instance, by: ☐ explaining the significance of these details/evidence to their overall idea ☐ exploring the relevance of these details/evidence to this part of their essay ☐ analyzing how these details/evidence echo, reinforce, or contrast with other moments in the text. ☐ offering personal interpretations or reflective questions that suggest deeper thinking and grapple with relevance.		☐ The writer's commentary offered thoughtful, nuanced insights into how evidence connects to larger ideas, perhaps by: ☐ exploring how evidence resonates across the text, pointing out patterns, echoes, or contrasts that illuminate the central idea in compelling ways ☐ revealing complexity—sometimes challenging assumptions, highlighting tensions, or drawing out subtleties that might not be immediately obvious. ☐ illuminating personal connections and insights
Craft				
☐ The writer included an introduction that names the title, author, and thesis. *(see next page for more)*		☐ The writer oriented their reader at the start of their piece, sharing essential information about: ☐ The author, title, and genre of the text they are writing about ☐ Their thesis, theory, or question *(see next page for more)*		☐ The writer oriented and engaged their reader at the start of their piece, introducing the text they are writing about and the idea they are exploring. *(see next page for more)*

Find the full rubric on our website: hs-guidetoteaching.org.

Celebrating and Planning for Next Time

As you work with writers, make some notes and gather some materials for the next time you teach, as well. Our kids' writing is feedback on our teaching, our curriculum. Were there some lessons that you could combine as micro-lessons because the kids picked them up quickly? Could you relegate some to teach only to your outliers—your most proficient or most novice writers? Did you need more or less time at any point? Was there any moment when students weren't writing enough? Did you wish you had previewed something earlier?

As you continue to reflect, you'll likely have some thoughts about which texts students especially had a lot to say. Think about if your students loved the texts they were writing about, and if they understood them well enough to write well. Might you add in some texts whose primary audience is teens? Might you consider some of the authors who are winning awards writing for teens right now? Might you think about podcasts or serials as fodder for literary analysis? Ultimately, kids' literary analysis reflects how deeply they've engaged with a text, so as you consider what you're thrilled about in kids' writing and what you'd still like to sharpen, you might consider opening up to more multimodal text choice as well.

You and your students will be more alert to literary analysis in the world after this. You'll find yourself sharing podcasts about books, and great video essays, and interesting reviews. And there is one more thing. Know this: By engaging your students in literary analysis, you have undoubtedly not only made your students better writers, you've made them better readers—more interpretive thinkers who attend to detail, who notice craft, who wonder about metaphor and implicit meaning. These young people, who are in your care as writers, will never really read in the same way for the rest of their lives.

Appendices
Sample Literary Essays

Appendix A: Spaces That Shape Us: Secrecy and Self-Expression in *The Poet X*

Sometimes, it can feel like the world is trying to silence you. In *The Poet X* by Elizabeth Acevedo, Xiomara, the protagonist, learns to navigate spaces in which she feels pressure to make herself small. Growing up in a strict religious household, Xiomara learns that certain thoughts, feelings, and desires must be kept hidden. Therefore, secrecy becomes a form of self-preservation. Across the novel, Xiomara is highly secretive, but the way in which she keeps and reveals secrets changes with the different spaces she inhabits, from her journal to the smoke park to her home to the stage.

For example, one space where Xiomara keeps and reveals secrets is in her journal. Her journal is more than just a place where she explores the world around her; it's also a place where she explores her own inner world. Xiomara details her secret feelings around the complicated emotions she feels about her body in her journal. For instance, early on in the text, in the poem, "Questions I Have," Xiomara describes herself as a "stew of mixed-up ingredients," reflecting on the confusion she feels about her identity and physicality (Acevedo 32). Later in the text, after a guy pulls on her bra strap and she curses him out, and after she shoves a senior into a locker for "trying to whisper into [her] ear," Xiomara describes her conflicting emotions: "I'm disgusted at myself/for the slight excitement/that shivers up my back/at the same time that I wish/my body could fold into the tiniest corner/for me to hide in" (47). Here, Xiomara engages in almost a form of self-deception, unable to process her own reactions. In this space—the pages of her journal—she works to conceal feelings not just from others but even from herself.

Beyond her journal, Xiomara both hides and reveals secrets at the smoke park. Unlike her journal, which is entirely private, the smoke park is a public space, but it feels semi-hidden, outside the control of her family, school, and church—a place where she goes to secretly spend time with Aman without her family knowing. It is here that she begins to share parts of herself with him. In their first visit at the smoke park, they sit in companionable silence, listening to a Kendrick Lamar album. While they don't say much, Xiomara admires his smell and lets her hand linger holding his. The next time they visit the park, Aman asks Xiomara to read him a poem, and she does. She reads him a "poem about Papi." It's the first time Xiomara reads her work to someone, and her heart is pumping in her chest. Xiomara writes, "when I'm done I can't look at Aman./I feel as naked as if I'd undressed before him" (112). In this moment, we see how vulnerable Xiomara feels, both exhilarated and terrified at the way she's shared a part of herself.

The smoke park serves as a sharp contrast to how Xiomara inhabits both her home, a space where she feels suffocated by rules and expectations. Unlike the smoke park, where she cautiously shares pieces of herself with Aman, home and church are spaces of enforced silence, spaces where Xiomara feels she must shrink herself to meet her mother's expectations. For example, after seeing a spoken-word video at school, Xiomara practices her poems at home, "[e]ven though [she doesn't] ever plan on letting anyone hear it" (79). When Mami hears Xiomara practicing in her room, Mami knocks on the door and asks Xiomara what she's doing. Xiomara responds, "Verses. I'm memorizing verses." Then, Xiomara thinks to herself, "I know she thinks I mean Bible ones" (79). Here we see how her secrecy shifts depending on where she is and who she is with—while she is willing to reveal parts of herself in the smoke park with Aman, she instinctively conceals them at home in the presence of her mother.

The space in which Xiomara is the most bold, however, is the stage. Xiomara first writes about the thrill of sharing her writing with an audience after the first day of poetry club. She writes, "I can't remember/the last time people were silent/ while I spoke, actually listening" (259). Next, Caridad, her best friend, and Twin, her brother, take her to an open mic night, and Xiomara gets on the stage and performs. Xiomara describes, "I let the words fill the room./I let the words carry me away" (279). Something inside Xiomara shifts that night, because as she leaves, she thinks, "I can't wait to do this again" (280).

Finally, as she gains confidence performing her poetry, the stage becomes a place that bridges the silence and secrets she holds at home. Near the end of the novel, when Xiomara is getting ready to present at the New York Citywide Poetry Slam, she practices her performance at home. As "Twin, Mami and Papi sit on the couch," Xiomara thinks, "I can't do this/I can't perform in front of them" (349), but finally, she opens her mouth and lets the poem flow out. Her family responds in encouraging ways—Twin smiles, Papi claps, and Mami gives her advice for the real performance. This, and the support of Aman, carry her through to the performance, where all of the people she is close to come to support her.

Throughout *The Poet X*, Xiomara's relationship with secrecy evolves as she navigates different spaces and chooses to reveal and conceal parts of herself. Her journal serves as a place where she records her deepest thoughts, but also attempts to hide her feelings, even from herself. The smoke park represents an opening, a place where she begins to share parts of herself and of her poetry with Aman. Home, for most of the novel, serves as a place where Xiomara conceals her biggest feelings, her most important thoughts. However, through poetry club and the stage, Xiomara learns to use performance to let herself be seen. In the end of the novel, the stage becomes a bridge to break the silence she experiences at home. Xiomara's journey shows the challenges we navigate as we move between different spaces, but ultimately, integrating and sharing different parts of ourselves is what helps us feel seen.

Appendix B: Why Does Xiomara Keep Secrets?

"This is a secret hope we share/that we are both good enough/for each other and maybe the world, too" (Acevedo 73). Usually, we think of secrets as scandalous or shameful, something we are hiding from the world for a reason, oftentimes a negative one. But secrets can also be positive forces—little kernels that we hold onto as just our own, at least for the time being. *The Poet X* demonstrates this perfectly in the way Elizabeth Acevedo depicts Xiomara's journey to find herself and her voice. Although she keeps secrets from everyone around her, those secrets are beautiful versions of her and her life, leading readers to ask: *Why does she keep secrets from her family, friends, and even from herself?*

Why does Xiomara keep secrets from her family?

Xiomara has beautiful things to share with the world, including her poetry and her budding romantic relationship with Aman, yet she chooses to keep those things a secret from the world, and especially from her family. Of course, it's easy to understand why she refrains from sharing with her religious, strict, hardworking (did I mention strict?) Mami. She has made it clear she isn't open to Xiomara dating, which means Xiomara has no choice but to conceal her relationship with Aman.

Even before she begins spending time with Aman, Mami accuses her of flirting with the boys on the block, but even though Xiomara was approached by the boys, she "bites her tongue and doesn't correct her" (Acevedo 6). Similarly, when Xiomara tries to reveal her hesitation about religion, she "uses her nerves like a pulley to lift [the words] out of [her] mouth." Immediately, Mami cuts her off and shuts her down, saying that she "will feed and clothe no heathen" (16). Maybe it's less that Xiomara doesn't want to share with her Mami, but that she is silenced by her mother in these moments … not to mention when her mother destroys her journals, literally burning her words up in flames. In this relationship, being vulnerable and sharing is met with interruption, accusation, and destruction. It isn't until the poetry slam that Xiomara opens up to Mami.

For everything Mami represents to Xiomara, Twin is the opposite. He finds the poetry club flyer and lays it out on Xiomara's bed, a gesture to show he knows about her poetry and believes in her. Then, "Twin says in barely a whisper, 'This world's been waiting for your genius for a long time'" (73). So, if Twin is supportive, does that mean Xiomara opens up to him? Not exactly. She remains close to him but closed off. It could stem from the fact that Twin and Xiomara are quite opposites—Twin "doesn't question the bible" and is "easier for Mami to understand" (43). Even though Xiomara is close to Twin, they clearly live their lives differently, perhaps leading her to keep things to herself.

On the other hand, it could be more about the power dynamics in their relationship. When Xiomara describes their differences, she describes Twin as an "alter boy … small, scrawny and … scarecrow skinny" (Acevedo 43, 98), while she describes "her hands [as] fists for him (45). Since Xiomara acts as Twin's protector, could this keep her from sharing secrets with Twin, even innocuous ones? Maybe she doesn't want to burden him with any of her emotions, since he is dealing with his own secrets. Interestingly enough, though, the secrets she's keeping from Twin are overwhelmingly positive: her relationship, her poetry, her dreams.

Why does Xiomara keep secrets from her friends?

Throughout the story, Xiomara doesn't spend a ton of time talking about friendship. In fact, when she talks about her high school, it's about blending in, not making any waves, and the desire to escape (35–36). And although she mentions being sexualized by guys at her school and in her neighborhood, the only friend she talks about is Caridad.

Caridad is Xiomara's best friend, though the two couldn't be more opposite. Similar to Twin, Caridad "recites bible verses and promotes peace, [Xiomara] curse[s] up a storm and [is] always ready to knuckle up" (30). Although the two of them act in opposite ways, Xiomara feels their friendship is powerful and enduring. But this is complicated when the two of them are whispering during Confirmation class, and Xiomara begins to reveal a secret, saying, "There's this boy at school …" Caridad replies with things like, "This is why your mom should have sent you with me to St. Joan's" and "It's wrong to lust, Xio. You know it's a sin" (71). Although Caridad is bringing her true self to the friendship, this is surely stopping Xiomara from sharing more about her feelings and relationship with Aman, forcing her to harbor secrets and show only some sides of herself. If Caridad was more open to the conversation, what might Xiomara have shared?

At the same time, Xiomara brushes this interaction off as she clearly knows Caridad is looking out for her, especially when Caridad says, "Sometimes I think I'm the only one/trying to protect you from yourself" (72). Although Xiomara isn't opening up about Aman, Caridad still demonstrates true friendship with her car and protectiveness. It just means that while Xiomara feels those things, she has to keep her thoughts and desires hidden from someone she should otherwise celebrate them with, leaving her with no one to share these feelings with but herself and her journal.

Why does Xiomara keep secrets from herself?

At times, reading Xiomara's journal is kind of like reading a tragic love story, only it's with herself. Constantly, her deepest desires are situated in ways that show her guilt. That, or she is trying to stuff her desires deep down inside of herself, not letting those parts of her feel loved. The poem "It's Only the First Week of Tenth Grade" showcases this beautifully when Xiomara reacts with "slight excitement that shivers up her back" as a teenage boy says, "we know what girls like you want" (46–47). She feels excitement at this moment but is "disgusted at [herself]" at the same time (46). Why does she do this? Why does she feel this guilt? It's likely external factors that lead her to this. Religion. Her family. Societal conditioning.

In the end, the people around Xiomara want to embrace her full self but have a hard time showing it. This, by default, leaves Xiomara alone with her own thoughts and emotions, a space that can sometimes lead to self-doubt and insecurity, that is, until her friends and family are the catalyst she needs to find herself. Caridad, despite trying to reign Xiomara in, is the one that signs her up to participate in the open mic night. Twin is the one that sees her, leaving the poetry club flyer on her bed. Even her mom listens to her rehearse and cheers her on. It's complicated because the same people that keep her voice stifled at times are also the ones that carve a path forward for her. Maybe that's how it goes. Those closest to us play both of those roles: Those we love push and pull in positive and negative ways because relationships are complicated, because understanding yourself is complicated. Xiomara has beauty to share with the world, from her relationship with Aman to her poetry, and those around her finally showed they were ready to listen.

Appendix C: Prisons of the Mind: Secrets in *The Catcher in the Rye* and *The Poet X*

Both *The Catcher in the Rye*, by the secretive-reclusive-sequestered J. D. Salinger, and *The Poet X*, by outspoken-spoken-word-poet Elizabeth Acevedo, are narratives of escape and liberation. *The Catcher in the Rye* tells the story of Holden, who escapes the confines of his boarding school and the generations of adult entrapment the school symbolizes to him, to the untamed freedom of New York City. *The Poet X* tells the story of Xiomara, who also yearns for escape, but hers is a longing for escape from the oppressive restrictions of her religious upbringing, the terror of her shifting femininity, and her tortured inability to express her dreams. Both young people are damaged by their own secrets, and both experience transformations, though the nature and result of these transformations are very different (perhaps mirroring the private/public nature of their authors).

Let's look at Holden first. The interesting thing about *The Catcher in the Rye* is that this theme of secrets imprisoning the self shows itself not only through the events of the story but also through the style of the prose, which presents a brash, supercilious voice, covering a subtext that reveals Holden's unprocessed grief and childhood trauma. Holden's narrative has defiance on the surface—like a teenager's cultivated persona that attempts to conceal what's underneath. Salinger quite literally writes prose that is confession—full of digressions and repetitions, so that it sounds urgent and unpolished, and it seems so genuine that you expect the story to be every bit as straightforward as the prose. But Holden is tricky. He keeps secrets from the reader.

When we're first introduced to Holden, he presents a straight-forward persona. "If you really want to hear about it, the first thing you'll probably want to know is where I was born, and what my lousy childhood was like … but I don't feel like going into it," Holden asserts on page 1. The rhythm of the words and the boundaries they establish seem to make Holden gleam with adolescent authority. He lets us know his childhood was lousy, while denying readers knowledge of it, or, at least, knowledge of how seriously that childhood has affected him. His childhood remains a secret that never fully reveals itself, like a Russian doll in which there is always something else hidden inside.

Holden also tells the reader that he lies. This seeming-truthtelling-while-actually-withholding is one of the most frustrating and fascinating aspects of Holden as a character and of Salinger's writing. You can never fully grasp Holden. Early in the novel, Holden asserts his practice with constructing elaborate lies. "I'm the most terrific liar you ever saw in your life," he confesses, almost proudly. "It's awful. If I'm on my way to the store to buy a magazine, even, and somebody asks me where I'm going, I'm liable to say I'm going to the opera" (16). The way Holden admits his deception makes Holden's lies seem inconsequential, even charming. It's interesting, though, to look at this simple lie. The lie is aggrandizing, mythologizing. He's not buying a magazine; he's going to the opera. Holden is a Don Quixote figure, tilting at windmills no one else can see, his lies and secrets his lance and shield.

Holden holds his childhood close. One way he does this is through his breezy tone. We encounter this breeziness, for example, when he describes his feelings as he walks toward Central Park. Holden remembers summer visits there with Sally Hayes. First, he says, "I got to feeling sad as hell. I got to worrying that I'd never go back to school again because I'd have to go home soon and then my parents would see it in the bulletin." But Holden follows that admission up closely with: "but I really wasn't worried. I really wasn't" (104). These lines, which alternate between anxiety and loneliness and breezy confidence, suggest the tension between Holden being about to reveal something, a true secret about his feelings, and his constant cover-up, that adds to his mythology of cool insouciance—Holden isn't a kid who cares about his own pain.

A lot of Holden's secretiveness seems to function as self-deception, and that self-deception seems to act as a way to avoid unprocessed grief. We see this emotion most starkly when Holden thinks about his brother, Allie's, death, which he alludes to in odd, unconnected moments of rumination. He thinks of his baseball mitt, on which Allie had written poems, and breaking windows in the garage in his grief, without ever fully describing how he feels about Allie or Allie dying. He sums up his feelings about Allie as "You'd have liked him. He was two years younger than I was, but he was about fifty times as intelligent.... God, he was a nice kid." There is a sense of affection and longing in Holden's words, but it is latent and quiet. Thinking about death overall, Holden says, "I started picturing millions of jerks coming to my funeral and all.... I almost wished I was dead" (154). There is so much submerged pain in Holden's words, though it is a pain that Holden simultaneously expresses and deflects.

Ultimately, Holden's spiral continues downward. His evasions lead to increasing isolation, his fragile defenses eventually collapse, and by the novel's end, he speaks from an institution, his future uncertain. "I could probably tell you what I did after I went home, and how I got sick and all, and what school I'm supposed to go to next fall … but I don't feel like it. I really don't" (213). Salinger's final pages offer no resolution, just as Holden's secrets remain unresolved, a cycle of avoidance that promises to repeat itself. Holden's personal mythology. The rebellion, the cynicism, the detachment was just that, a mythology. It was an illusion—a façade of superiority and independence that concealed his profound pain, about which he can barely speak and therefore never fully heal.

When we are first introduced to Xiomara in *The Poet X*, she seems like and unlike Holden. She is like Holden in how she defines herself by other's perceptions. Xiomara's secrets are not just about hiding actions; they're about protecting identity, desire, and selfhood. Xiomara is unlike Holden in that Holden denies his constant secrecy and how it affects him, while Xiomara acknowledges it. In this one way, Xiomara is much less secretive than Holden: She knows her secrets are hurting her.

One site of Xiomara's secrets is her burgeoning relationship with Aman. Xiomara hides this relationship from her mother, knowing it would be forbidden. In "Mira, Muchacha," for example, Xiomara says of her mother, "she better not hear about me hanging out like a wet shirt on a clothesline just waiting to be worn or she would go ahead and be the one to wring my neck" (6). Xiomara's words show her awareness of her mother's pressure, a pressure that denies her sexuality and maturity, and drives her into secrecy. But more deeply, Xiomara also hides how *important* Aman is to her emotionally and sexually. In "Stoop Sitting … with Aman," for instance, Xiomara longs to stay with Aman, to be intimate with him physically and emotionally, but then she pulls her hand from his, tells him she doesn't feel great. She's split between craving tenderness and fearing judgment. The secrecy creates distance not only between Xiomara and her mother but also between Xiomara and her full, unashamed self. In this way, Xiomara is much like Holden. They both feel real affection for others, and mask it, to be careful.

Xiomara also keeps secrets about her body and her feelings about her body, and these secrets are chaotic. Xiomara writes in her journal: "While some girls are pretty/ and some are pretty smart,/I got a body that makes grown men turn their heads,/ and girls call me conceited" (5). The economy of Xiomara's words and their brutal honesty reveal Xiomara's dilemma, suggesting the way she is caught between self-loathing and the possibility of self-love. In "Unhide-able," Xiomara describes how "The other girls call me conceited. Ho. Thot. Fast. When your body takes up more room than your voice you are always the target of well-aimed rumors, which is why I let my knuckles talk for me" (5). She builds a wall of pride and potential violence between herself and others, but also between herself and her body.

Xiomara keeps other secrets—about her loss of faith in religion, about her rejection of confirmation class. But one of the most interesting of her secrets, which is different from any of Holden's, is the one she shares with her brother, whom she calls Twin. As Xiomara comes to understand Twin's secret sexuality, she shares a secret that can damage Twin by being revealed and is damaging Twin by being kept secret. In "Fights," for instance, Xiomara sees Twin for the first time with Cody, a boy who looks at Twin with love in his face, and she thinks, "I came to knock my knuckles into someone's face. To redeem his black eye. To let them know Twin isn't alone" (174.). Xiomara recognizes that Twin's love can lead to violence, and she is willing to use violence to defend him. But it's harder for her to use words to defend him. In "Gay," Xiomara regrets how her silence makes Twin feel more alone. Her reflectiveness and regret feel more revelatory than Holden's. Xiomara changes on the page as she comes to accept Twin.

Ultimately, Xiomara puts her words out there in a way that Holden never does, so that the novel ends with the possibility of Xiomara achieving full expression, if not peace. Xiomara is fully aware that her words will create trouble, and she knows that her words are part of her. In "Burn," she asserts to her mother, even as her mother burns her journal, "This is where the poems are," I say, thumping a fist against my chest" (308). In the final citywide poetry slam, Xiomara states, "There is power in the word" (353). Xiomara breaks free of her secrets and her boundaries through her poetry. She is not free of trouble, but she is free to seek new futures.

The way in which Xiomara and Holden trust in the power of words to shape relationships may reflect their author's personae. Salinger chose a life of seclusion and privacy, refusing interviews, rejecting commentary on his novels place in the world. Acevedo lives as a spoken-word performer, her performances manifesting as activism and integration in the world. In her 2016 TEDx talk, titled, "I Use My Poetry to Confront the Violence Against Women," Acevedo comments on the many kinds of violence that daughters experience, and how her poetry explores those themes. She describes how her writing engages with the urgent social issues that shape girls, just as Xiomara's writing manifests those qualities. In contrast, Salinger seems to have rejected self-salvation, in his characters and through his own reclusivity (Wei, 2019). Like the authors who shaped them, Xiomara and Holden outgrow their secrets or hold onto them, in ways that ultimately shape and contain their liberation.

References

Acevedo, Elizabeth. *I Use My Poetry to Confront the Violence Against Women | TEDxMidAtlanticSalon*. TedX, 2016. https://www.youtube.com/watch?v=SJOG1iCLzCA.

Acevedo, Elizabeth. The Poet X. First paperback edition. New York, NY: HarperTeen, 2020.

Salinger, Jerome D. *The Catcher in the Rye*. 1. Back Bay paperback ed. New York: Little, Brown and Co, 2001.

Wei, He. "A Research on J. D. Salinger's Disillusionment of Self-Salvation." *International Journal of Science* 6, no. 3 (2019).

Acknowledgments

We have been reveling in literary criticism since we could read book reviews in *In the Middle,* listen to Terry Gross talk with authors on *Fresh Air*, or devour reviews of *Ted Lasso* and *Bridgerton.* We are grateful to all of these mentors who have inspired others to read, watch, and listen with attention.

Inside of this book, we strive to situate literary analysis inside of the writing process. For instilling writing workshop and writing process in schools and inspiring generations of writing teachers, we honor the groundbreaking work of Don Murray, Don Graves, Lucy Calkins, Nancie Atwell, Penny Kittle, Ralph Fletcher, Linda Rief, Katie Wood Ray, Felicia Rose Chavez, and Katherine Bomer.

For deepening criticality, destabilizing oppressive power dynamics inside of writing workshop, and questioning how to make writing instruction more congenial for more learners, we especially honor Tom Newkirk, Felicia Rose Chavez, Ofelia García, Colleen Cruz, and Carla España.

For innovating grammar instruction and linguistic consciousness, we delight in the work of Jeff Anderson, Vicki Vinton, Roy Peter Clark, Jamila Lyiscott, and April Baker Bell—all writing teachers who love language, promote linguistic justice, and abhor rules.

For contributing to the thinking and the lessons in this book, we thank all of our colleagues with whom we've collaborated with over the years through and beyond our early work together at Teachers College—in particular, Kate Roberts's beautiful thinking about literary analysis; Kate and Chris Lehman's work on close reading; Katy Wischow, Audra Robb, and Heather Burns's work on interpretation and writing about reading; and Phil Seyfreid, whose innovative thinking about AI helped shape all our AI lessons. We also thank our friends in high school classrooms who have shared ideas and student work over the years (and which appears here), especially Jenny Killion and Lauren Freer at the American School of Barcelona; Christen Klewicki and Shehnaz Khalfan-Washington at Rye School District, New York; Sharon Larpenteur of Beaverton, Oregon; the teachers and leaders at Columbia High School in Maplewood, New Jersey; and Laura Bonilla and the ELA team at STEMCivics for innovating alongside us. Jordan Kravitz and Todd Shy, when they were together at Avenues, created a hotbed of innovation in literary analysis, and you'll see their influence in these pages, as well as the influence of Elisa Zonana, Chantal Francois, and Mark Federman from our gorgeous time working with them at East Side Community High School.

countless emails. Thank you to Sam Meagher for offering your wisdom and expertise. Thank you to Monica Cohen whose thoughtful design work brought our vision to life across these lessons. Our book is better because your eyes were on it. Thank you to Pamela Hunt for copyediting so patiently. Thank you to Liz Spicer and the production team for taking our vision and making it come to life! Your attention to detail and patience is unmatched.

And we can never say enough about our editor, Terry Thompson. Thank you for your patience as we perfected every last chart and lesson. Thank you for your dedication to culturally responsive teaching and representation. Thank you for holding our hands, and for kicking our asses. We appreciate you.

References

Abdelmahmoud, Elamin. "Ted Lasso, and the Fantasy of Soft Masculinity." *The New York Times*, May 31, 2023, sec. Style. https://www.nytimes.com/2023/05/31/style/ted-lasso-masculinity.html.

Acevedo, Elizabeth. *I Use My Poetry to Confront the Violence Against Women | TEDxMidAtlanticSalon*. TedX, 2016. https://www.youtube.com/watch?v=SJ0G1iCLzCA.

Acevedo, Elizabeth. *The Poet X*. First paperback edition. New York, NY: HarperTeen, 2020.

Bomer, Katherine. *The Journey Is Everything: Teaching Essays That Students Want to Write for People Who Want to Read Them*. Portsmouth, NH: Heinemann, 2016.

Chavez, Felicia Rose. *The Anti-Racist Writing Workshop: How to Decolonize the Creative Classroom*. Chicago: Haymarket Books, 2021.

Clark, Roy Peter. *How to Write Short: Word Craft for Fast Times*. Little, Brown Spark, 2013.

Clark, Roy Peter. *Writing Tools: 55 Essential Strategies for Every Writer*. Revised Little, Brown paperback edition, 10th anniversary edition. New York: Little, Brown and Company, 2016.

Corrigan, Maureen. *So We Read On: How the Great Gatsby Came to Be and Why It Endures*. New York: Little, Brown and Company, 2014.

Ehrenworth, Mary, and Philip Seyfried. *AI-Enhanced Literacy: Practical Steps for Deepening Reading and Writing Instruction*. New York: Routledge, 2025.

España, Carla, and Luz Yadira Herrera. *En Comunidad: Lessons for Centering the Voices and Experiences of Bilingual Latinx Students*. Portsmouth, NH: Heinemann, 2020.

Feldman, Joe. *Grading for Equity: What It Is, Why It Matters, and How It Can Transform Schools and Classrooms*. Second edition. Thousand Oaks: Corwin Press, 2024.

Fitzgerald, F. Scott. *The Great Gatsby: The Original 1925 Edition*. United States: Amazon, 2021.

Frey, Nancy, John Hattie, and Douglas Fisher. *Developing Assessment-Capable Visible Learners, Grades K–12: Maximizing Skill, Will, and Thrill*. First edition. Thousand Oaks, CA: Corwin Literacy, 2018.

García, Ofelia, Susana Ibarra Johnson, Kate Seltzer, and Guadalupe Valdés. *The Translanguaging Classroom: Leveraging Student Bilingualism for Learning*. Philadelphia: Caslon, 2017.

García, Ofelia, and Tatyana Kleyn. "Translanguaging Theory in Education." In *Translanguaging with Multilingual Students*. New York: Routledge, 2016.

Grady, Constance. "Nickel Boys Review: Colson Whitehead's Novel Is Spare and Riveting." Vox, July 18, 2019. https://www.vox.com/culture/2019/7/18/20696706/nickel-boys-colson-whitehead-review.

Graham, Steve, and Michael Hebert. *Writing to Read: Evidence for How Writing Can Improve. Carnegie Corporation Time to Act Report*. Washington, DC: Alliance for Excellent Education, 2010. https://www.carnegie.org/publications/writing-to-read-evidence-for-how-writing-can-improve-reading/#:~:text=Writing%20to%20Read%20is%20a,reading%20skills%20and%20content%20learning.

Guskey, Thomas. "Making High School Grades Meaningful." *Phi Delta Kappan* 87, no. 9 (2006): 670–75.

Guskey, Thomas R., Nancy Frey, and Douglas Fisher. *Grading with Integrity: A Research-Based Approach Grounded in Honesty, Transparency, Accuracy, and Equity*. Thousand Oaks, CA: Corwin, 2024.

Hattie, John. *Visible Learning, the Sequel: A Synthesis of over 2,100 Meta-Analyses Relating to Achievement*. First edition. London; New York: Routledge, 2023. https://doi.org/10.4324/9781003380542.

Hattie, John, Douglas Fisher, Nancy Frey, and Shirley Clarke. *Collective Student Efficacy: Developing Independent and Inter-Dependent Learners*. Corwin Teaching Essentials, vol 1. Thousand Oaks, CA: Corwin, 2021.

Hochman, Judith, and Natalie Wexler. *The Writing Revolution: A Guide to Advancing Thinking through Writing in All Subjects and Grades*. First edition. San Francisco: Jossey-Bass, 2017.

Howard, Jaleel R., Tanya Milner-McCall, and Tyrone C. Howard. *No More Teaching Without Positive Relationships*. Portsmouth, NH: Heinemann, 2020.

Jackson, Michael R. "Opinion | Is 'Wicked' Really a Resistance Musical?" *The New York Times*, March 2, 2025, sec. Opinion. https://www.nytimes.com/2025/03/02/opinion/wicked-resistance-anti-authoritarian.htm.

Johnston, Howard. "Best Practices in Grading. Research into Practice." *Education Partnerships, Inc.* Education Partnerships, Inc, December 2011. https://eric.ed.gov/?id=ED538743.

Kakutani, Michiko. "Book Review: An Epic Showdown as Harry Potter Is Initiated into Adulthood." *The New York Times*, July 19, 2007, sec. Arts. https://www.nytimes.com/2007/07/19/arts/19iht-19potter.6726208.html.

Kermode, Mark. "Moana Review—Sail of the Century from Disney." *The Guardian*, December 4, 2016, sec. Film. https://www.theguardian.com/film/2016/dec/04/moana-review-disney.

Kittle, Penny. *Write Beside Them: Risk, Voice, and Clarity in High School Writing*. Portsmouth, NH: Heinemann, 2008.

Marchetti, Allison, and Rebekah O'Dell. *Beyond Literary Analysis: Teaching Students to Write with Passion and Authority About Any Text*. Portsmouth, NH: Heinemann, 2018.

Mollick, Ethan. *Co-Intelligence: Living and Working with AI*. New York: Penguin Random House, 2024.

Muhammad, Gholdy. *Unearthing Joy: A Guide to Culturally and Historically Responsive Teaching and Learning*. New York: Scholastic Inc., 2023.

Pecheone, Ray, and Columbia University TCRWP. "Think Tank on Performance Assessments." Teachers College, Columbia University, October 2015.

Reeves, Douglas B. "The Case Against the Zero." *Phi Delta Kappan* 86, no. 4 (December 1, 2004): 324–25. https://doi.org/10.1177/003172170408600418.

Ritchhart, Ron, Mark Church, and Karin Morrison. *Making Thinking Visible: How to Promote Engagement, Understanding, and Independence for All Learners*. First edition. San Francisco: Jossey-Bass, 2011.

Rosenblatt, Professor Emeritus Louise M. *The Reader, the Text, the Poem: The Transactional Theory of the Literary Work*. Carbondale, IL: Southern Illinois University Press, 1994.

Salinger, Jerome D. *The Catcher in the Rye*. Back Bay paperback ed. Little, Brown and Co, 2001.

Swift, Taylor. *Taylor Swift—Bad Blood Ft. Kendrick Lamar*, 2015. https://www.youtube.com/watch?v=QcIy9NiNbmo.

Thomas, Angie, and Amandla Sternberg. *The Hate U Give*. New York: Harper Collins Publishers, 2022.

Tolentino, Jia. "Pure Heroines." In *Trick Mirror: Reflections on Self Delusion*, 95–129. New York: Random House, 2022.

Warner, John. *More Than Words: How to Think Aabout Writing in the Age of AI*. New York: Basic Books, 2025.

Warner, John. *Why They Can't Write: Killing the Five-Paragraph Essay and Other Necessities*. Baltimore: Johns Hopkins University Press, 2020.

Wiggins, Grant, and Jay McTighe. "Put Understanding First." ASCD, May 1, 2008. https://www.ascd.org/el/articles/put-understanding-first.

Wiggins, Grant P., and Jay McTighe. *Understanding by Design*. Expanded 2nd ed. Alexandria, VA: ASCD, 2024.

Index